W9-ARM-705

PARK & RECREATION
MAINTENANCE
MANAGEMENT

THIRD EDITION

Robert E. Sternloff and Roger Warren
North Carolina State University
Raleigh

ALLYN AND BACON
BOSTON LONDON TORONTO SYDNEY TOKYO SINGAPORE

To our parents and our wives

CONTENTS

CHAPTER 6

GENERAL OUTDOOR MAINTENANCE   175

CHAPTER 7

GROUNDS MAINTENANCE   209

PREFACE

Park and recreation maintenance management is a multidisciplined field that developed during an era when park and recreation facilities were increasing tremendously, both in number and variety. The knowledge needed to solve park and recreation maintenance problems must be derived from a wide variety of disciplines if park and recreation administrators and maintenance superintendents are to manage the areas and facilities under their jurisdiction intelligently and effectively. Maintenance management presupposes knowledge of many fields, including landscape architecture, horticulture, turf management, forestry, ecology, plant pathology, hydrology, civil, electrical, mechanical, and chemical engineering, as well as business and personnel management. Maintenance managers do not have to be experts in all of these fields, but they must have some knowledge of each. They must know when to seek the advice of experts, and they must be able to discuss pertinent problems intelligently with such specialists.

This book was written originally and has been updated for this third edition to fill a void in professional park and recreation literature. We have compiled information from a variety of disciplines directly related to maintenance/management problems because at present, there is no comprehensive literature in the field of park and recreation maintenance management attempting such a synthesis.

We have chosen to approach the subject of park and recreation maintenance from the standpoint of management. We have not attempted to describe how to do a job or use a material but, instead, have dealt with such questions in general terms, evaluating the techniques and materials and other alternatives. For example, this book does not deal with the various methods of constructing check dams to control gully erosion or of maintaining a variety of specific floor coverings that might be used in a community center—such detailed information is available from other sources when and if the maintenance manager has a need for it. We instead provide an overview of the total maintenance program that must be developed in a variety of park and recreation settings if the program is to be successfully planned and operated.

In this text we deal with principles that are broadly applicable to a variety of areas and facilities. For example, park and recreation professionals should have little difficulty applying the principles of building maintenance discussed in this book to a community center, a resort lodge, a swimming pool bathhouse, or a family campground restroom. The principles discussed in the chapter on general outdoor maintenance can easily be applied to park and recreation facilities ranging from a neighborhood park to a picnic area in a national forest.

Throughout this book, we have used evaluative criteria to illustrate how maintenance managers can make judgments necessary to operate an effective maintenance program. We believe that the technique of using evaluative criteria is a valuable one and that maintenance managers who use this concept when making value judgments in the day-to-day operation of their departments will do a better job. We encourage maintenance managers to constantly ask "Why?" They should always have a substantive basis for performing a particular maintenance function in a certain way or for selecting a particular material, supply, or piece of equipment to do a job.

Changes in this third edition include the following: an important new chapter dealing with computer applications to maintenance management; increased emphasis on the environmental impact of parks and recreation and the manager's responsibility for land stewardship; increased emphasis on recycling as a means of solid waste disposal; a new section on wood preservation; considerable expansion of the material pertaining to trails, including an emphasis on greenways; a new section dealing with urban forestry; and a comprehensive updating to reflect recent changes in all aspects of park and recreation maintenance management.

As in the previous edition, review questions follow each chapter, allowing students to review and apply information.

We hope this textbook will be a valuable resource for a variety of individuals involved in the park and recreation field. It is intended for park and recreation students in both two- and four-year colleges and universities. This book is designed to give students the understanding necessary to function in a supervisory or management position in a maintenance department, or as a general park and recreation supervisor or administrator dealing with the maintenance function and perhaps coordinating the efforts of the entire park and recreation agency. The book also will be of value to professionals managing physical plant maintenance operations for private institutions and parks, school districts, and military bases.

Acknowledgments

We wish to recognize the contribution of the regents and instructors of the Park and Recreation Maintenance Management School, whose monographs on various aspects of maintenance management have been a great help to practitioner/students attending the school. Much of the information contained in those pieces has been utilized as a guide in preparing this text. For example, Steven S. Plumb of the School Board of Regents recently prepared the monograph "Computer Applications to Park Maintenance," which was helpful in developing Chapter 3.

We would like to thank the following individuals, who reviewed the third edition manuscript, for their help: Dr. Russell L. Stubbles of South Dakota State University; Dr. Leslie M. Reid of Texas A & M University; and Dr. Robert W. Douglass of The Ohio State University. The text is greatly improved as a result of their constructive suggestions.

Robert E. Sternloff
Roger Warren

CHAPTER 1

MAINTENANCE PRINCIPLES

I n the United States, we tend to think that the organized park and recreation movement is quite young. Viewing it historically, the development of park and recreation facilities is actually quite old. Descriptions of the early Babylonian, Assyrian, Persian, and Indian gardens antedate the birth of Christ by many centuries. Historical records indicate that many of these early parks and gardens were quite elaborate, with floral displays and fountains. Many provided sanctuaries for wild animals and were established as private hunting grounds for the nobility.

During the Greco-Roman era, gardens, parks, and recreation facility development became considerably more elaborate. In and around Rome, villas were developed with elaborate gardens, courts for ball games, and baths. Most of these were privately owned and used; however, some were opened for public use at a later date.

Subsequently, large parks and gardens such as the Tuileries, Luxembourg, and Versailles near Paris; Kensington, Victoria, and Hyde Park in London; Friedrickshain in Berlin; and Central Park in New York were developed. With few exceptions, early parks and gardens were developed for aesthetic reasons. Roads, trails, and benches provided access to these areas so people could stroll leisurely, ride, or sit quietly, enjoying the beauty. The development of facilities in parks for intensive recreation use is, for the most part, a recent phenomenon.

Historical records reveal little insight into the maintenance practices carried out in these early parks and gardens. There are occasional references to "groundsmen" and "gardeners," and it must be assumed that maintenance was performed by people we would call horticultural and urban forestry specialists. At any rate, the tools and equipment used by park maintenance personnel were primitive. It is safe to assume that much hand labor was employed in maintaining the grass, trees, shrubs, and flowers grown in these parks and gardens. When we compare the maintenance tasks needed to maintain early gardens and parks used for recreation with maintenance requirements for modern park and recreation facilities, the differences are astounding.

1

Today's park and recreation maintenance manager must be concerned with maintaining indoor recreation facilities—gymnasiums, bowling alleys, community centers, museums, art galleries, auditoriums, theaters, dance pavilions, and arenas. Outdoor recreation facilities, such as tennis courts, athletic fields, picnic areas, family campgrounds, ice skating rinks, multiple-use game courts, swimming pools, public beaches, archery ranges, shooting ranges, stadia, toboggan slides, ski slopes, golf courses, zoos, amphitheaters, and marinas, must also be maintained. When one considers the tremendous variety of facilities to be maintained, with the inherent maintenance problems associated with each of the facilities, the maintenance manager's job becomes seemingly impossible. Indeed, park and recreation maintenance management is a complex job, and as new types of facilities and new equipment are developed, the job becomes more complex.

This chapter will examine the principles of park and recreation maintenance management. Maintaining a particular type of facility, a family campground, for example, will be dealt with in general terms. When the principles related to establishing maintenance objectives and standards, planning and organization, personnel, general outdoor maintenance, grounds maintenance, computer applications, maintenance of vehicles and equipment, building maintenance, and public relations are understood, application of these principles to specific park and recreation facilities can be made by the recreation professional.

THE ROLE OF PARK AND RECREATION SERVICE

Any park and recreation maintenance department that does not have a sound understanding of the purpose, aims, and objectives of the park and recreation agency of which it is a part cannot operate at peak efficiency. Maintenance is a service function and must be geared to help meet agency goals. The maintenance department that functions as a separate and independent entity, unresponsive to the agency's needs, is not performing its assigned function within the agency. In the past, many maintenance units have assumed this independent role, creating havoc as the maintenance and program functions tug in opposite directions. For this reason, it is important to consider the role of park and recreation service today.

To understand the role of park and recreation service, we must first consider the concept of leisure and recreation. *Recreation* is defined as an experience that takes place during leisure (discretionary time) and is self-gratifying to the individual who participates. A great many of an individual's recreation experiences occur at a facility especially provided for that purpose—a golf course, a gymnasium, a community center, a hiking trail, a ski slope. Unless the facility is constructed, maintained, and operated in the best possible manner, the individual's chances of experiencing self-gratification are significantly reduced. The desire to provide the highest quality experience for each individual who participates in park and recreation programs should be the basic, underlying goal of every park and recreation agency and each employee within that agency from the director to the building custodian.

Next, we must examine some of the changes taking place in the use of leisure in American society. This examination in turn will give us some indication of the trends expected in the park and recreation movement in the future.

The most important change affecting park and recreation service is the increase in U.S. population. The total population has increased from 76 million in 1900 to 250 million in 1990.[1] In addition to gross growth in population, distributional and compositional changes must be considered. Some sections of the United States are growing rapidly (e.g., the Sun Belt), while other sections of the country (e.g., the Northeast and Midwest) are experiencing static or declining populations. One of the most significant compositional changes is the growth of older persons in the population. An aging population can be expected to increase the demand for facilities for picnicking, golf, social activities, travel, and other less strenuous forms of recreation. Another rapidly growing segment of the population is small children, indicating a need for playground equipment and child care facilities in the near future. The growth of minority groups should also be monitored because cultural factors may play a major role in an individual's selection of recreation pursuits. Although the Bureau of Census projections indicate a slowing in population growth between 1990 and 2010, the U.S. population will increase by 32 million people during this period (more than the 1990 population of California).

The United States has become an increasingly urbanized nation. According to 1990 census data, 82 percent of the population lives in urban areas compared with 40 percent in 1900.[2] Population densities are rising annually; a majority of the states east of the Mississippi River have population densities of more than 100 people per square mile.

Our large cities present serious problems concerning the delivery of leisure services. The pressures of urban living present problems that have only recently been recognized and are still being studied by sociologists and psychologists. Most cities, large and small, have not met (or are just beginning to meet) the challenge to provide and preserve open space. Park and recreation facilities remain far behind the demands and needs of the people. Previously, recreation has been provided primarily by public agencies. Now a much broader leisure service system is in force, whereby many agencies—public, private nonprofit, and private for profit—combine to provide leisure services on the local level.

Changes in energy and transportation may have a profound effect on the way Americans use their leisure. The automobile has typically been used to gain access to recreation sites. Mass transportation, particularly air travel, will become more important. Many current forms of recreation consume energy. Boating, use of ATVs, golf carts, and water skiing are examples of recreation that consume, when aggregated, significant amounts of energy. In the future, these and other forms of recreation may be curtailed or drastically modified.

Affluence is a factor that directly affects the recreation movement. Although estimates vary according to what is included, Americans spend over $300 billion annually for leisure. Americans spend one dollar out of eight for sports equipment, vacation travel, golf and tennis outings, admission to movies and spectator sports events, and a variety of other recreational pursuits. Present indicators demonstrate that Americans place a high priority on recreation spending. In spite of great affluence in the United States, millions of Americans live at poverty or near-poverty levels, causing a difficult dilemma for agencies seeking to provide recreation service for everyone.

Social change has major implications for park and recreation agencies. Increased crime and delinquency, changing sexual mores, changing family patterns, religious influence, and the loss of primary group contacts must be considered by any agency seeking to provide park and recreation services. The emergence of new values and life styles will influence future recreation demand.

The changing nature of work, both in qualitative and quantitative terms, is a vital issue. With industrialization, automation, cybernation, and the rapid growth of service-related jobs, millions of men and women in recent decades have been forced into dull, monotonous jobs that provide little challenge and even less satisfaction. The growth of health, fitness, and wellness programs in the 1980s may reflect an escape from monotony. Traditional patterns of park and recreation services reflect the five-day, forty-hour work week with heavy use of facilities on weekends and during summer vacation periods. With the advent of changing work patterns, such as the four-day work week, flex time, early retirement, longer vacations, dual-spouse wage-earning families, and sabbaticals, these traditional patterns are changing.

Scientific and technological change has provided the opportunity for additional leisure through such labor-saving devices as microwave ovens, dishwashers, snow blowers, and prepared food. Medical advances have produced healthier individuals who live longer and are physically more active. Science and technology have also provided the knowledge to produce facilities and equipment that improve our recreation. Examples of these changes include artificial ice rinks, snow-making machines, lightweight materials for hang gliding and backpacking, and home entertainment equipment, such as the VCR and compact disc. The aerospace industry has produced materials that have been adapted for use in tennis racquets, golf clubs, fishing rods, and sailboat masts. Sports clothing is lighter weight and offers improved warmth, better durability, and better freedom of movement.

Changes in education have the potential to produce profound changes in leisure use patterns. The need to educate for leisure-centered living is now being realized and translated into programs at all educational levels. The adult education movement is gaining momentum in terms of professional and personal opportunities. Modern communications technology makes home study a reality, and cable television provides an avenue all park and recreation agencies must explore for new programming concepts.

The environmental movement, born in the 1960s, continues to gather public attention. The American public has developed a land ethic, and park and recreation agencies as primary landholding agents of the people will be expected to exhibit responsible stewardship for land under their jurisdiction. This is particularly important in urban areas where natural areas are quickly disappearing. The continuing demand for more and better outdoor recreation opportunities indicates the need for educational programs that will stress intelligent and responsible use of our natural resources.

Many of the changes discussed suggest an increase of leisure available to masses of people and the need to use this leisure wisely. Indicators such as increased population spending and the increased use of a great variety of recreation facilities show that increased leisure is indeed a reality. Leisure is neither good nor bad. Unwisely used, leisure is dehumanizing and leads to boredom and anxiety. Conversely, the individual who learns to use leisure in a wholesome manner can add a new dimension to his or her life. The wise use of leisure can add an exciting, dynamic quality to life, transforming the human mind and spirit.

The challenge to the park and recreation professional is to provide an opportunity for individuals to experience the positive rather than the negative side of leisure. Although the park and recreation professional cannot ensure a positive leisure experience (the individual's freedom of choice predicates this assumption), he or she has the responsibility of leading the public to these experiences by providing facilities and programs in which such experiences may occur. The recreation specialist has the further responsibility of making the facility and program opportunities as attractive and appealing as possible.

MAINTENANCE AND OPERATION DEFINED

For the purposes of this book, *park and recreation maintenance* is defined as keeping park and recreation areas and facilities in their original state or as nearly so as possible. In this definition, maintenance includes routine, recurring work; repair work (both major and minor); and minor construction work. Areas and facilities where maintenance is performed include properties owned or under the jurisdiction of a park and recreation agency.

Park and recreation operation deals with park and recreation programs and with the organization and/or regulation that allows optimum public use of areas and facilities. Park and recreation agencies deal with two types of program opportunities for people: directed and self-directed programs. With directed programs, park and recreation agencies plan and organize programs and may provide direct leadership. Examples of directed recreation programs include day camps, playground programs, Little League and other youth baseball pro-

FIGURE 1-1 Good maintenance helps to ensure a safe playground.

grams, and arts and crafts instruction. With self-directed programs, an area or facility is provided by a park and recreation agency and use is unplanned and unorganized. Custodial leadership may be provided, but the participant need not have any direct contact with an agency employee. Examples of self-directed recreation programs include picnicking, hiking, free play in a gymnasium or game room, and golf.

Park and recreation agencies need to provide opportunities for both directed and self-directed recreation. If, however, the agency is to provide for the mass recreation needs of the community, state, or nation, efforts must be aimed more and more toward self-direction. For example, swimming instruction classes are offered so the individual who participates can enjoy swimming at a pool or beach on his or her own.

More is involved in operating a self-directed recreation facility than just constructing the facility and opening it to public use. An agency must follow three basic steps: (1) establish operating principles—for example, determine who may use the facility, hours of operation, and under what conditions; (2) provide supervision to ensure that the established policies are carried out; and (3) maintain the facility according to established maintenance standards.

Fortunately, the era of "Keep off the grass" signs in our public parks is largely over. Parks should be aesthetically pleasing, but they are also provided for people to use. The maxim "Parks are for people" accurately reflects the thinking of today's park and recreation professional. Maintenance and operating policies must be geared to provide optimum use, and the professional should be concerned both with the quantity and quality of the recreation experience. Quantity of use is ensured by providing an adequate number of areas and facilities for public use. Quality is provided through good management, that is, by operating and maintaining areas and facilities according to the highest possible standards.

The park and recreation professional has a dual responsibility: (1) to provide an opportunity for the finest possible recreation experience for people, and (2) to protect the resource, natural or man-made. Both of these obligations are vitally important, and to some, they seem diametrically opposed. This, however, is not the case—they go hand in hand. Unless both goals are achieved, the park and recreation professional has not done a good job.

GUIDELINES TO ESTABLISHING A MAINTENANCE PROGRAM

Each recreation agency has problems and needs that are unique. The maintenance operation of every agency is different because of geography, facilities to be maintained, recreation programs provided, whether the agency is public or private, budget, and public being served. Despite these differences, certain principles or fundamental truths are basic to any effective maintenance operation. The following principles are designed as general guidelines to establishing a

FIGURE 1-2   Good design minimizes maintenance problems.

maintenance program. These principles provide a basis upon which the entire maintenance operation of a department should be developed. These principles can also be used as standards to measure the effectiveness of an existing maintenance program. A breach of any one principle can cause a serious disruption in providing high quality recreation service by a park and recreation agency.

1. Maintenance objectives and standards must be established.

The first step in establishing a maintenance program is to form general objectives, which are statements of the purposes and goals of a park and recreation maintenance department. Although maintenance standards may vary from one department to another, the general objectives of park and recreation maintenance will vary little. The general objectives of park and recreation maintenance may be stated as:

1. Park and recreation areas and facilities should have a clean, orderly appearance at all times.
2. Areas and facilities that are aesthetically pleasing should be developed and maintained or identified and protected.
3. Areas and facilities should be maintained to create a healthful environment.
4. Areas and facilities should be maintained to create a safe environment.
5. Maintenance should promote good public relations by providing areas and facilities where people have an opportunity for an enjoyable leisure experience.

A standard is a yardstick or criterion by which particular maintenance practices may be gauged. Maintenance standards are the stepping-stones used to accomplish the general maintenance objectives. Obviously, these standards can be established only after the general objectives for the department have been formulated.

Factors that affect how maintenance standards are achieved include intensity of use, weather, topography, quality and quantity of supervision, types of programs, and vandalism.

Although objectives are general in nature, maintenance standards must be established for specific areas and facilities contingent on the criteria previously listed. Maintenance standards describe the conditions that will exist when maintenance tasks have been successfully completed. They provide a means to compare conditions as they are found by inspection or observation and the accepted standards for the particular area or facility. Maintenance standards should be established for all areas and facilities, including grounds, signs, fences, buildings and other structures, roads, parking lots, trails, utilities, and specific facilities, such as picnic areas, campgrounds, and ballfields. The quality of the maintenance program is established as standards are determined. A maintenance standard is established for guidance in developing and carrying out a maintenance plan for the park and recreation department. Examples of maintenance standards are given in the appendix to Chapter 5.

2. **Maintenance should be performed with economy of time, personnel, equipment, and materials.**

Economy of time. All maintenance tasks should be done as quickly as possible. Every effort should be made to accomplish maintenance work as soon as possible after a legitimate request has been made. Month-old requests for repairs and service are irksome to the staff member making such requests, and they lead to conflicts between maintenance and program personnel. It is also important that maintenance work not interfere with a program function. For example, grass cutting or building maintenance at a facility where a day camp program is held should be performed when the camp program is not in session. That is, the maintenance on such a facility should be performed early in the morning before the campers arrive or late in the afternoon when they have departed for the day.

Economy of personnel. The optimum number of workers should be assigned to perform various maintenance functions. Each maintenance task, whether it be mowing a golf green, winterizing a swimming pool filter system, or maintaining a baseball diamond, can best be performed by one, two, three, or a dozen people determined by experience in doing the job. A conscious effort should be made to determine the optimum number of workers required to perform the task. Economy of personnel also implies using workers trained to do a particular job. Assigning workers to a job they cannot efficiently perform because of lack of skill or training is wasteful.

Economy of equipment. It is important to have the proper equipment necessary to do the job. In attempting to do the maintenance job in the most economical manner possible, the use of mechanized equipment plays a vital role. Historically, many maintenance tasks have been performed with hand tools and backbreaking labor. Considering its high cost, hand labor should be reduced to a minimum. Switching from hand labor to power equipment is not the total solution to the problem. Modern maintenance operation implies having the right power equipment to do the job.

Economy of materials. Along with adequate equipment to do a job, proper materials are also necessary. Workmen must be provided with appropriate cleaning materials and chemicals to accomplish their tasks. Economy of materials is particularly applicable to all types of repair work. Communication between the person requesting work to be done and the maintenance department supervisor assigning the task to a work crew is essential. If proper assessment of the job is made initially, the work crew can take all tools and materials needed to accomplish the task rather than have to return to the shop or storeroom for additional supplies once they see what has to be done.

Maintenance costs continue to rise each year as the cost of personnel, equipment, and materials increases. One way the maintenance department can combat these rising costs is to do the job more economically and more efficiently.

3. Maintenance operations should be based on a sound, written maintenance plan.

Every maintenance department should have a detailed, comprehensive maintenance plan. The values of a maintenance plan are (1) to provide a systematic approach in accomplishing the work of the department, (2) to provide a sound method of justifying budget requests, and (3) to serve as a communication device for persons higher or lower in the organization.

The maintenance plan should never be the work of one individual (although one individual can best coordinate the actual writing of the plan). It should be a cooperative, coordinated effort encompassing the entire maintenance staff. The plan must be dynamic, that is, subject to constant revision as conditions change and/or better ways of accomplishing certain tasks are found. Above all, the maintenance plan should allow no substitute for quality. If compromises must be made because of a lack of personnel or equipment, these should be made after the plan has been completed and not incorporated into the plan. A detailed discussion of how the maintenance plan is formulated is presented in Chapter 2.

4. Scheduling maintenance work must be based on sound policies and priorities.

The decision of *when* to do *what* is vital in a well-managed maintenance department. When assigning work priorities, value judgments are constantly being made by administrative and supervisory personnel. For example, someone must make the decision whether first to fix a leak in a golf course irrigation system or at a drinking fountain in a picnic area. While the elimination of these value judgments might at times seem desirable, pragmatically it is impossible to eliminate this responsibility. Part of a maintenance supervisor's job is to make these decisions. Although these value judgments cannot be eliminated, guidelines can be established, which will be helpful in the decision-making process. Every maintenance department should carefully consider the criteria upon which maintenance scheduling decisions are to be made. Once criteria have been established, work scheduling gains consistency, and judgments made can be evaluated in terms of their conformity to the criteria. For a more complete discussion of this topic see Chapter 2.

5. All maintenance departments should place high emphasis on preventive maintenance.

All maintenance departments should stress preventive maintenance. Preventive maintenance is defined as continuous attention and care to prevent damaging wear and costly repairs. The purpose of a program of preventive maintenance is to get optimum life from facilities and equipment used by a park and recreation agency. A maintenance department can get into the rut of constantly trying to catch up with needed maintenance and repair, while little attention is given to preventive maintenance. Careful planning and scheduling is necessary to prevent such a situation.

Preventive maintenance is an important consideration in all aspects of maintenance work. In relation to all types of equipment, it means daily, weekly, and seasonal attention to lubrication, changing oil, and replacing worn parts before they fail rather than when the machine breaks down. In relation to buildings, the concerns must be for care of mechanical systems, care of floor coverings, and a painting schedule. Preventive maintenance applies to maintaining all recreation surfaces in top notch condition, for example, tennis court resurfacing or maintaining adequate ground cover in a picnic area to prevent costly and unsightly erosion. It may involve a spray program to prevent insect and disease damage to turf or shrubbery. In short, preventive maintenance is good maintenance management to prevent damage before it occurs. The advantage of such a system is being able to schedule maintenance conveniently rather than responding to breakdowns in the system that are likely to occur at times when the maintenance department is understaffed or extremely busy.

6. The maintenance department must be well organized.

The purpose of departmental organization is to see that the maintenance function is carried out in the most efficient manner possible. Basically, good organization involves making the most efficient and effective use of personnel, equipment, materials, and time. There are no easy solutions to the problem of effective organization. Organizational structure must be tailored to the needs and particular requirements of each park and recreation agency. The problems of organizational structure are discussed in detail in Chapter 2.

7. Park and recreation agencies must provide adequate fiscal resources to support the maintenance program.

Although there is a great variation among park and recreation agencies, maintenance costs are a major expenditure for all. In a typical state or national park with a heavy emphasis on outdoor facilities, maintenance costs may represent 60 to 80 percent of the annual operating budget. Municipal park and recreation departments may easily spend 50 to 60 percent of their operating budget on facilities and maintenance. If ways can be found to do the maintenance job more efficiently and more economically, more fiscal resources can be made available for new programs and facilities. Unfortunately, too often the maintenance section of the park and recreation budget has become the "whipping boy" for uninformed boards, city councils, and administrators, so inadequate fiscal resources are provided to accomplish the needed maintenance. One of the prime responsibilities of the head of any maintenance program must be to sell budget needs to superiors. This can best be accomplished by well-documented evidence of previous years' expenditures and projected needs for the coming year(s).

One of the most important and often neglected aspects of the maintenance budget is equipment replacement. A separate, adequate fund, which can be drawn upon as needed, should be established for this purpose. The merit of this system is that equipment can be replaced at the optimum time rather than when money has been budgeted for that fiscal year, or waiting two years beyond optimum replacement because funds for replacement are not available. In order for an agency to have the equipment needed to get the job done, some workable system of equipment replacement is essential. A more complete discussion of this topic is found in Chapter 8.

One essential policy for all recreation agencies should be "If you can't maintain it, don't build it." Too often funds for capital improvements are secured and facilities constructed with no regard for the funds needed to operate and maintain them. Operating facilities with inadequate program, supervisory staff, and funds for maintaining the facilities may seem to be beneficial when considering only short-term needs, but ultimately it is costly and poor management practice.

8. Park and recreation agencies must provide adequate personnel to carry out the maintenance function.

Because of low wages, park and recreation agencies have traditionally hired unskilled laborers for maintenance work. While the unskilled nature of the work may provide a legitimate reason for low wages, today the conditions have changed. Personnel used in maintenance work should be skilled technicians rather than laborers. This change has come about primarily because of the use of sophisticated mechanical equipment.

When maintenance labor is approached positively with the idea of providing work that is important, meaningful, and essential to the success of a park and recreation agency, a successful maintenance operation is likely to result. When maintenance labor is viewed as demeaning work that must be accomplished despite its unpleasantness, failure will be the probable result.

The positive approach to maintenance labor is predicated upon (1) hiring quality personnel (the implication here for adequate wages is obvious), (2) a good orientation program to sell an individual on the importance of his or her job and the overall importance of what the agency is seeking to accomplish, (3) adequate initial and in-service training to do the job for which the employee has been hired, (4) good supervision that is responsive to the needs of the employee, and (5) good communication at the upper administrative levels to articulate the importance of the job the maintenance staff is doing.

9. The maintenance program must be designed to protect the natural environment.

Park and recreation professionals must accept responsibility as stewards of the natural environment for the public. Park and recreation agencies, particularly in urban communities, often have under their jurisdiction a high percentage of the open space and natural areas remaining in a community. Stewardship of this land must be viewed as a serious responsibility. This stewardship responsibility extends to private landholders as well as to public holdings. Private agencies,

Durham Parks and Recreation Department, Durham, N.C.

FIGURE 1-3 Good stewardship means preserving natural beauty.

for example, country clubs, family campgrounds, and resorts, manage valuable natural landholdings. If we expect the general public to take seriously the environmental crisis confronting our nation and the world, the park and recreation profession must accept a leadership position through good environmental management of lands under their jurisdiction. This is particularly applicable to the way in which we develop and maintain land for recreation use. The impact on the environment should be carefully considered in all aspects of park and recreation management.

Park and recreation professionals should act in a number of ways to protect the natural environment. First, they are preservers. Park managers must preserve all park resources from encroachments and seek to acquire more open space to ensure parkland for the future. They must act as preservers of natural beauty in those areas now controlled and acquire land to preserve areas that are perceived as beautiful for present and future generations. The aesthetic value of park and recreation areas cannot be overstated. Developing areas where people observe beauty in a spirit of contemplation may indeed be one of the highest forms of recreation. Beauty is inherent in an environment where people can breathe clean air, swim, or fish in clean, unpolluted lakes and streams. Beauty is also inherent where urban populations can enjoy greenery and open space. This beauty should be available and accessible to people as long as access does not destroy the natural resource. Carrying capacities for each facility should be established so that fragile resources can be protected from overuse. Management techniques must be developed to realize the goal of

FIGURE 1–4   Well-designed and maintained parkways provide vistas of
scenic beauty for many Americans.

natural resource protection more fully.

Park managers must ensure the protection of the natural resource during
the design and construction phase, when areas for intensive recreation use are
developed. Picnic areas, campgrounds, athletic fields, and any other facility,
which because of poor design and/or construction destroy the environment, are
a disgrace to the profession. Facilities must be planned and constructed to blend
with rather than intrude on the natural landscape.

When a park and recreation agency develops and adheres to high standards
of maintenance, it has taken an important step toward preservation of the natural environment. The preserver's role extends to providing litter-free picnic
areas, well-maintained restrooms, and vandal-resistant facilities. A well-maintained facility is essential if individuals are to achieve the full potential from
their recreation experience.

The maintenance manager must be concerned with ecological processes
and the impact of the park and recreation visitor on those processes. A conscious effort must be made to plan for and carry out the management of natural
and cultural resources in a manner suited to protect them now and preserve
them for future generations. These considerations must be included in the maintenance management plan (discussed in detail in Chapter 2).

Second, the park and recreation professional should help create natural
beauty where none now exists. Unfortunately, in many urban neighborhoods little, if any, natural beauty remains. Formal gardens, attractively kept parkland,

FIGURE 1–5 This picnic shelter was designed to blend
into the natural environment.

well-landscaped and maintained roads and streets, and aesthetically designed
play areas provide an opportunity to increase the quality of life for everyone.
Opportunities must also be provided for the urban dweller to experience the
natural environment by maintaining access to large natural areas.

People need places to go to escape from the stresses of modern life. Park
and recreation professionals should provide parks and greenways for adoles-
cents to escape from their parents and to contemplate what life is all about,
for senior citizens to enjoy the beauty of spring wildflowers, for anyone who
needs quiet, and for dating couples to walk beside clear streams planning their
lives together.

Of course, the park and recreation professional cannot be expected to solve
all environmental problems, but he or she can and should make a positive contribution in many areas.

10. The maintenance department must assume the responsibility for public and em-
ployee safety.

The maintenance department has a primary responsibility for public safety,
which should, of course, be shared by the entire park and recreation agency. The
responsibility for the conduct of participants in the recreation program is largely
a matter for the program staff; however, providing areas and facilities that are
safe for recreation use must be carried out by the maintenance department.

Public safety is a relative matter. It is not possible to restrict the public's activities to the point of making an area or facility totally safe. When children and adults play, accidents will happen, and some will be hurt. Realizing the inherent dangers associated with many types of recreation activities, the park and recreation professional must make sure that facilities are as safe as possible so that the equipment and facilities provided are not the cause of accidents. With the emphasis on liability in current society, public safety is a more important consideration than ever before.

A program designed to reduce accidents must begin with accurate accident reports and periodic review of these records. Accident records may be required by law or by the agency's insurance company. But, lacking either of these mandates, the agency should nonetheless keep good records for internal use.

When accidents occur and agency facilities or equipment are at fault, action should be taken immediately to prevent additional accidents. This may involve immediate repair of the equipment or facilities at fault, or it may mean closing an area or facility until repairs can be made. An analysis of accident reports on a periodic basis will reveal accident-causing areas, and action can be taken to prevent future occurrences.

The maintenance staff should be trained to routinely observe and report any conditions that they feel may endanger public safety. Many times, an individual performing a maintenance function may be the only staff person to come into contact with remotely located facilities for a long period of time. In addition to routine observation by staff, periodic inspection tours should be conducted by individuals trained to look for hazardous conditions. When possible, a safety engineer should be hired to carry out periodic inspections.

Public safety should be carefully considered during planning and construction stages. Errors made with regard to public safety are much easier to correct at this stage than after the facility has been constructed.

The maintenance program must also emphasize employee safety. Comprehensive accident prevention and safety programs should be developed.

One of the most constructive steps toward improving employee safety was taken with the passage of the Williams-Steiger Occupational Safety and Health Act of 1970 (OSHA). The OSHA program has had, and will continue to have, far-reaching effects on the improvement of employee safety, including the establishment of safety standards for many maintenance activities directly related to park and recreation work. In addition, states have established employee safety standards for governmental employees.

The recognition of safety problems by agency administrative personnel and the desire to correct them are basic requisites for a workable safety program. Putting up a few posters is not enough; the department must be dedicated to preventing accidents. Expert help, essential for establishing a worthwhile safety program, is available in most communities through a variety of sources, including insurance company safety engineers, industrial safety engineers, local safety councils, the National Safety Council, or the Occupational Safety and Health Administration. It is irresponsible not to take advantage of these sources of assistance. The details of how to establish an employee safety program are discussed in Chapter 4.

11. In the design and construction of park and recreation facilities, maintenance should be a primary consideration.

There is no truer maxim for the park and recreation professional than "Build it right from the start." In these days of high construction costs, it is easy to rationalize cutting corners to make a construction project economically feasible. Compromising the principle of good design and construction from the beginning is, in the end, more costly than doing it right from the beginning.

One of the most important factors in good construction is the use of appropriate building materials. Materials used in park and recreation facility construction should be (1) durable, (2) easy to maintain, (3) easy to repair, and (4) easy to replace. Good planning and choice of materials can ease the task of replacement when necessary. These factors are critical from the standpoint of maintenance and should be carefully evaluated along with other considerations, such as aesthetics, safety, cost, and function.

Using rustic materials in parks or materials that blend with rather than protrude from the environment is not incompatible with high quality, easy-to-maintain materials. Careful design and selection can accomplish both objectives.

The importance of maintenance input into the planning process should not be overlooked. The time to prevent mistakes that will be costly in terms of maintenance time and effort is during the planning process. When maintenance department employees have an opportunity to review plans for new buildings and facilities, potential problems can be averted by adopting alternatives that are acceptable to the designer, program staff, and maintenance staff. One way to ensure maintenance input is to have a maintenance engineer on the planning staff. In addition, there should be consultation with the operational maintenance staff when planning new facilities, particularly those with which the maintenance staff has had some experience. Designing facilities that are functional as well as aesthetically pleasing should be the goal of every park and recreation agency.

There is no such thing as a maintenance-free facility, but some types of facilities are easier to maintain than others. Attention to minor details of the plan can ease the maintenance burden. For example, adequate numbers and placement of electrical outlets and water faucets can avoid the need for long extension cords and hoses when maintaining the facility.

The use of temporary structures should be discouraged and avoided whenever possible. Temporary structures have a way of becoming permanent, and they usually represent high overhead maintenance headaches.

12. Maintenance employees are responsible for the public image of the park and recreation agency.

Every maintenance employee is responsible for maintaining the public image of the park and recreation agency. Many park and recreation professionals do not think that maintenance employees have a role in public relations for the department; however, the maintenance staff can be a fine public relations emissary. As the public uses the park and recreation facilities, the only contact they may have with an agency staff person is with a maintenance employee—for example, a building janitor, a crew picking up trash in a picnic area or campground, or an individual raking a sand trap on a golf course. When this happens, it is important that the image presented to the public be a positive one.

Good public relations begins simply with the maintenance department doing a good job in its routine work. Clean, well-kept facilities create a good public image. Public relations extends to the clean, neat personal appearance of all employees, including maintenance workers. Uniforms, although not essential, are very helpful in conveying the desired impression.

Good public relations on the part of maintenance employees does not just happen because the responsibility appears in the individual's job description. It is the result of a concerted effort on the part of the department. It begins with an orientation program designed to instill pride in working for the agency and is continued with in-service training opportunities designed to help the employee meet people while on the job. Employees should be able to answer questions, even foolish ones, commonly asked by the public, and when they do not know the answers, they should make the proper referral.

Conscious efforts by program staff can and should be made to involve some of the maintenance staff with the public when appropriate. For example, a gardener with a knowledge of plant propagation and care would make a welcome addition to a garden club tour. Not only would the gardener be a valuable asset to the group by virtue of the information he or she could provide, but also the experience would provide an invaluable boost to the individual's morale by letting him or her know that the job is worthwhile.

REVIEW QUESTIONS

1. Define maintenance and operation.
2. Differentiate between maintenance objectives and standards.
3. What is a maintenance principle?
4. Why is good maintenance important to the park and recreation agency?
5. Discuss some of the ways good or bad design and construction can affect maintenance.
6. What is preventive maintenance?
7. Discuss the park and recreation professional's responsibility toward the natural environment.
8. Describe the maintenance employee's role in public relations.

CHAPTER BIBLIOGRAPHY

Hoffman, Mark S. (Ed.). *World Almanac and Book of Facts 1991.* New York: Pharos Books, 1992.

Kraus, Richard. *Recreation and Leisure in Modern Society.* 4th ed. Glenview, IL: Scott, Foresman/Little, Brown, 1990.

MacLean, Janet R.; Peterson, James A.; and Martin, W. Donald. *Recreation and Leisure: The Changing Scene.* 4th ed. New York: Macmillan, 1985.

Naisbitt, John, and Aburdene, Patricia, *Megatrends 2000.* New York: William Morrow, 1990.

U.S. Census Bureau, *Current Population Reports,* Series P-25, No. 1017. Washington, DC: U.S. Government Printing Office.

NOTES

1. U.S. Census Bureau, *Current Population Reports,* Series P-25, No. 1017.
2. Ibid.

CHAPTER 2

PLANNING AND ORGANIZING MAINTENANCE PROGRAMS

I nadequate funding for maintenance may be the most critical problem facing park and recreation agencies. Too many ribbon-cutting ceremonies have been conducted for new recreation facilities without some reasonable guarantee of adequate maintenance service being provided by the proud, facility-dedicating officials. More than a few frustrated managers are asking the question: "Why buy and develop park land or build recreation facilities if we don't have the means to maintain them?"

Deferred maintenance inevitably results in gradual but accelerating deterioration, which goes unnoticed by the occasional visitor, until the condition becomes quite intolerable or dangerous to the user. At this point, corrective maintenance assumes the proportions of an expensive, major repair project.

The inadequacy of today's maintenance funding problem began in the past, prior to the time when accelerating costs of wages, energy, vandalism, and liability insurance put a great strain on available financial resources for maintenance. Managers and their agencies willingly took on added maintenance responsibilities for new facilities with reasonable assurance that additional maintenance funds would be forthcoming. However, today's climate of scarce dollars and increased competition for these dollars from other public service agencies, together with a tax-cutting fever, further threaten already strained budgets. Beyond question, we have failed to calculate and communicate, in advance of acquisition and development, the projected costs of maintaining areas and facilities. Our decision makers have only been aware of the first half of total expenses, the initial investment for capital improvements, and have been relatively unaware that almost forty cents of every local park and recreation dollar is spent on maintenance for these same facilities. Yet, park maintenance remains one of the least understood functions of local government, with park and recreation facilities often perceived as inefficiently managed.

Maintenance management today requires not only effectiveness and effi-

21

ciency in achieving maintenance objectives, but also financial accountability. As never before, managers are expected to prove the worth of maintenance expenditures and tie these closely with available revenues. The responsibility of park and recreation managers is to calculate and communicate so that they can sell decision makers and the public on the importance and magnitude of costs involved in maintaining a facility over its life cycle before the acquisition and development decision is made.

A technique for accomplishing this task is the development of a maintenance impact statement[1] detailing financial expenditure forecasts and maintenance level expectations that will serve as a guide during the decision-making process relative to proposed facilities. A sample maintenance impact statement appears as Appendix 2A at the end of this chapter.

When the decision to acquire and develop is "go," we must recognize that recreation areas and facilities are the "precious jewels" of our kingdoms and will depreciate far too rapidly if emergency and "crisis maintenance" is a continuing condition.

The maintenance of recreation areas and facilities, with their accelerating public use, cannot tolerate a situation in which emergencies and crisis maintenance are a regular and continuing condition. Instead, the maintenance program must function on a planned, systematic basis according to maintenance standards—a plan that anticipates deterioration and breakdown rather than reacting to them. To be effective, such a planned maintenance program cannot remain static; it must be evaluated continually and modified according to changing visitor use. It must be evaluated not only in terms of changes in the frequency of maintenance service, but also in terms of improved program management—for example, by selecting better materials and by improving the utilization of personnel.

If we would refuse to cross a busy thoroughfare blindfolded, then we should refuse to conduct a park and recreation maintenance program without a systematic plan that is designed to anticipate problems and promptly respond to emergencies.

The development of an acceptable, realistic maintenance plan should include the following:

1. A complete inventory of park and recreation areas, facilities, and equipment to be maintained.
2. A written routine maintenance plan including:
   a. Maintenance standards written for all areas, facilities, and equipment items identified in the inventory.
   b. Identification and listing of specific routine maintenance tasks necessary to achieve the maintenance standard set for each facility.
   c. Procedures describing the most efficient methods to accomplish routine maintenance tasks.
   d. Maintenance task frequency.

   e. Personnel necessary to accomplish tasks.

   f. Material and consumable supplies necessary for each task.

   g. Tools and equipment required to accomplish tasks.

   h. Accurate task time estimates.

3. A means for accomplishing nonroutine, nonrecurring maintenance work. (Repair work and preparation for special events are examples of such work.)

4. Preventive maintenance for conditions that may accelerate wear and deterioration, as determined by systematic, scheduled inspections.

5. A schedule for assigning responsibility for each maintenance job. This includes designating an individual, crew, or contractor to do the job, and the supervisory staff to see that it is done properly.

6. A system for job design and planning, accurate scheduling of maintenance work, and workload control.

7. A system of cost analysis and controls.

FACILITY AND EQUIPMENT INVENTORY

If the areas and facilities of a park and recreation system are to be routinely maintained according to general objectives and established standards, a definite plan for accomplishing this must be developed and followed. Such a plan must include a detailed inventory of existing areas, facilities, and equipment indicating the extent and time of their use by days, weekends, holidays, and seasons. The detailed inventory must also denote the types, sizes, special features, and condition of each area and facility, which in turn allows decisions to be made as to the scheduling of work and the need for specialist personnel, proper maintenance equipment, and supplies.

A worthwhile addition to the descriptive inventory would be a measurements compilation for all areas and facilities together with a corresponding site map reduced to appropriate legible size. Key numbers or letters appearing on each map can illustrate graphically the level and frequency of maintenance required for that particular site. The maintenance plan for parks in Ann Arbor, Michigan,[2] utilizes such an inventory format. A sample of this format appears as Appendix 2B to this chapter.

ROUTINE MAINTENANCE PLANS

"Keep it short and simple" (KISS) is one of the first lessons learned by those who are successful in communicating with others. Keeping it short and simple certainly applies to a park and recreation manager who is anxious to institute a

FIGURE 2–1   The maintenance plan must be easily interpreted
by field personnel.

new routine maintenance plan. Unfortunately, the history of parks and recreation is replete with examples of meticulously written, lengthy plans going unused because they were difficult to interpret and did not capture and hold the attention of the supervisor or worker quickly enough.

A routine maintenance plan can be painstakingly developed in narrative form. However, this approach often leaves maintenance employees dismayed and discouraged at trying to remember what was written about the maintenance standards, tasks, and frequencies appearing earlier in the text of the plan. A most important consideration in developing a routine maintenance plan for any park and recreation system is to recognize from the outset that the plan must be easily and clearly interpreted by both the field personnel who supervise and those who do the prescribed maintenance work.

One maintenance plan found to be an effective means of interpreting routine maintenance responsibilities to field personnel is a written instruction manual with companion illustrations or photographs for specific developed areas or facilities. An excellent example of this method appears in *Cleaning Recreation Sites,* a manual published by the USDA Forest Service Equipment Development Center, San Dimas, California.

A major problem, however, with the combination written-illustrated maintenance plan is cost. A great majority of park and recreation systems simply do not have the resources to produce a written maintenance plan with photographs or illustrations for each developed area, facility, or equipment item to be routinely maintained.

The search has been under way for years to find an alternative maintenance format easily understood by field personnel that could be used by recreation systems unable to provide costly illustrations and photographs. The table format presented in Figure 2–2 is the product of refinements that have been made during several years' use by the annual Park and Recreation Maintenance Management School held at Oglebay Park, Wheeling, West Virginia. The capstone requirement for all second-year students at the school is to develop a routine maintenance plan for a hypothetical park.

This table format has also been required for students at North Carolina State University who are enrolled in the park maintenance course. In addition, the table format has been reviewed and critiqued by maintenance managers in the field. The following criteria were used in developing the table format:

1. Presentation of all elements of the routine maintenance plan for each developed area, facility, or equipment item on a single sheet to avoid the need to refer to previous or following sections of the plan.
2. Presentation of basic information (necessary to successfully carry out the plan) in logical, systematic order in adjacent columns on a left to right read-out basis.
3. Provision of readily accessible information through columns and tabulations for the following determinations and uses:
   - Maintenance standards.
   - Tasks necessary to achieve the standards.
   - Personnel requirements (general and specialized) to carry out the plan.
   - Supply and material requirements (to allow for advance ordering and purchase).
   - Equipment requirements to carry out the plan (availability—on hand, purchase, rental, or contract).
   - Maintenance task frequencies and task time estimates for maintenance scheduling purposes.
   - Appropriateness of maintenance work to be done "in house" or by contract.
   - A basis for maintenance budget requests.
4. Easy access to appropriate sections of the plan by means of a table of contents that identifies specific areas, facilities, and equipment items by sheet number.
5. Use of an 11- by 17-inch table plan. There are several advantages to this size:
   - Two facing 8½- by 11-inch sheets provide sufficient space for handwritten or typed information in the various column categories.
   - Facing sheets (constituting one table plan page) can be linked together in a standard three-ring loose-leaf binder cover.
   - The binder cover provides physical protection for the table plan document when used in the field.

FACILITY OR EQUIPMENT ITEM: _____

Maintenance Standards	Routine Maintenance Tasks	Procedures for Maintenance
"Standards" must clearly and accurately describe conditions that should exist following maintenance work.	Use terms such as the following to describe "tasks":	"Procedures" are descriptions of *How to Do* the Maintenance "Tasks" and should cover such things as:
Examples for building housekeeping: Wastebaskets and ash trays—empty and clean. Radiators, desks, cabinets, louvers, exhibit cases, panels, displays—clean and dusted. Examples for restrooms, washrooms: Restroom and washroom areas—free of odors and clean. Soap, paper, and towel racks—filled. Mirrors—clean of fingerprints; shelves—clean, polished, and free of debris.	Cleaning, lubricating, adjusting, painting, litter and trash removal, planting, fertilizing, watering, mowing, etc.	Soil and turf improvement; care of lawns, trees, shrubs, indoor and outdoor recreation surfaces, floors, walls, windows, roofs. Housekeeping tasks. Information source: observations of several workers doing the same task, consultation with experienced colleagues in the field, job sampling, or time-motion study.
Example for Baseball Field		
Fields, outfields, dugouts, and spectator areas free of debris and trash.	Remove debris and trash.	Pick up debris and trash by systematically walking the area. Empty all trash containers.
Replenish skinned infield soil lost during previous season with adequate slope (15°) for drainage away from pitcher's mound.	Truck in soil from storage yard.	Dump soil at pitcher's mound, and drag spread toward base lines. Anchor pitcher's rubber at proper height.
Eliminate holes on infield surface.	Fill holes.	Add extra soil, rake, and tamp firm.
Smooth infield surface.	Drag infield.	Drag infield by circling pitcher's mound and rotating in from base lines.
Wet infield to minimize dust and loss of soil due to wind.	Wet infield.	Dampen infield surface with hose spray or broadcast calcium chloride.

FIGURE 2-2   "Table" format for planning routine maintenance.

From facilities inventory, giving location and I.D. No. if available. That is, athletic fields, lawns, trees, shrubs, structures, trails, parking areas, picnic grounds, pools, equipment items, etc.

Frequency	Calendar												Personnel
	J	F	M	A	M	J	J	A	S	O	N	D	
Daily, Weekly, Biannual, Annually, Cyclical, Periods exceeding one year.													Optimum (minimum) personnel required to do the job with indication of technical skills required— i.e., groundskeeper, carpenter, electrician, plumber, or specialist crews. Information from labor-estimating guide. Preferably developed from in-house historical records.

Example for Baseball Field

Frequency	J	F	M	A	M	J	J	A	S	O	N	D	Personnel
Daily			✓	✓	✓	✓	✓						2 person grounds crew
Daily		✓	✓	✓	✓	✓	✓	✓	✓				2 person grounds crew
Annually		✓											2 person grounds crew
Daily, before games				✓	✓	✓	✓	✓					1 groundskeeper
Daily, before games			✓	✓	✓	✓	✓	✓					1 groundskeeper
Daily, before games				✓	✓	✓	✓	✓					1 groundskeeper

FIGURE 2–2 *(Continued).*

Materials and Consumable Supplies	Tools and Equipment	Task Time Estimate
Fertilizer and seed quantity. Cleaning agent and supplies, lubricants, paint-type, etc. Information sources: suppliers, manufacturers representatives, in-house testing of various products.	Trim mower, housekeeping equipment, blower, vacuum motorized equipment, type and size, etc. Information sources: dealers, manufacturers representatives. Colleagues in the field who are involved in similar situations.	Time for completion based upon in-house historical records, work-load cost tracking data, job sampling, or time estimating guides developed elsewhere. Record man-hours M/H estimate for *each* task application and total annual (yearly) task hours in parentheses below this figure. Example: One M/H per application and 240 applications per year: One M/H (240 M/H)
Example for Baseball Field		
	2 stick punches, 2 shoulder bags.	1 M/H (75 M/H)
		1 M/H (120 M/H)
	Tractor with box trailer.	
	Dump truck, tractor with blade, drag mat, rake hoe, shovel.	24 M/H (24 M/H)
Approx. 10 yards 60%–40% sand/soil mixture		
Extra soil	Tractor with box trailer, shovel, rake, tamper.	1/2 M/H (75 M/H)
	Tractor with drag mat.	1/2 M/H (75 M/H)
Calcium Chloride	Hose with nozzle, broadcast spreader.	1/2 M/H (75 M/H)

FIGURE 2–2 *(Continued).*

• The loose-leaf feature allows for easy removal of outmoded material and replacement with updated, refined information. Refining the written maintenance plan should be viewed as a continuing process.

A reproduction of a table plan, together with an example of how the table might be used to describe routine maintenance for a baseball field, is illustrated in Figure 2–2.

There are pitfalls to avoid in developing a routine maintenance plan using the table format. During the use of the table plan over the past several years, certain problem areas were consistently noted. Unless these are understood and avoided, the final routine maintenance plan may confuse those who will depend on it for guidance. The following problem areas have been identified:

1. Maintenance standards which describe conditions that should exist following satisfactory maintenance work are routinely misunderstood, primarily because they are poorly written and lead to misinterpretation by those who are responsible for supervising and performing the necessary maintenance work. A standard by its very nature is the minimum acceptable level of maintained condition for an area, facility, or equipment item. There is no latitude for negative error here. To minimize misunderstanding, the written maintenance standard must clearly and precisely describe conditions that should exist following minimally acceptable maintenance work. A clear understanding of written standards can best be accomplished by the use of descriptive terms and phrases such as "empty and clean," "clean of fingerprints," "free of deposits on surfaces," "clear of obstructions," "free of dirt and grease," "straight and secure," "secure and drip-free," "free of loose boards and loose nails," and "bright, free of holes and blemishes."

2. Routine maintenance tasks are best described by the use of terms such as cleaning, lubricating, adjusting, painting, litter and trash removal, planting, fertilizing, watering, and mowing.

3. Procedures for maintenance are simply descriptions of how to do the maintenance tasks in the most effective and efficient manner possible. The table column covering procedures is a short-hand method of providing procedural information that is otherwise included in a detailed jobsheet for a routine operation.

The "Procedure for Maintenance" statement should clearly describe the manner in which the job should be approached, based on the job procedure that works best in any particular situation. Should there be doubt as to what is the best method, it would be well to study the job being done several times by different workers to identify the "best" way. Consulting with colleagues in other situations is also helpful. Job procedure information will be modified from time to time as more effective and efficient ways of doing a job are identified.

For example, a procedural statement for cleaning picnic tables, as found in the Forest Service manual *Cleaning Recreation Sites* gives the following description: "(a.) Apply a liberal amount of disinfectant-deodorant-detergent solution to the table top and benches. Let the detergent work for a short time. (b.) Scrub the table top and benches with a scrub brush to remove soil or stain. Clean possible soil between planks. (c.) Use water sparingly to rinse off cleaning solution and soil. (Excessive water will result in muddy conditions around and under the table.) (d.) Squeegee excess rinse water from surfaces to promote quick drying and prevent spotting. (e.) Wipe remaining excess water from plank edges and other surfaces with a sponge or clean rag."[3]

4. Personnel assigned to accomplish routine maintenance work are probably the most critical part of maintenance planning and organization. It is imperative that the optimum (minimum) number of workers be hired, trained, and assigned to perform the various routine maintenance functions. We simply can't afford to assign three competent (trained) workers to a job that can and should be performed by only two.

5. Accurate task time estimates are critical to the success of a maintenance manager in job planning and scheduling. Maintenance task time estimating in many park/recreation organizations begins with informal estimates based upon experience and general advice from supervising and worker personnel. In other situations, national or regional maintenance task time manuals developed by outside sources are used.

Developing internal maintenance task time standards is also important. National or regional time standards are always crude averages that include wide variations in productivity and working conditions. Therefore, these should be replaced with "in-house" work time rates for specific routine maintenance jobs as soon as a substantial "in-house" historical work file is accumulated.

Maintenance plans should also be established for specialized equipment and mechanical systems, including heating, ventilating, and air conditioning. Routine maintenance plans are also necessary for utilities, such as water systems, sewer systems, irrigation systems, liquid fuel systems, electrical distribution systems, radio systems, fire alarm systems, and street and area lighting systems. For small park/recreation organizations, much of the maintenance for the systems mentioned will, because of its highly specialized nature, be delegated to others outside the park/recreation organization on a contractual basis. Nevertheless, these systems are an integral part of the maintenance operation and should be included, at least in general terms, in the overall written maintenance plan so as not to overlook them. Normally, the major portions of maintenance data included in the written maintenance plan regarding specialized equipment are quite general in nature, with the admonition that those responsible for such maintenance consult detailed information and instructions provided by the manufacturer or other sources of specific maintenance information.

The written maintenance plan, then, should be simplified and condensed for easy reference and use, while at the same time, it must cover detailed, specific maintenance requirements by reference to other sources of specialized information.

ACCOMPLISHING NONROUTINE, NONRECURRING MAINTENANCE

Nonroutine, nonrecurring maintenance work includes such repairs as replacement of broken insect screen wire; replacement of a broken door closer, hinge or lock; or possibly the replacement of a cracked section of pipe in the golf course irrigation system. Nonroutine, nonrecurring maintenance work also includes such nonroutine tasks as the set up and removal of audience chairs for a band concert, the temporary mounting of artificial lighting fixtures for a special event, or the installation of a temporary public address system for a Fourth of July celebration.

The Work Order System

An effective maintenance program depends to a great extent on a work order system that receives all work requests, initiates action, and follows the project through to completion.

Work Control Desk

A large park and recreation organization should establish a work control center to effectively coordinate its work order system. In a small system, work control might be assigned to a clerk or to the maintenance manager. It is important to designate a person and place for receipt of work requests and complaints. All operating personnel should be aware of a telephone number for reporting maintenance problems.

Work Order Request Form

Work requests come from a variety of sources: building occupants, operational personnel, security officers, skilled workers, and preventive maintenance mechanics. In a well-managed maintenance division, most requests should come from department employees trained to identify and report problems during normal work rounds. Such training helps the division keep on top of maintenance problems and frees program personnel and their administrators to concentrate on recreational functions.

Work request forms should, however, be distributed to all major operational and program offices to facilitate maintenance requests. A properly designed work request form, such as the one shown in Figure 2–3, aids the individual requesting service to provide complete and accurate information essential for analyzing the request and issuing a work order. Work request forms also serve as a reminder that the maintenance division carries responsibility for handling maintenance problems.

WORK ORDER REQUEST

METROPOLITAN RECREATION DISTRICT
Maintenance Division
Repair & Control Section

Dept. No. ____________
Control No. ____________

Date ______________________

The following work is requested for ______________________________________
(Area where work is to be done)

Requested by: ______________________________________
(Name)

Division: ______________________________ Phone: ____________________

Description of Desired Work: ______________________________________

____

____

____

Draw sketches if needed on reverse side of this form.

Special Instructions: ______________________________________

____

Received by: ______________________ Date ______________ Time ____________

DISPOSITION: Action 1, 2, or 3

For Maint. Div. Repair & Control Section Only

ADDITIONAL WORK ORDER

Trade	W.O.

1. Work Order = ______________________ written.
2. Assigned to Prevent. Maint. ______________________
(Date)
3. Returned to Requesting Division with explanation ______________________
(Date)

Original — Maintenance Division
Duplicate — Requesting Office

FIGURE 2–3 Work request form.

Some recreation systems attempt to combine the work order request form with the work order form in hope of reducing paperwork. This procedure results in improperly described work and fails in the effort to deal with complex work requiring several trade crews and compound work orders.

When work requests come to the work control desk via telephone, the work order clerk can, with well-designed forms, take from the caller all necessary information in order to translate the layperson's work description into the language of the supervisor and workers on the work order form.

Work requests must be analyzed to determine which will not need to become work orders. If the request is a familiar one and the job elements are simple tasks with clearly established time standards, the clerk can quickly estimate time, assign work order numbers, and work them into the maintenance schedule. If questions remain about the nature and extent of a job, a supervisor must investigate and make an analysis to decide whether the request should be rejected or accepted. This final decision should be noted in the bottom section of the work request form entitled "Disposition."

Work Order Form

When a request is accepted as a legitimate job order, the clerk or supervisor assigns a number and completes a work order form. The number is, of course, one of the key elements in the whole system. It follows the job through scheduling, completion, and final recording.

The work order analyzes and estimates the work in detail, serves as a means for coordinating various work elements within the maintenance division, collects cost estimates for labor, equipment, and material, and authorizes the work to be done. Figure 2–4 illustrates an acceptable work order form.

There should be at least three copies of the work order; the first and second copies go with the worker assigned to the task. On this form, he or she notes the hours spent and records or attaches receipts for the materials, parts, and supplies used. Upon completion, the worker returns the first copy to the work control clerk.

The third copy remains with the clerk until the worker's copy returns. From the work copy, the clerk compiles all the costs involved—labor, equipment, materials, and overhead. The clerk then compares the actual totals with the estimates on his or her form, notes any significant discrepancy, clips the two forms together, and files them in the file for the facility involved. In some situations, periodic reports of work accomplished are required by supervisors.

The historical cost file is one advantage of the work order system. From these records, planners can project maintenance costs for the next year and maintenance unit costs for similar facilities in the planning stage.

PREVENTIVE MAINTENANCE

A system of preventive maintenance to minimize unscheduled shutdowns, major breakdowns, and costly repairs should be a continuing concern of every maintenance organization. The adage "A stitch in time saves nine" describes the overall objective of preventive maintenance in all aspects of maintenance work.

Preventive maintenance and its specific applications to buildings and structures, certain aspects of general outdoor maintenance items, grounds maintenance, and maintenance equipment are detailed in Chapters 5 to 8.

METROPOLITAN RECREATION DISTRICT
Maintenance Division
WORK ORDER   Repair & Control Section

W.O. No. _____
Date _____

TO: _____ Department
(person to whom work is assigned)

You are to do the following described work at _____
(location of job)

Description of Work to be Done

_____
_____
_____
_____
_____
_____
_____

Priority: Emergency [   ]   Routine [   ]   Standing [   ]

Job is scheduled for starting on _____ , _____ , _____ M
                                    (day)   (date)   (time)
Work is to be completed by _____ , _____ , _____ M
                             (day)   (date)   (time)

COST RECORD

	POSITION, TITLE, GRADE AND SURNAME	EST. M/DAYS	DAILY RATE	EST. COSTS	ACT. M/DAYS	ACTUAL COSTS
PERSONNEL						

	EQUIPMENT TYPE	EST. HRS./MIS.	RATE'	EST. COSTS	ACT. HRS./MIS.	ACTUAL COSTS
EQUIPMENT						

	ITEM	EST. COSTS	ACTUAL COSTS
MATERIALS AND OTHER			

COST ACCOUNT	PERSONNEL SERVICES	EQUIPMENT COSTS	SUPPLIES AND MATERIALS	OTHER	TOTAL

Use other side for remarks, sketches, etc. ON RECEIPT OF THIS FORM FROM WORK CONTROL CENTER, ENTER ON LOG BOOK AND ASSIGN WORK PARTY, AUTHORIZE MATERIAL DRAW, OR ORDER MATERIALS, ALL IN TIME TO PERMIT WORK TO BE STARTED AND COMPLETED IN TIME.

First two copies to Department performing work. Third copy is retained in Control Center. Original copy is returned to Control Center after completion of work.

DATE COMPLETED: _____ VERIFICATION _____
                                                         (signature – requesting dept.)

FIGURE 2–4   Work order form.

Maintenance of recreation surfaces, adequate cover in a picnic area to prevent costly erosion, or a spray program to prevent insect disease damage to turf or shrubbery is often described as preventive maintenance. However, such maintenance work is normally accomplished by inclusion in the routine maintenance plan or through the work order system for accomplishment of nonroutine, nonrecurring maintenance work.

Regardless of the manner in which preventive maintenance is accomplished, the essential prerequisite for an effective program is a systematic inspection procedure to identify small, but accelerating, problems and promptly doing the necessary preventive maintenance work.

ASSIGNING RESPONSIBILITY FOR MAINTENANCE WORK

Criteria for Determining Maintenance Organization

Organization of the maintenance operation will depend upon many local factors, such as visitor or participant use of each of the units or facilities within the system broken down by time (weekend, weekday, and holiday), the size of the area to be maintained, and the types of facilities and equipment within the units to be maintained.

Only after considering each of these factors can a maintenance work responsibility be assigned and a workable maintenance organization be developed. The maintenance organization must be designed specifically to meet the requirements for each park and recreation system because no two are alike. Considerable variation is to be found in areas, buildings, other structures, program offerings, and numbers of visitors.

Methods for Assigning Maintenance Work

Unit Maintenance

In utilizing this method, each unit within the park and recreation system would perform its own maintenance. A neighborhood park would, for example, have its own maintenance crew responsible for all of the maintenance tasks necessary to completely maintain the facilities found in that unit, including building maintenance, lawn and shrubbery care, maintenance of ball fields, and so forth. The advantages of the unit method of maintenance organization are the following:

1. Maintenance personnel become familiar with the facility.
2. It is relatively easy to determine responsibility when maintenance service is not properly performed.
3. The director of the unit controls both the maintenance and program staff, resulting in a potentially better coordinated effort.
4. Maintenance personnel tend to develop a loyalty to their particular unit and

often take more pride in their work.

The disadvantages of the unit method of maintenance organization include the following:

1. Unit maintenance personnel must learn to perform a variety of jobs and use a variety of equipment in a satisfactory manner.
2. The supervisor must also be familiar with the various jobs and equipment necessary to perform these jobs.
3. Unit maintenance does not make the most efficient use of expensive equipment.

The application of the unit method of maintenance work functions best when there is enough work to justify the assignment of maintenance personnel to a unit on a full-time, year-round, or on a full-time, seasonal basis. The unit method of maintenance is appropriate when the equipment needed to do the job is relatively simple to operate and not too expensive.

Specialized Maintenance Crews

In utilizing the specialized-crew method of maintenance, each crew is trained to do a job, such as grass cutting, shrubbery care, floor care, window cleaning, lighting fixture cleaning or replacement, and other specialized work. The specialized crew is scheduled to move from one unit to another to perform their specialized work. The advantages of the specialized crew are as follows:

1. The crew becomes extremely proficient in their specialized type of work.
2. Expensive equipment is used on a regular basis so as to make the cost of the equipment justifiable.

The major disadvantages of the specialized-crew method of maintenance are the following:

1. The repetition of the job tends to make it monotonous for the crew.
2. There is loss of travel time from area to area.

The most appropriate application of the specialized-crew method of maintenance is when the required skill involved is difficult to learn, when specialized equipment is involved, or when a number of small areas and facilities are involved, making the use of full-time unit maintenance personnel impractical.

Maintenance by Contract

The third basic method of maintenance is to arrange for maintenance service by an outside contractor. Conceivably an entire maintenance function could be handled by contractors who would perform the various maintenance jobs. The advantages of maintenance by contract are as follows:

1. There is no capital investment in equipment.
2. Well-trained specialists for each job can be hired.
3. There are no in-house personnel problems.

The disadvantages of maintenance by contract are the following:

1. There is loss of control as to when and how well jobs will be completed.
2. The cost may be higher because the contracting firm must make a profit.

The best applications of contractual maintenance are in very remote areas where travel time is excessive, with jobs that require specialized equipment and trained operators, when the job is not done routinely, and when the agency has a relatively low demand for the job to be done. Tasks that would be appropriate for maintenance by contract in many small park and recreation agencies include tree trimming and the cleaning and replacement of outdoor lighting fixtures.

Safeguards to follow when contracting maintenance work should include the following:

1. *Choose reputable firms.* Recognize that the low bid does not necessarily represent the most competent contractor. If the low bid from an unknown contractor cannot be justified by economy, technique, or method, investigate the contractor's previous work and client satisfaction.
2. *Develop complete and detailed specifications.* Bids may be received on an overall sum basis and/or on time and materials. Accurate detailed specifications will protect the recreation organization in either case. Specifications should be reviewed annually and revised when appropriate. Appendix 2C is a sample specification for contract exterior painting.
3. *Inspect the contractor's work.* Usually in-house workers inspect the work of contractors to determine specification compliance before the final contract payment is made. However, it is recommended that the maintenance manager check the work of a new, relatively unknown contractor.

Few park and recreation agencies exclusively use any one of the three basic methods of organizing the maintenance work. Rather, a combination of each of the three methods of assigning maintenance work is most common.

Figure 2–5 presents a hypothetical organization chart for a park and recreation system of several thousand acres of park land, a number of buildings, and sufficient manpower and equipment to accomplish the maintenance work.

PLANNING AND SCHEDULING JOBS

Successful annual, seasonal, weekly, and daily maintenance planning and scheduling is dependent upon knowledge of work requirements coupled with adequate personnel to do the work according to established standards.

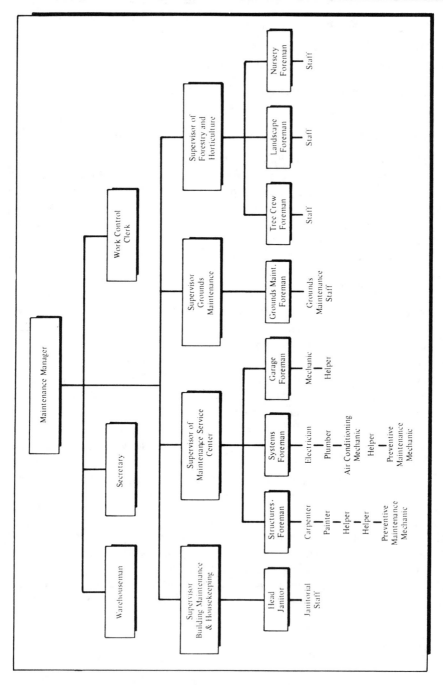

FIGURE 2–5 Sample organizational chart for the maintenance division
of a park system serving a population of approximately 100,000.

Work Requirements

The sources of information necessary to determine maintenance work requirements are as follows:

1. A carefully detailed routine maintenance plan for all areas and facilities within the system indicating the frequency of maintenance as dictated by the extent and time of use.

2. The need for repairs, either determined by a systematic inspection procedure or dictated by breakdowns that may or may not require immediate emergency repair, depending on their urgency and effect upon overall operation. (The repairs ought to be communicated by means of a standardized repair order request and work order system.)

3. A standardized job method that outlines the best way of doing the job; the correct selection of tools, equipment, and materials for the job; and an estimate of work time, thus minimizing the necessity for repeated maintenance job analysis.

Personnel Requirements

For the sake of economy, the optimum number of workers should be hired, trained, and assigned to perform the various maintenance functions. Job standardization will indicate the minimum number and types of competent personnel necessary to accomplish a particular maintenance job. In the absence of job standardization or previous experience doing a particular job, estimates will have to be made as to number and types of competent personnel required with future work force adjustments made, based upon that experience.

Fundamentally, job scheduling requires a comparison of estimated hours of workload with actual labor-hours available. The objective is to maintain necessary personnel such as skilled laborers, shop personnel, roving crews, unit crews, and janitorial personnel in order to accomplish the work according to standards and within acceptable time limits.

A procedure must be established to determine the need to increase or decrease the number of competent personnel assigned to particular maintenance jobs in which experience indicates that the work assigned is consistently not accomplished or when the work force exceeds work requirements.

One method for making such a determination is keeping detailed, factual records of the work backlog for each maintenance group according to supervisor and area of responsibility.

Work Order Log

To keep track of work backlog, the work control clerk should keep a work order log. Such a record is simple to maintain and can reveal unusual delays, identify unproductive crews, and show dollar value of work done during any time period.

The most informal log is one the supervisor keeps on a clipboard, listing work order number, date assigned, estimated completion date, and projected costs. Several simple yet efficient alternatives are listed below:

1. A general hook file holding all uncompleted work orders.
2. Separate hook files for the work orders assigned each trades group or maintenance force, whether it be for trails, grounds, buildings, utilities, automotive, equipment, or shops.
3. A general list of all work orders assigned, noting date assigned, group responsible, estimated time, and cost of completion.
4. Separate lists for each trades or maintenance group.

Alternatives 3 and 4 require more paperwork. The clerk must copy pertinent information from each work order form when first assigned and when returned after completion. However, these alternatives do provide a more accurate account of the current backlog and a record of productivity and expense.

Workload Control

The purpose of workload control is to match the work force with the workload. Perfect control results in no work orders waiting for workers and no workers waiting for maintenance problems to develop. Unfortunately, this optimum situation rarely occurs because unforeseen maintenance problems and emergencies inevitably arise in random sequence. A backlog of work orders, therefore, should not be regarded negatively but, rather, as a necessary hedge against days when emergencies do not occur and extra work is needed to complete work schedules. A maintenance organization with personnel consistently sitting around waiting for work orders is, more than likely, overstaffed.

A moderate backlog is ideal, but it is difficult to define in the abstract. However, when the rate of new work orders consistently exceeds the rate of job completions, an immoderate backlog exists.

When the backlog accumulates past the maximum time limit allowed for completing all work orders, including low priority tasks, then workload control is breaking down. The next symptom is skipping low priority jobs in the rush to remedy emergency and high priority demands. The final stage of an "out of control" overload takes two forms: (1) work orders are written only for the most critical problems, or (2) all work orders are given the highest possible priority, unduly delaying many legitimate, high priority tasks.

Recommended remedies include the following:

1. Hiring temporary help to alleviate the backlog.
2. Hiring a private contractor to handle selected backlogged work orders.

3. Increasing the labor force permanently.

The perfect solution depends upon the conditions causing the backlog. Hiring temporary help or contractors is especially appropriate when a sudden increase in workload can be diagnosed as a passing phenomenon due to a seasonal overload or an unusual number of problems. Increasing the permanent work force is a solution only when it is clear that the backlog will otherwise continue unchecked.

Estimating Time

A major advantage of the work order system is more accurate time estimates for future work orders. An organized approach to estimating requires analyzing each problem according to its basic job elements and assigning a time value for each element. Theoretically, the sum of these values gives the total time estimate. A highly sophisticated approach involves further analyzing the elements into work units and applying internally established work standards for each unit.

Maintenance task time estimating at a small recreation system, however, often begins with informal "guesstimates" by the work order clerk. At this stage, the clerk must rely heavily on the experience and general advice of the maintenance supervisors and workers. To set up the first, rough time standards for work units, the clerk might utilize maintenance manuals developed by the United States Army, Navy, and Air Force.

As historical records accumulate via the work order system, internal work standards can be developed to replace personal intuitions and national standards. With a task time standards list, a capable clerk can quickly and accurately estimate the time requirements for the majority of jobs to be scheduled. The importance of developing internal work standards cannot be overemphasized. National standards are always crude averages that account for wide variations in productivity and working conditions. Although helpful for a start and for comparison with in-house work rates, they should be replaced as soon as a substantial historical file is accumulated.

Each recreation organization should develop maintenance task time standards for those jobs performed most frequently according to their records. For example, a survey of workers' task performance for a recreation organization might result in maintenance task personnel and time requirements as indicated in Table 2–1.

WORK TIME STUDY VIA WORKLOAD/COST TRACKING

A good workload/cost tracking system, either manual or computerized, allows the manager to collect, record, and evaluate information about maintenance

TABLE 2–1 Time and labor estimating guide for work orders.

Trade	Number of Workers	Travel Allow (hr)	Labor Time (hr)	Total (hr)
Carpentry				
Repair door surface closer	1	½	½	1
Repair concealed door closer	2	½	1	3
Repair door damage at shop	1	1	3	4
Repair and replace screens	1	½	½	1
Replace broken glass	1	½	½	1
Repair and replace ceiling tile	1	½	½	1
Repair small dry-wall damage	1	½	1	1½
Repair and replace sash balance	2	½	1½	4
Change lock on door	1	½	1	1½
Paint				
Repaint 20' x 15' room, 1 coat	2	1	16	34
Repaint small bathroom, 1 coat	1	½	8	8½
Repaint exterior window	1	½	2	2½
Clean and paint graffiti, sign 30" x 18"	1	Shop	2	2
Plumbing and Steamfitting				
Clear stopped water closet	2	½	1	3
Clear stopped basin	1	½	1	1½
Replace leaking radiator valve	2	½	2	5
Clear external sewer stoppage	2	½	4	9
Install replacement valve, faucet, or trap	2	½	3	7
Electrical				
Replace fluorescent lamp ballast	1	½	1	2
Reset fire or security alarm				
Replace fractional HP motor	2	1	3	8
Replace blown fuse or reset circuit breaker	1	½	1	1½
Repair exterior light damage	2	½	1	3
Control circuit problems	2	1	2	5

Source: A Basic Manual for Physical Plant Administration (Washington, DC: The Association of Physical Plant Administrators of Colleges and Universities, 1974), p. 117. Reproduced with the permission of The Association of Physical Plant Administrators of Colleges and Universities.

task times, travel time and distance from one job site to another, and facility visitor use. Such information provides the basis for more accurate and appropriate job scheduling. A data collection system designed specifically for park and recreation agencies was developed by Chrystos D. Siderelis, of North Carolina State University.[4]

Siderelis recommends the following considerations prior to adopting any workload/cost tracking system:

Simplicity: How can the agency collect the type and quantity of data as simply as possible?

Level of Detail: Given your agency size and capability, how much data can you realistically process and use?

Easy to Understand: How should information derived from the system be formulated so as to be understandable to park personnel and decision makers?

Interpretation of Data: Will the system fit with agency's information systems, both operational and planned?

The Park Maintenance Management Manual,[5] developed by the Bureau of Recreation and Conservation of the State of Pennsylvania, suggests a systematic process for initiating a workload/cost tracking system that involves six phases.

First: Inventory and categorize the various types of maintenance work functions and facilities you are maintaining. Examples: *Work Functions:* carpentry, field preparation, leaf collection, mowing, plumbing, snow removal. *Facilities Maintenance:* ball fields, beaches, campgrounds, electrical systems, football/soccer fields, gymnasiums, horseshoe courts, ice skating rinks, lakes, lighting systems, picnic grounds/shelters, roads, swimming pools, tennis courts, water systems.

Second: Determine your information needs, such as what documentation you need for maintenance budget requests and what maintenance information you need to make proper managerial decisions regarding work force allocation, job setup and breakdown time, and equipment down time.

Third: Develop a data collection report form with your staff (you will need their support and total commitment) which will provide the information necessary in the second phase of the process.

Fourth: Train your key supervisory staff first in the data collection methodology and then have them provide training for the remaining staff.

Fifth: Pilot test your workload/cost tracking system for a minimum of one month; then make changes needed for full implementation.

Sixth: Evaluate reported data each month and note reasons for unusual patterns or variations.

JOB SAMPLING—A POTENTIAL SUBSTITUTE FOR WORKLOAD/COST TRACKING

Unless an agency already has a workload/cost tracking system in place, the manager might want to consider substituting job sampling.

Sampling is a technique that may be employed to collect and analyze information and to draw conclusions regarding a mass of data when the mass is too large or too expensive to study in its entirety. Job sampling provides data for analysis on the basis of randomly sampled work only at certain times and at certain locations rather than through continuous data collection (workload/cost tracking), which is time consuming and more expensive.

Measurement by sampling has the following appropriate applications and advantages:

1. It has good application for indirect maintenance jobs in which standardized methods are not defined.
2. Sampling technique can be easily learned.
3. Sampling is a good do-it-yourself technique for the manager.
4. It is a relatively inexpensive process when compared with workload/cost tracking.
5. It measures utilization of labor.
6. It can provide periodic data over a long time frame.
7. It allows for simultaneous study of a variety of situations.
8. It requires no description or methodology training of the maintenance staff, as is the case with workload/cost tracking.

The main disadvantage of work sampling is that its best and most appropriate application is to work that is highly repetitive, that is, when the work or job is done in excess of thirty times per year. Much park and recreation maintenance work simply does not occur this often. For example, turf mowing in most parks is done no more than a dozen times per growing season and therefore is best studied on a continuous data collection basis via workload/cost tracking. In contrast, garbage and trash collection in some parks is done with much greater frequency and therefore might best be studied by means of work sampling, which requires direct observation only on an occasional random basis.

The theory and use of job sampling is explained fully in the publication *A Guide to Work Sampling Procedures* by Walter W. Erwin[6] of North Carolina State University.

GROUP TIMING TECHNIQUE

An adaptation of random work sampling is group timing technique (GTT). The difference between random work sampling and GTT is based on the use of a different statistical technique to analyze data collected. Fewer observations are necessary for the same accuracy.

GTT is a work measurement tool that has been useful to study groups of employees at the same time. Unlike time study, which requires one observer to study two to fifteen employees simultaneously, GTT operates by making continual observations of a group at fixed intervals and recording the observations as tally marks on an observation sheet in predetermined categories of activity. A GTT study resembles other work sampling studies because GTT (like all sampling) is based on drawing conclusions about the whole by only looking at a portion of the whole. GTT requires fixed intervals between observations, whereas a work sampling study consists of random intervals between observations.

Some of the advantages of GTT are as follows:

1. A GTT study requires less time and fewer observations than a work sampling technique for a given level of accuracy.

2. One observer can "time" a *group* of employees in a continuous manner, similar to a time study.

3. A more accurate performance rating can be obtained because the observations are continual rather than taken quickly at random.

Disadvantages in using GTT include those listed below:

1. Workload fluctuations are not reflected as in work sampling because a GTT study is usually conducted over a short one- or two-day period.

2. The observation is continual, therefore, the observer is limited to the study of a single situation.

3. Unlike time study or MTM (time and motion), detailed analysis of the job methodology is not determined.

GTT is particularly valuable for studying maintenance activities conducted by crews in which individual members of the crew can be observed simultaneously. GTT is useful in identifying problem areas for future detailed analysis; as a basis to correct allowances for worker fatigue and delay; setting production standards for repetitive activity or for determining correct equipment or personnel requirements.

As with work sampling, the major limitation found in the application of GTT to park maintenance is that much park maintenance work is not done often enough to provide sufficient random sampling opportunities. Therefore, workload/cost tracking or continuous data collection is most appropriate for maintenance work activities that occur less than thirty times in a given year.

Detailed explanation of the correct procedure to follow in initiating a GTT study is presented in *A Guide to Work Sampling Procedures.*[7]

MAINTENANCE WORK SCHEDULES

The key to successful maintenance operations is a carefully planned and faithfully followed work schedule. When developing any maintenance work schedule, the following should be considered: priority of work items, anticipated visitor use, capabilities of maintenance personnel, labor available, season of the year, and availability of materials.

Priority of Work Items

Simply stated, those maintenance jobs most critical to ongoing operations should be scheduled first and the least critical last.

Priorities should be established solely on the basis of critical need and not favoritism. The most effective safeguard against bias and favoritism is a clearly defined priority policy that can be readily understood and easily interpreted by everyone—supervisors, workers, clerks, complainants, foremen, and tradespeople. At least two or, at the most, three priority classes are needed:

1. *Emergency.* Problems that create safety hazards or seriously disrupt recreation operations take preference over all other work. Ruptured water mains, backed-up sewers, or electrical outages require immediate repair.
2. *Routine.* Problems less serious than emergencies are placed into the work schedule on a first-come, first-served basis. With leaking roofs or malfunctioning air conditioners, it may be practical to delay repair so the regular routine or preventive work can continue as scheduled.
3. *Standing.* A miscellaneous category is necessary for (a) shop work not easily assignable to specific work orders, and (b) seasonally recurring jobs that can be performed to level peaks and valleys in the workload schedule.

Anticipated Visitor Use

Priority scheduling should be given to routine maintenance of visitor use areas and facilities during those seasonal periods of greatest use. Major maintenance and new construction generally should be avoided during periods of heavy visitation.

Capabilities of Maintenance Personnel

The capabilities of maintenance personnel are determined by skill, experience, and supervision. The productivity and quality levels of performance are influenced greatly by training and motivation. Only when the maintenance manager thoroughly knows the capabilities of the personnel can he or she organize them into teams or crews and make realistic schedule assignments.

Labor Available

The number and types of maintenance personnel together with the methods of organizing and conducting maintenance work vary considerably from system to system because of variations in size, the character of development, and the intensity of visitor use. Therefore, labor requirements must be carefully calculated as the basis for staffing so as to allow for efficient personnel scheduling.

Season of the Year

Park and recreation maintenance is seasonal. The season of greatest visitor load depends upon the kinds of recreation areas and facilities provided and the section of the country in which these are located. In some areas of the country, cold temperatures, extreme heat, and high levels of precipitation during certain seasons of the year limit the kinds of maintenance and construction work that can be performed during those seasons. Under such circumstances, the work schedule must be carefully planned so that work hours are utilized to the fullest, doing those jobs, both indoor and outdoor, that are not adversely influenced by weather.

Availability of Materials

A variety of maintenance materials must be provided in order to accomplish the work. Too often, materials are not immediately available and thus create a delay in scheduling work. An adequate materials inventory record system is required to provide information on the depletion of materials on hand and to fix responsibility for advance ordering of required stock materials for delivery prior to total depletion.

DAILY MAINTENANCE SCHEDULING

The scheduling of maintenance work involves the sequencing of maintenance jobs according to priority on a *daily planning and schedule form*. Each day's schedule should provide for a full day's work for all craft personnel or maintenance groups with another job waiting upon completion of the previous one.

Depending upon the size of the operation, the daily maintenance work schedule may be developed by the park and/or recreation manager, a maintenance manager, or a group of craft supervisors. The schedule may include both routine and repair maintenance jobs. Routine maintenance job scheduling should be dictated by a detailed annual maintenance plan, while repair orders indicate repair work that must also be scheduled.

The daily planning and schedule form is usually prepared during the afternoon of the previous day to facilitate an immediate start the following work day and also to allow time for review and approval by a superior in a larger organization.

The last job listed on the daily schedule may be underscored or otherwise noted for easy identification of additional jobs that are added to the schedule after appraisal. The purpose of such identification is to allow for investigation to determine the reasons for the breakdown in the daily scheduling process.

Effective job planning and scheduling proceeds from the simple to the complex in direct proportion to the growth of the operation. In a small operation, the manager will "wear" many hats and may be required to develop the maintenance plan, inspect areas and facilities for preventive maintenance, handle maintenance emergencies, establish maintenance priorities, schedule maintenance jobs, supervise maintenance work, participate in actual maintenance work, and rely to a considerable extent upon contractual maintenance service. At the other extreme, in a large, highly organized operation, the manager will function through in-house engineers, supervisors, and crews to accomplish the maintenance function without outside assistance.

COMPUTERIZED MAINTENANCE WORK ORDERING AND SCHEDULING

As the size of the maintenance operation increases, manually establishing efficient work schedules for a large work force becomes an almost impossible task. Contributing to this difficulty are unpredictable variations in visitor use, routine maintenance plan neglect, and various unpredictable crises that occur in random sequence. In addition, increased vehicle fuel costs have made it necessary to sequence jobs so as to minimize travel distance from one job site to another. The human mind simply cannot cope effectively with diverse problems of such complexity on a continuing basis.

MS2, a computerized maintenance scheduling and management system, was devised by Chrystos D. Siderelis at North Carolina State University to cope with such situations.[8]

MAINTENANCE COST ANALYSIS AND CONTROLS

The maintenance operating budget that is soundly established and properly used will provide valuable information regarding changes in conditions and trends. However, it must be recognized that in the absence of sufficient cost analysis and trend analysis, the operating budget, when used for coordination and comparison, is quite incomplete and may well give misinformation. It is only through sufficient cost analysis and trend analysis, which includes the study of cost variations from the normal, that we can determine the true reasons for variations or deviations from the estimated expenditure for each budget item. Such examination serves the purposes of developing more accurate future budgets and also serves as a basis of action to eliminate or change inefficient or undesirable conditions.

Achievement of Maintenance Cost Controls

Park maintenance costs can be controlled if maintenance activity is carefully budgeted before work begins and regulated during the course of maintenance work that is done.

The first step in achieving an adequate maintenance cost control program is the acceptance and application of the following two basic principles:

1. Direct maintenance labor and supervision must be related to definite quantities of measured work.
2. Responsibility for each item of maintenance expense must be assigned to a specific individual.

A program designed to control direct labor and supervisory expense for recreation maintenance requires careful preplanning to ensure that the maintenance activity is carried out on a standardized basis. Only then can a "standard cost" be established and thus provide knowledge of what the work should cost. A comparison of the standard cost and the actual cost of a given maintenance operation may then be determined. The variation or difference between the two represents that part of the total expense that can be controlled.

Cost control of maintenance then is really concerned with the amount of money required for the maintenance operation that is in excess of that which would have been spent to get the work done on a standard basis. The underlying concept in this maintenance cost control approach is to first determine what the work should cost and, knowing this, plan future activities based upon that standard.

Cost Accounting

Considerable effort has gone into the development of methods to determine unit costs of park programs and services. It has been speculated that if adequate cost records are kept, meaningful comparisons between services and facilities can be made on the basis of costs per participant. Unfortunately, cost data relates largely to quantitative aspects of efficiency and not to the qualitative aspects of performance. The most valid application of cost accounting at present is when it is applied to an identical facility, activity, or service. It is only within this realm of identical comparisons that cost accounting has validity.

Cost Record System

Separate cost figures for each function performed by the maintenance division should be recorded, and the cost of each function should be broken down according to an object and a functional classification in the recording of expenditures. If the cost data is to be meaningful and useful, expenditures must be directly related to work accomplished. If this is done, it is necessary to keep separate accounts for each function.

When cost records are kept according to function or separate facilities, the maintenance cost must be recorded for each. It will be necessary to keep record of the time spent on each maintenance job and the materials and supplies used, so that maintenance costs can be charged against each maintenance function and facility.

When maintenance work is accomplished by contract, or when other governmental departments supply maintenance service, the costs must be charged to each function, if not to each facility.

If figures are to tell a true story of the cost of a particular function or facility, they must include all of the cost items involved. Otherwise, the cost data are incomplete, misleading, and valueless for comparative purposes.

Documenting Maintenance Costs

A procedure is needed that will allow for the accurate estimation of maintenance costs of a given program or facility. For such a procedure, there are two possibilities: (1) investigating costs for situations in which no historical cost information exists from comparable programs, and (2) workload/cost tracking that provides historical cost information.

Investigating costs can be accomplished by contacting nearby colleagues in the field who have comparable maintenance requirements, labor, and material costs. Maintenance equipment and materials suppliers can also provide valuable information relative to costs and can often provide equipment use time standards.

Workload/cost tracking systems allow a manager to collect, record, and evaluate information relative to the use and cost of specific programs or facilities.

Siderelis[9] cautions that before any workload/cost tracking system is adopted, careful consideration should be given to *integration of data,* that is, will the tracking system mesh with the informational needs of maintenance managers? This point is relevant to the importance of the cost data produced by the workload/cost tracking system. Cost accounting should identify not only direct costs (variable with volume) but also indirect or overhead (fixed) costs. Examples of direct costs are salaries, employee benefits, lumber, hardware, and utilities. Examples of indirect costs are insurance, data processing, administrative salaries, depreciation for both equipment and facilities, and security patrol costs. A guide to grounds maintenance cost estimating, which includes worksheets for calculating direct and indirect costs for grounds maintenance, has been developed by the Professional Grounds Management Society.[10]

Unit Costs and Standardization

It is true that economy may be effected and unit costs may be decreased through standardization. However, it must be understood that if in effecting economy through standardization the unique values for which the recreation area or facility was initially established are subverted or lost, then the profit or saving means very little. Unfortunately, decisions affecting recreation areas are sometimes made only on the basis of a financial measure, with no test of their influence on the unique characteristics of the particular park or recreation area. There is no substitute for the careful, considered judgment of the park manager who is dedicated to maximizing the total value of the park to the public.

REVIEW QUESTIONS

1. Describe a maintenance impact statement, its purpose, and justification.
2. Outline the steps that should be followed in developing a recreation park maintenance program.
3. Describe the purpose of a descriptive inventory of areas and facilities, indicating the various considerations to be included in such an inventory for maintenance purposes.
4. Describe the advantages to be gained in developing a routine maintenance plan utilizing the table format.
5. Explain the purpose of a work order system.
6. Identify and explain the elements included in an acceptable work order system.
7. Identify three basic personnel organization methods for assigning maintenance work.
8. Describe the several methods available to the maintenance manager to estimate maintenance job time.
9. In the overall job of maintenance work scheduling, describe the techniques that might be utilized to keep track of work backlog.
10. Describe the purpose of preventive maintenance and its source of supporting information.
11. Hiring temporary help, hiring a private contractor, or increasing the labor force permanently are possible remedies to alleviate maintenance and repair work backlog. Cite justifications for each of the three remedies.
12. In developing an effective maintenance work schedule, what factors should be considered as the schedule is being developed?
13. Contrast the purposes, methodology, and appropriate applications of (1) workload/cost tracking, (2) job sampling, and (3) group timing technique (GTT).

14. What is a standard cost for a given maintenance operation and what potential use is a standard cost to the maintenance manager?

15. Describe the purpose of cost accounting and indicate the most valid application of cost accounting at present.

16. What is the greatest potential danger to a particular recreation area or facility when standardization and unit cost comparisons are exclusively relied upon to effect economies?

NOTES

1. USDA Heritage Conservation and Recreation Service, *Maintenance Impact Statement Handbook.* Prepared by the Division of State Planning and Technical Assistance, Pacific Southwest Regional Office, San Francisco, California, 1980.

2. *Park Maintenance Plan* (Ann Arbor, MI: Department of Parks and Recreation, 1981).

3. USDA Forest Service Equipment Development Center. *Cleaning Recreation Sites—An Update* (San Dimas, CA: USDA Forest Service, 1980), 42–44.

4. Chrystos D. Siderelis, "Workload Cost Tracking," *Trends* (Winter 1979): 31–36.

5. State of Pennsylvania, *Park Maintenance Management Manual.* Prepared by the Bureau of Recreation and Conservation, Harrisburg, Pennsylvania, January 1979.

6. Walter W. Erwin, *A Guide to Work Sampling Procedures* (Raleigh, NC: Industrial Extension Service, School of Engineering, North Carolina State University, 1978).

7. Ibid., 67–68.

8. Chrystos D. Siderelis, "Maintenance Scheduling and Management System," *Trends* (Winter 1983): 7–12.

9. Siderelis, "Workload Cost Tracking," 32–36.

10. Professional Grounds Management Society, *Guide to Grounds Maintenance Estimating,* 2d ed. (Pikesville, MD: The Society, 1982).

APPENDIX 2−A

A Sample Maintenance Impact Statement for Landscape Maintenance

PUBLIC SERVICE DEPARTMENT
MAINTENANCE IMPACT STATEMENT
FOR THE RUDGEAR PARK ADDITION PHASE II

Description

Increases present developed area by 2.60 acres, consisting of tennis courts, parking area, picnic area, game court, tables, benches, drinking fountain, turf and associated tree and shrub plantings. Adjoins a park area already intensely used and highly maintained (e.g. ballfield, tot lot etc.).

Expenditure Item

I.   Salaries and Fringe Benefits

    A.   38 mowings—80 hours/year

    B.   Turf Maintenance—23 hours/year

    C.   Landscape Maintenance—199 hours/year

    D.   Irrigation Maintenance—84 hours/year

    E.   Other Maintenance—30 hours/year

        Total: 416 hours/year @ $10.08/hr   = $4,193

    F.   Fringe benefits—30%   = 1,258

        Total salaries/benefits $5,451

II.   Materials and Supplies

    A.   Equipment Usage $ 385

    B.   Materials, supplies, small tools   329

        Total materials/supplies   714

      Total estimated annual maintenance costs $6,165

Date Service to Begin   July 1, 1993

Alternatives/Recommendations

To keep turf maintenance costs down, we have recommended extra paving. (Costs reflect this adjustment.)

    Contract grounds maintenance has been considered and appears cost effective. However, because we expect the area to be intensely used, staffing by full time employees seems wiser. In the interest of public relations, we therefore recommend that funding for the additional full time staff be appropriated, or that full time staff hours be transferred from other less critical sites, (e.g. possibly through greater reliance on contract median maintenance).

APPENDIX 2−B

Sample of Inventory Format—Ann Arbor, Michigan Area and Facility Inventory with Site Map.

BURNS PARK AND SENIOR CENTER

CLASSIFICATION:	Area-wide Park (School/Park)
LOCATION:	Wells and Baldwin (Park);
	1320 Baldwin (Senior Center)
TOTAL ACREAGE:	15.0 Acres (two sites)
DATE COMPILED:	August, 1980

Park Site (14.68 Acres)

Map Key	Facilities/Equipment/Installations	Linear Feet	Area (Square Feet)
1.	*Public Buildings* Maintenance building w/small shelter, water fountain, restrooms (1620 Wells; •F•E•W•)	75 x 35	2,625
2.	*Tennis Courts* 5 Green asphalt courts (no lights) 36 ft nets	221.5 x 120.5	26,690
	1 Practice board w/asphalt half-court	44.5 x 18	800
			27,490
3.	*Hard Surfaced Game Courts* Asphalt basketball court w/2 baskets	73 x 41	2,993

4. *Walks and Trails*

West perimeter	722	x 5	3,610
Surrounding maintenance building	70	x 3.5	245
			3,855

5. *Horticultural and Landscaped Areas*
   None

6. *Playground Equipment*

Woodchipped play area with:	100 ft diameter	6,900
1 wood play structure w/		
1 tire swing		
1 10 ft slide		
1 horizontal ladder		
1 wood tire swing		
1 bounce pad		
1 swing set (3)		
1 tether ball pole		
1 gym climber		
1 set chinning bars (2)		
1 set parallel bars		
1 balance beam		
Sand play area with:	35 x 60	2,100
1 wood play structure w/		
1 wide 8 ft slide		
1 horizontal ladder		
1 wood play structure w/		
1 10 ft slide		
1 horizontal ladder		
1 slide pole		
1 bounce pad		
1 swing set (3)		
Concrete wading pool	60 ft diameter	2,825
(1518 Wells; •W•)		
1 Timberform fountain/play structure		
Miscellaneous play equipment: 2 soccer goals		11,825

7. *Park Roads and Parking Areas*

Asphalt access road (maintenance building)	20 x 300	6,000
Asphalt parking lot (Baldwin St.): 23 spaces	(23) 10 x 45	10,350

1 drive	25	x	30	750
1 turnaround	25	x	15	375

(Does not include 9 spaces
and access to Senior
Center)   17,475

8. *Picnic Areas*
   2 picnic grills   1.0 acre
   2 picnic tables

9. *Ball Diamonds*
   1 60 ft baseball w/backstop
   (16'-16'-16') x 12 ft   13,640
   1 60 ft softball w/backstop
   (0'-10'-0') x 10 ft   5,000
                                                                             18,640

10. *Bridges and Site Amenities*
    7 benches
    5 trash receptacles
    3 wood signs (multiple pieces)
    2 auto gates
    6 single light fixtures
    (5 D.E., 1 P&R)
    4 double light fixtures (P&R)
    2 drinking fountains
    3 water supply

11. *Fencing*
    10 ft chain link fence
    (surrounding tennis courts)   400

12. *Turf Areas of Park Site*
    Total non-turf area:
    83,900 sq. ft (1.93 acres);   13% of total area
    Total turf area:
    555,500 sq. ft (12.75 acres);   87% of total area

13. *Winter Sports*
    Non-supervised sledding   60   x 200   0.4 acres
    Ice hockey rink (on tennis
    courts)   120   x 220   26,400 sq. ft.
    Natural ice rink
    (1224 Baldwin; •W•)   120   x 220   26,400 sq. ft.

Senior Center Site (0.32 Acres)

Map Key	Facilities/Equipment/Installations	Linear Feet	Area (Square Feet)
1.	**Public Buildings**		
	Senior Citizens Center:		
	original	94 x 36	3,384
	addition	30 x 15	450
	Barrier free		
	(1320 Baldwin; •F•E•W•)		3,384
2.	*Tennis Courts*		
	None		
3.	*Hard Surfaced Game Courts*		
	None		
4.	*Walks and Trails*		
	Concrete walk to main		
	entrance	30 x 5	150
	Concrete walk to side		
	entrance	20 x 5	100
			250
5.	*Horticultural and Landscaped Areas*		
	Shrub planters along perimeter of building	6 x 150	900
	Shrub hedge	6 x 40	240
			1,140
6.	*Playground Equipment*		
	None		
7.	*Park Roads and Parking Areas*		
	Asphalt parking lot (Baldwin St.)		
	(Access from Burns Park parking lot)		
	Service ramp	12 x 25	300
8.	*Picnic Areas*		
	None		
9.	*Ball Diamonds*		
	None		

10. *Bridges and Site Amenities*
       1 Single-light fixture (D.E.)

11. *Fencing*
       6 ft wood-slat screen fencing   10 ft

12. *Turf Areas*
       Total non-turf area:
          7,775 sq. ft (0.18 acres);   56% of total area
       Total turf area:
          6,225 sq. ft (0.14 acres);   44% of total area

13. *Winter Sports*
       Non-supervised sledding   60   x 200   0.4 acres
       Ice hockey rink (on tennis
          courts)   120 x 220   26,400 sq. ft.
       Natural ice rink
          (1224 Baldwin; •W•)   120 x 220   26,400 sq. ft.

   Turf Areas for Both Sites:
       Total non-turf area:
          91,675 sq. ft (2.10 acres);   14% of total area
       Total turf area:
          561,725 sq. ft (12.90 acres);   86% of total area

MAINTENANCE STANDARDS SYMBOLS KEY

1. **Public Buildings**
   Class A—Recreation Center
   Class B—Full Service Center
   Class C—Open Shelter
   Class D—Maintenance and
              Miscellaneous Use

2. **Tennis Courts**
   Class A—Tournament
   Class B—Recreation
   Class C—Neighborhood

3. **Hard Surfaced Game Courts**
   Class A—Recreational
   Class B—Neighborhood

4. **Walks and Trails**
   Class A—Hard Surfaced Major
              Routes
   Class B—Hard Surfaced Moderate
              Routes

8. **Picnic Areas**
   Class A—Group Reservation
   Class B—Popular
   Class C—Occasional

9. **Ball Diamonds**
   Class A—Tournament
   Class B—League
   Class C—Neighborhood

10. **Bridges and Site Amenities**
    Class A—Major Circulation Routes
    Class B—Minor Circulation Routes

11. **Fences**
    Class A—Chain Link
    Class B—Woven Wire
    Class C—Temporary
    Class D—Other

Class C—Non-Hard Surfaced Major
    Routes
Class D—Non-Hard Surfaced
    Minor Routes

5. **Horticultural and Landscaped Areas**
Class A—Horticultural Displays/
    Gardens
Class B—Park Landscape
Class C—Natural

6. **Playground Equipment**
Class A—High Use Playgrounds
Class B—Moderate Use
    Playgrounds

7. **Park Roads and Parking Areas**
Hard Surfaced Roads/Lots:
    Class A—Heavy Use
    Class B—Moderate Use
Gravel Roads/Lots:
    Class A—Heavy-Moderate Use
    Class B—Light Use

12. **Turf Areas**
Class A—Premium
Class B—Play
Class C—Field
Class D—Meadow

13. **Winter Sports Areas**
Class A—Sites With Amenities
Class B—Sites With Limited
    Amenities
Class C—Natural Conditions Only

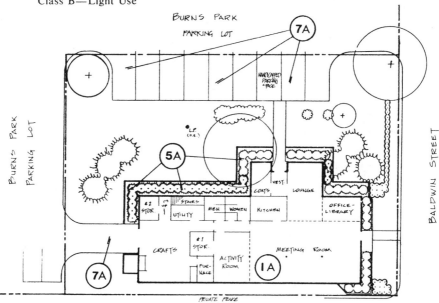

FIGURE 2B-1   Burns Senior Center.

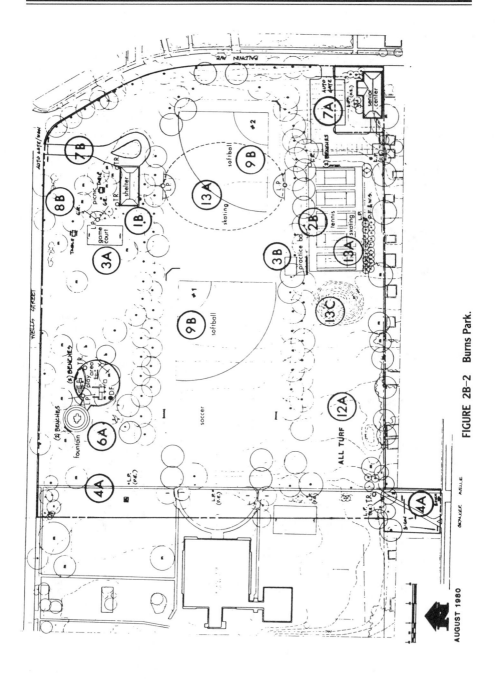

FIGURE 2B-2 Burns Park.

APPENDIX 2−C

Sample Specifications for Exterior Painting of Various Buildings

_____   _____   **PARK/RECREATION SYSTEM**

MAINTENANCE DIVISION   **DATE** _____

SECTION 1 SCOPE OF THE WORK

1-01 The Contractor is to furnish all labor, equipment, materials, and so on, necessary to accomplish the painting of the exterior trim of various buildings as listed on the Bid Proposal Form [page 64], and in strict accordance with these specifications.

1-02 Bidders *must* examine the buildings and acquaint themselves with the exact nature of the work to be done and all the conditions and obstacles likely to be encountered in their performance and completion of the work.

1-03 The submission of a bid shall indicate that the Bidder thoroughly understands the specifications and the scope of the work.

1-04 The Park/Recreation System reserves the right to award a contract on any single bid, or combination of bids, whichever is considered to be in the best interest of the Park/Recreation System.

SECTION II MATERIAL AND WORKMANSHIP

2-01 Storage facilities for the painting contractor will be provided in the buildings if requested by the Contractor and will be designated by the system representative. Generally, the storage of flammable materials within buildings is not permitted for reasons of fire safety. The rooms to be furnished will be such that they may be locked by the Contractor for the protection of equipment and materials. The room must be kept clean and orderly. Oily rags, waste, and the like, must be removed from the building at the close of each working day. Smoking or the use of matches in paint storage space will not be permitted.

Source: A Basic Manual for Physical Plant Administration (Washington, D.C.: The Association of Physical Plant Administrators of Universities and Colleges, 1974), pp. 123-27. Modified and reproduced with permission of the Association of Physical Plant Administrators of Universities and Colleges.

Storage of thinners in the paint storage space *will not be permitted.*

2-02 All materials must be delivered at the job site in factory sealed containers, clearly marked so as to fully identify the contents. Delivery shall be refused if not so shipped.

2-03 No thinners may be added to any manufactured painting material.

2-04 Each coat of paint shall be tinted a different shade from the final approved color. Each coat of paint shall be inspected and approved before succeeding required coats are applied.

Unless otherwise specified, all surfaces to be painted shall be cleaned free of loose paint, blisters, runs, dirt, grease spots, and all scotch tape is to be removed and spots cleaned with Varsol. All protruding nails and similar items are to be "set" or removed. All holes, cracks, or indentations are to be spackled or plaster pointed and sanded smooth. All nail holes and small cracks in the woodwork are to be puttied and sanded smooth.

2-05 All materials must be evenly spread and smoothly flowed on without runs or sags; woodwork to be finished with enamel shall be sanded with fine sandpaper to produce an even, smooth finish.

SECTION III SPECIFICATIONS FOR PAINTING

3-01 In general, all exterior surfaces presently painted shall receive two coats of paint specified. Those areas previously unpainted are not to be painted at this time. This applies particularly to unpainted window guides. These should be given an additional heavy application of linseed oil and painting contractor shall be responsible that all double-hung windows are operable, that is, not painted shut.

3-02 Extreme care shall be taken to adequately prepare all exterior wood and metal surfaces on buildings which are to be re-painted. The woodwork and metalwork should be cleaned and sanded where paint has chipped and blistered. A full-time inspector from the System will be present on this contract work, and work considered to be unsatisfactory must be repainted by the Contractor at no additional expense to the Owner.

3-03   All loose caulking and putty shall be completely removed and replaced with Number M-242 Elastic Glazing Compound as manufactured by the Pecora Paint Company, Inc., Philadelphia, Pennsylvania, or an approved equal.

3-04   All exterior wood surfaces are to receive a good primer or base undercoat and an oil base finish coat. The paint used shall be highest quality white exterior house paint as manufactured by O'Brien, Benjamin Moore, Dutch Boy, or approved equal.

3-05   Paint shall be non-chalking of the variety guaranteed by the manufacturer not to run down and discolor red brick exterior walls.

_____ PARK/RECREATION SYSTEM

(Address)

MAINTENANCE DIVISION _____ Date _____

Gentlemen:

You are invited to submit a proposal for furnishing all labor, equipment, materials, etc., necessary to accomplish the work described in the attached drawings and/or specifications, for the project noted below:

PROJECT NO: _____

PROJECT TITLE: _Exterior Painting of Various Buildings_

LOCATION: _____

ARCHITECT: _____

ENGINEERS: _____

DEPOSIT: _____

BIDS DUE: Time: _____ Date: _____

Bids will be received and publicly opened at the following address:

Bidders must visit the site prior to the submission of a bid, and are requested to contact the individual(s) noted below to arrange for an appointment and to clear up any questions relative to the drawings and/or specifications. The submission of a bid shall indicate the bidder thoroughly understands the drawings and/or specifications, and the scope of the work.

_____ Phone: _____

Bidders must allow sufficient time for all bids, either mailed or hand carried, to reach this office by the date and time indicated for the bid opening. LATE BIDS, including those postmarked prior to the bid opening date, WILL NOT BE CONSIDERED.

Sincerely,

_____ , Manager
                    Maintenance Division

Enclosures

FIGURE 2C-1   Sample bid proposal form.

_____ PARK/RECREATION SYSTEM

_____
(Address)

MAINTENANCE DIVISION _____ Date _____

We propose to furnish all labor, equipment, materials, etc., necessary for EXTERIOR
PAINTING of various buildings of the _____
Park/Recreation System of the _____ of _____
all in accordance with the specifications for the following LUMP SUMS:

BUILDING NUMBER and/or BUILDING NAME	COST	CALENDAR DAYS TO COMPLETE
_____ _____	$_____	_____
_____ _____	$_____	_____
_____ _____	$_____	_____
_____ _____	$_____	_____
_____ _____	$_____	_____
_____ _____	$_____	_____
_____ _____	$_____	_____
_____ _____	$_____	_____
GRAND TOTAL (All Buildings)	$_____	_____

Enclosed with the Proposal is a Bid Bond in the amount of five percent of the total
amount of the above Bid Proposal. It is understood that the Park/Recreation System
reserves the right to award this contract in its entirety, or any portion thereof.

_____
Firm Name

The manufacturers and identifying trade or brand names or numbers of the paints
which we intend to use for the work specified are:

WOODWORK . . . . Base Coat _____
                                        Finish Coat _____
METAL SURFACES. . . . . ._____

FIGURE 2C–2   Bid proposal for exterior painting of buildings.

_____ PARK/RECREATION SYSTEM
Maintenance Division

JOB INSPECTION OF MATERIALS; This requirement is included in order to insure
that the Paint Bid shown in this specification is actually used throughout the job.
Park system inspectors reserve the right to withdraw one gallon of paint at any time
which may be laboratory tested to insure compliance with this requirement of the
specification. Contractors found guilty of substitutes of unapproved materials will be
required to remove all unapproved material and apply that originally approved and
may disqualify themselves in bidding further work for the _____
Park/Recreation System.

Should the Park/Recreation System desire to extend the contract to other work on a
"Time and Material" basis. the following proposal shall apply with overhead and profit
percentages applied separately to the material and labor costs:

FOR MATERIALS: OVERHEAD AND PROFIT TOTAL..... _____%

FOR LABOR:

	PAINTER FOREMAN	PAINTER
Pay Scale..................	S _____/hr.	S _____/hr.
Welfare Benefits	S _____/hr.	S _____/hr.
Social Security	S _____/hr.	S _____/hr.
Insurance	S _____/hr.	S _____/hr.
Overhead & Profit on Labor	S _____/hr.	S _____/hr.
Other Items (Specify)		
_____.....	S _____/hr.	S _____/hr.
_____.....	S _____/hr.	S _____/hr.
_____.....	S _____/hr.	S _____/hr.

TOTAL LABOR CHARGE PER HOUR S _____   S _____

CONTRACTOR'S LICENSE NO.:   Signed: _____

_____   Firm: _____

BID PROPOSAL MUST BE   Address: _____
SUBMITTED IN
TRIPLICATE   Phone: _____

FIGURE 2C-2 _(Continued)._

CHAPTER 3

COMPUTER APPLICATIONS IN PARK MAINTENANCE

Along with the corporate and industrial sectors, the park and recreation profession is experiencing an incredible growth in information and technology. The volume of data and information available is increasing at an overwhelming rate.

As the amount and quality of information increase, the demand for better management and more efficient manipulation of data for planning and monitoring purposes also becomes greater. Therefore, transforming data (facts and records) into meaningful information (statistics, reports, knowledge) is increasingly necessary to ensure better control and accurate predictions within public maintenance operations.[1] More and more, computers are necessary to assist maintenance managers in managing the large quantity of changing information and data that is continually available.

Today, computers are readily available to even the smallest recreation agency or maintenance department. Inexpensive microcomputers, which are extremely simple to operate, can be purchased virtually anywhere. The proliferation of easy-to-use software has also removed most of the difficulty associated with program development. All that is necessary for an agency or department to become computerized is commitment.

The purpose of this chapter is to provide information about a wide variety of management-oriented computer applications that can be implemented in either large or small agencies. Topics that will be discussed include software and hardware selection, basic applications, specific computer applications, and networks and information services.

SOFTWARE AND HARDWARE SELECTION

The selection of appropriate software and hardware is a critical step in ensuring a successful computer operation within an agency or department.

Ideally, an agency should first investigate software when considering the implementation of a particular computer application. The hardware should be selected secondarily because most software will run only on certain types or sizes of hardware. In reality, an agency often has to locate and purchase software that will operate on existing hardware, which in some circumstances may limit alternatives.

Several important concerns should be addressed when considering the purchase of software:

1. Will the software satisfy and provide for current and future needs?
2. Are other agencies using the software and are they satisfied with it?
3. Will the software be adequately supported; are other users satisfied with levels of service?
4. Is the software documented completely?
5. Is there a user's group for developing new applications?[2]

After the most effective software solutions have been determined, examine the hardware on which the appropriate software will run and begin the selection process for necessary components. Primary concerns that should be considered when purchasing hardware include the following:

1. Is it easy for software suppliers to work with?
2. Is the hardware "user friendly?"
3. Is the hardware technology relatively current?
4. Can the hardware be expanded to meet future needs?
5. What is the availability and cost of service?
6. Is the manufacturer financially stable?

BASIC COMPUTER APPLICATIONS

Several common computer applications, while not specifically maintenance-oriented, can be effectively used in park and recreation maintenance operations. Four applications are discussed here.

Word Processing

Word processing is a type of computer program that allows the user to type, record, organize, print, display, and edit documents, letters, and reports. Most word processing programs also permit the user to create files, develop indexes, check spelling and word meanings, set up forms, and perform a wide variety of other functions. Some word processing programs also provide personal services, such as a daily schedule, telephone directory, "to do" list, meeting calendar, and similar functions. Most word processing programs can be easily used by any person who can use a typewriter.

Word processing is useful in large and small maintenance operations. For larger operations, in which administrative assistants or secretaries complete most of the necessary typing, word processing can help those individuals to speed up the processing of documents considerably. In smaller operations, word processing can be used by managers and supervisors directly, thereby eliminating the need to draft letters and reports by hand. This allows the manager and supervisor to become more efficient and also reduces the turn around time for reports, letters, and other documents.

Numerous word processing packages are on the market. Some of the more universally available programs include MICROSOFT WORD, WORDPERFECT, and WORDSTAR. An effective word processing package can be purchased locally.

Spreadsheets

Spreadsheet programs enable users to perform a variety of mathematical functions on the computer. They have proven useful for people in accounting and other aspects of business. They can calculate columns, plan departmental forecasts, and perform many other numbers-based analyses. Spreadsheets are particularly helpful with "what if" questions because numerous scenarios can be quickly developed by changing a few numbers.[3]

Spreadsheets also have an assortment of applications for maintenance managers. Several examples of spreadsheet applications on LOTUS 1-2-3, a widely used packaged software program, are shown in Figures 3–1 through 3–4.

Figure 3–1 shows a sample Change Order Log for a major facility expansion. This spreadsheet is a combination of text and numbers. The use of mathematical formulas in the cells under the "Amount" and "YTD Total" columns causes the total amount to change automatically when an individual amount changes.

An employee performance evaluation in which an employee is rated by three different supervisors is detailed in Figure 3–2. This spreadsheet calculates averages, then automatically multiplies the average rating by a weighting factor to get a total.

Figure 3–3 is an example of a complex budget backup sheet in which employee wages are automatically spread among eight budget functions by using mathematical formulas in appropriate places within the spreadsheet.

An expense fund recap sheet in which balances are calculated automatically is illustrated in Figure 3–4. This function enables the user to update the spreadsheet on a regular basis without having to refigure totals.

Spreadsheets vary tremendously in their range of features and ease of use. One of the most comprehensive and widely used spreadsheet programs is LOTUS 1-2-3. Many other spreadsheet programs are available that have differing capabilities.

Database Management

Database management software programs have a wide range of applications for maintenance managers. They can be used for recordkeeping, but they also can be used effectively as tools for managing projects, monitoring budgets, tracking expenditures, developing forecasts, and many other functions.[4]

FIGURE 3-1 Change order log.

Chg Order Number	Date	Amount	YTD Total	Description	Originator
1	2/27/89	184.80	184.80	replace door hardware	H&R
2	2/27/89	9,459.45	9,644.25	remove unsuitable fill	Hurley
3	3/12/90	9,520.00	19,164.25	add column covers	H&R/Poulos
4	4/20/90	3,759.67	22,923.92	storm drain support	City
5	2/27/89	4,327.00	27,250.92	construct balance tank	H&R/Poulos
TOTAL CHANGE ORDERS			27,250.92		

FIGURE 3-2 Employee performance evaluation.

RATING ITEM	RATING A	RATING B	RATING C	AVERAGE RATING	WTG FACTOR	TOTAL POINTS
PAGE 1						
completes reports and projects	7	6	7	6.67	2.00	13.33
communicates w/ Mgt Board	7	6	6	6.33	2.50	15.83
completes work schedules	6	8	6	6.67	2.00	13.33
maintains records	7	7	7	7.00	4.00	28.00
present new ideas	7	8	8	7.67	2.00	15.33
establish goals and objectives	7	7	7	7.00	2.00	14.00
PAGE 2						
formulate policy and philosophy	7	9	8	8.00	4.00	32.00
develop policies and procedures	8	6	7	7.00	3.00	21.00
develop and revise safety manuals	8	7	7	7.33	5.00	36.67
review and develop statistical data	6	4	6	5.33	0.50	2.67
enforcement of safety rules	6	9	8	7.67	1.50	11.50
investigate accidents	7	9	8	8.00	1.50	12.00
TOTAL JOB RESPONSIBILITY					30.00	215.67

Database programs are used in three major ways to manage data: specific queries, data analysis, and report generation.

Specific Queries

One of the purposes of database management is to rapidly and efficiently retrieve data that meet certain criteria. For example, a maintenance manager wants to know the number of linear feet of paved trails within his or her jurisdiction, or a supervisor needs to know how many tennis nets remain in the department's inventory. Through customized menu-driven screen prompts or simple commands, a database program can quickly search the data and summarize the information from a database file that is designed for particular situations, eliminating paper searches or manual calculations by the user.[5]

Figure 3–5 shows a sample database program that allows a maintenance manager to ask questions about dates and locations for specific work tasks. The

FIGURE 3–3   Budget backup sheet.

FUNCTION/FUND:
LINE ITEM:
ACCT NO: 10 -   - 400/402/406

ELMHURST PARK DISTRICT
FUND SPREAD SHEET
1991-92

ITEM	TOTAL	G&A	FLEET	GRNDS	BLDGS	HORT	GEN	FAC	PI
ADMINISTRATORS									
Employee 1	34,994	34,994							
Employee 2	22,445	22,445							
Employee 3	28,350	2,835		8,505	2,835	2,835	2,835	5,670	2,835
Employee 4	28,733	2,873	1,437	8,620	5,747		1,437	8,620	
SUBTOTAL	114,522	63,147	1,437	17,125	8,582	2,835	4,272	14,290	2,835
BOOKKEEPERS									
Employee 5	6,699	6,699							
Employee 6	7,147	7,147							
SUBTOTAL	13,846	13,846	0	0	0	0	0	0	0
HORTICULTURISTS									
Employee 7	46,377					46,377			
Employee 8	34,951					34,951			
SUBTOTAL	81,328	0	0	0	0	81,328	0	0	0
MAINTENANCE WORKERS									
Employee 9	24,975			12,488	2,498		2,498	7,493	
Employee 10	29,116			11,646	2,912			14,558	
Employee 11	28,193			8,458	5,639		2,819	11,277	
Employee 12	18,575			9,288	1,858		1,858	5,573	
Employee 13	28,349	2,835	2,835	2,835	8,505		2,835	8,505	
Employee 14	19,497			9,749	1,950		1,950	5,849	
Employee 15	21,060			8,424	4,212			8,424	
SUBTOTAL	169,765	2,835	2,835	62,887	27,572	0	11,959	61,678	0
TRADESMEN									
Employee 16	20,610				14,427			6,183	
Employee 17	23,378		1,169		10,520		1,169	10,520	
Employee 18	25,171		22,654	2,517					
SUBTOTAL	69,159	0	23,823	2,517	24,947	0	1,169	16,703	0
TOTAL	448,620	79,828	28,094	82,529	61,100	84,163	17,399	92,671	2,835

manager enters a primary and secondary task code into the computer, and a comprehensive listing of dates and locations is generated.

Data Analysis

Besides their quick retrieval capability, some database programs also manipulate data through counting, grouping, averaging, summing, aggregating, and extrapolating. Such functions allow maintenance managers to do sophisticated types of calculations, projections, and analyses for a selected group of data.[6]

A sample database that can be sorted in a variety of ways is detailed in Figure 3–6. In this example, the database has been sorted by the number of uses (column 4) from highest to lowest. The table could also be rearranged by sorting data in each of the other columns.

FIGURE 3–4 Expense fund recap.

CAPITAL IMPROVEMENT FUND EXPENSE RECAP

PROJECT	LOC	ACCT	1990-91 BUDGET	YTD EXPENSES	PROJECTED EXPENSES	12/31/90 BALANCE
1. TRAILS/PASSIVE ACTIVITIES						
renovate prairie	WMT	900	200	43	0	157
develop exhibit	WMT	901	1,000	267	0	733
remove woody growth	WMT	903	200	0	0	200
replace gazebo	WMT	904	3,500	0	0	3,500
2. FAMILY PLAY/FITNESS						
renovate play area	YC	905-001	40,000	42,293	0	(2,293)
replace swing	CV	905-002	1,300	1,462	0	(162)
renovate W play area	EL	905-003	15,000	17,496	0	(2,496)
replacement parts	MISC	905-010	4,000	3,522	0	478
replace border	MD	906-001	2,084	2,319	0	(235)
replace border	EE	906-003	3,346	3,346	0	0
replace border	SC	906-004	2,723	2,958	0	(235)
replacement timbers		906-009	500	424	0	76
fitness trail repairs	WMT	908	500	5	0	495
3. PICNICKING						
replace tables/grills		916	1,500	3,013	0	(1,513)
4. RACKET GAMES						
repair cracks	BE	919-002	8,000	6,500	0	1,500
replace tennis supplies		919-004	1,500	90	0	1,410
repair lighting systems		919-005	2,000	897	0	1,103
repair tennis fence	BU	919-008	2,000	1,110	0	890
5. DIAMOND SPORTS						
renovate league fields		922-001	2,000	4,892	0	(2,892)
renovate practice fields		922-004	2,000	6,116	0	(4,116)
renovate ballfield	SC	922-005	1,000	334	0	666
renovate backstop area	VV	922-006	500	265	0	235
construct ballfield	BW	922-007	10,000	11,177	0	(1,177)
replace inserts	BE	924-002	600	0	0	600
replace players benches		924-003	400	128	0	272
replace bleacher boards		924-004	600	875	0	(275)
repair lighting systems		924-005	5,000	7,466	0	(2,466)
relamp ballfields	BE	924-006	4,000	1,550	0	2,450
replace backstop 1	BU	924-007	10,000	4,980	0	5,020

FIGURE 3-5 Sample database query.

SUMMARY OF MANHOURS BY DAY AND ACTIVITY

PRIMARY CODE	SECONDARY CODE	DESCRIPTION	LOCATION	DATE	TOTAL MANHOURS
001	0013	Soccer Fields - aerate,overseed	BE	03-31-91	13.00
			BE	04-03-91	16.00
			BE	04-05-91	4.00
			BE	06-28-91	5.00
			BE	06-29-91	14.00
			BE	07-14-91	8.00
			BE	08-30-91	14.00
			BE	08-31-91	4.00
			BE TOTAL		78.00
			BU	04-14-91	4.00
			BU	04-24-91	1.00
			BU	06-30-91	8.00
			BU	08-31-91	4.00
			BU TOTAL		17.00
			EE	07-03-91	4.00
			EE	09-22-91	1.50
			EE	09-26-91	2.00
			EE TOTAL		7.50
			WC	04-05-91	2.50
			WC	07-03-91	4.00
			WC TOTAL		6.50
			PN	04-05-91	2.00
			PN	07-03-91	4.00
			PN TOTAL		6.00
			GRAND TOTAL		115.00

FIGURE 3-6 Sample database analysis.

SUMMARY OF SERVICE AREAS
SORTED BY NUMBER OF USES

Items	(1) Program Revenue $	(2) Operating Expense $	(3) Capital Expense $	(4) No. of Uses	(5) Revenue Per Use $	(6) Cost Per Use $
MISC PARK USE	61,330	571,700	97,764	817,830	0.07	0.82
BASEBALL FIELDS	5,437	62,417	10,287	118,122	0.05	0.62
SWIMMING POOLS	203,244	353,452	91,382	106,615	1.91	4.17
SOCCER FIELDS	3,435	42,702	5,951	82,156	0.04	0.59
BUILDINGS	21,130	208,728	27,795	70,847	0.30	3.34
TENNIS COURTS	1,653	19,594	17,978	51,192	0.03	0.73
GREENHOUSE	15,370	132,966	8,262	38,424	0.40	3.68
LAGOON	252	2,392	0	29,800	0.01	0.08
FORMAL GARDENS	1,977	20,468	0	28,800	0.07	0.71
DEPOT FOUNTAIN	727	8,420	0	17,300	0.04	0.49

Report Generation

Most database programs can develop management reports that summarize complicated data into a two-dimensional table format. Depending on the type of report and its subject, content, and audience, a management report can be classified as assembled or analytical.

Assembled reports simply compile, calculate, and summarize raw data, such as budget expenditures, project progress, and inventory counts. *Analytical reports* represent more significant types of information through data comparisons, trend forecasts, and expenditure projections.[7]

Figure 3–7 illustrates the type of report that can be generated by a typical database management program. A wide variety of database management programs are available. One of the most widely used is dBASE.

Graphics

Of the four basic computer applications discussed here, graphics may be the least useful to maintenance managers. A tremendous variety of graphics programs are available, with a wide range of features and applications. One of the most common applications is the development of charts, graphs, and tables. For many of the graphics packages, special printers, plotters, and storage capabilities are needed. A sample of one type of graph that can be developed on many of the available software programs is illustrated in Figure 3–8.

SPECIFIC COMPUTER APPLICATIONS

In addition to the basic applications discussed in the previous section, many specialized computer programs are available to recreation professionals and maintenance managers. Several of the most useful applications are described below.

FIGURE 3–7 Sample database report.

OPEN WORK ORDER REPORT   MAY 1991

ORDER NUMBER	PRIORITY	REQUEST DATE	DUE DATE	TYPE	LOCATION	TASK DESCRIPTION
814	2	10-17-89		GC	CV	raise catch basin by hydrant
938	2	01-19-90		LA	BE	remove stumps in picnic area 4
1342	1	07-28-90		CA	BE	repair bathroom door closer
1495	2	10-31-90		GC	WM	barricade trail entrance
1497	2	10-31-90		LA	GL	remove lilacs
1588	1	02-06-91	06-17-91	CA	GH	rebuild polyhouse west wall
1611	1	03-20-91		GC	CF	remove metal edging

FIGURE 3-8   Sample graph.

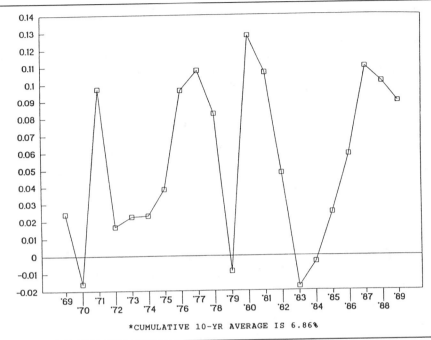

*CUMULATIVE 10-YR AVERAGE IS 6.86%

Maintenance Management

Maintenance management is a critical function to the recreation professional and one that should be initiated by every public agency. A properly designed maintenance management system should benefit managers in many ways, especially in planning, scheduling, and decision making. Customized and packaged software programs are available. These programs include such features as labor and cost tracking, inventory control, work scheduling, work order development, and monitoring of items such as overtime, vandalism, and employee leaves.

Maintenance management programs are usually database management programs that will organize, store, retrieve, and sort information in standardized formats. Many maintenance management programs also will manage information about the inventories of commodities, such as equipment, supplies, and parts.[8]

Some maintenance management programs are capable of developing work orders and schedules. A few generate alternative schedules, which consider elements such as weather, available personnel, and equipment breakdowns, and allow the supervisor to choose among the various schedules. The major benefit of work order generation is that routine tasks can be entered into the computer for retrieval at the appropriate time without the danger of losing, forgetting, or overlooking some necessary job.

An important benefit of using a maintenance management program is that it provides the ability to develop performance standards. The program may enable managers to identify sectors of high and low productivity within their department and to establish standards for productivity. Furthermore, by providing a method of accounting for the number of hours and amount of materials historically associated with various tasks, maintenance managers can relate budgetary constraints to levels of service and plan schedules in advance.[9]

Figures 3–9 through 3–12 are examples of the types of reports that can be generated by a maintenance management program. Figures 3–9 and 3–10 illustrate two different types of labor tracking reports: 3–9 shows task projections and accomplishment and 3–10 tracks personnel. Figures 3–11 and 3–12 show two types of work orders that can be generated by maintenance management programs.

Project Management

Most maintenance managers have, at one time or another, been involved with the planning, monitoring, and implementation of a major design, development, or construction project. Project management is a computer application that is now available to managers.

FIGURE 3–9   Maintenance management system report, no 1.

```
                        E L M H U R S T   P A R K   D I S T R I C T
                              PMMS MONTH END REPORT NUMBER 3
                        M A N H O U R S   B Y   P R I M A R Y   T A S K
          CURRENT PERIOD 7                                                    PAGE 1

                                         MONTHLY    MONTHLY      YTD        YTD
          CODE         T A S K          PROJECTED   ACTUAL   PROJECTED    ACTUAL

          001   ATHLETIC FIELD MTC          464.00   564.00   1,824.00   1,950.50
          002   WALK MAINTENANCE             16.00     4.00     160.00      40.50
          003   PARKING LOT AND ROAD MTC     24.00    13.00     210.00     146.50
          004   TENNIS COURT MAINTENANCE     70.00    38.00     317.00     126.50
          005   PLAY AREA MAINTENANCE        76.00   213.00     382.00     613.00
          006   FOUNTAIN AND HYDRANT MTC     32.00    37.50      94.00      88.00
          007   MISCELLANEOUS FACILITY MTC   86.00   225.00     589.00     557.50
          008   ICE RINK AND SLED HILL MTC    0.00     0.00     255.00     727.00
          009   PARK MOWING                 960.00   792.50   2,910.00   3,269.00
          010   TURF AREA MAINTENANCE        88.00    89.00     240.00     346.00
          011   SHRUB MAINTENANCE           326.00   246.50     801.00     734.50
          012   TREE MAINTENANCE            242.00   428.00     745.00   1,101.50
          013   BUILDING MAINTENANCE        395.00   149.50   1,593.00   1,153.50
          014   OFF-SEASON POOL MAINTENANCE  50.00     0.00   1,802.00   1,991.50
          015   SEASONAL POOL MAINTENANCE   184.00   154.50     360.00     313.00
          017   BICENTENNIAL FOUNTAIN MTC    41.00    15.00     164.00     295.50
          019   GREENHOUSE & CONSERVATORY MTC 485.00  352.00   2,404.00   2,264.50
          020   FLOWER BED MAINTENANCE       58.00   169.50     406.00     504.50
          021   FORMAL GARDEN MAINTENANCE   108.00   150.00     456.00     562.00
          022   EQUIPMENT REPAIRS           170.00    98.50     945.00     850.00
          023   PREVENTATIVE EQUIPMENT MTC  110.00    63.50     670.00     763.00
          024   ALL PARKS MAINTENANCE       696.00   647.00   2,692.00   2,813.50
          025   MAINTENANCE CENTER MAINTENANCE 202.00 186.00   1,202.00   1,044.50
          026   MISCELLANEOUS MAINTENANCE   180.00    99.50     477.00     443.00
          027   ADMINISTRATION AND TRAINING  78.00    58.50     761.00     823.50

                         **** TOTAL  5,141.00  4,794.00  22,459.00  23,522.50
```

FIGURE 3-10   Maintenance management system report, no 2.

```
                            ELMHURST  PARK  DISTRICT
                            PMMS MONTH END REPORT NUMBER 4
                    BREAKDOWN  OF  AVAILABLE  MANHOURS
   08-01-91   CURRENT PERIOD 07

                                 MONTHLY    MONTHLY      YTD        YTD
              TYPE OF LABOR       PROJECTED  ACTUAL     PROJECTED  ACTUAL

      091     REGULAR LABOR         2,038.00  1,747.50  14,740.00  13,643.00
      092     CETA LABOR              213.00    420.50     582.00     990.00
      094     SEASONAL AND PART TIME LABOR  3,028.00  2,817.50   8,224.00   9,024.00
      095     OVERTIME LABOR           62.00     71.00     662.00     790.00
      096     VACATION LEAVE          338.00    262.50   1,149.00   1,204.00
      097     SICK LEAVE               45.00    205.50     296.00     535.00
      098     OTHER LEAVE             149.00    359.50     681.00   1,623.50

                      **** TOTAL   5,873.00  5,884.00  26,334.00  27,809.50
```

Project management programs give managers the ability to list and sequence activities; establish completion dates; and track costs, resources, and personnel. Some programs offer the Program Evaluation and Review Technique (PERT) and/or Gantt charts, which are helpful in planning projects that require the monitoring of sequential, dependent, or concurrent activities. Some examples of projects that require extensive planning, and for which project management programs could be used, include planning a referendum or a major park renovation, development of a play area, or constructing a building or facility.[10] Some of the more widely used project management programs are TIMELINE, HARVARD TPM, INSTAPLAN, MICROSOFT PROJECT, and SUPERPROJECT.[11]

Vehicle and Equipment Maintenance

Because of the large number of businesses that use vehicle fleets (UPS, Federal Express, trucking companies) and the increasing need for more efficient fleet management, computerized vehicle and equipment maintenance programs have proliferated recently. Some of the more notable applications available to maintenance managers include maintenance scheduling, gasoline consumption and management, vehicle replacement schedules, and equipment inventories and histories.

Preventive Maintenance Scheduling

One of the more important fleet management applications involves the development of preventive maintenance standards and schedules for both vehicles and equipment. Standards can be developed for each individual vehicle or groups of similar vehicles. Simple schedules that indicate the month or week a vehicle is due for servicing can be developed, as well as more complex schedules that detail specific tasks, repairs, and parts. Many programs also have the capability to print preventive maintenance work orders.[12]

Other available features can assist the maintenance manager in controlling fleet maintenance budgets, component costs, parts and labor costs, inspection schedules, inventory levels, and productivity. Figure 3–13 illustrates a simple preventive maintenance standards and schedule outline.

Gasoline Consumption and Management

Many of the fleet management programs track gasoline consumption and mileage for vehicles and equipment. Where turnkey gasoline monitoring systems are used, gasoline reports are generated automatically. However, if an agency does not have access to a computerized gasoline monitoring system, a simple spreadsheet can be developed easily. A gasoline monitoring spreadsheet is shown in Figure 3–14.

FIGURE 3–11 Sample work order, no. 1.

```
          WORK   ORDER  —  1177
                  REPRINT


   MAJOR CODE      RAN32    RAND PARK POOL
   EQUIPMENT CODE  POO
   PART NUMBER     XX       RAND POOL-SEASONAL
   JOB NUMBER      13       OPENING CHECKLIST

   SCHEDULED DATE  05/01/91              FREQUENCY  Y01   USER CODE
   LAST SCHEDULED MAINTENANCE           LAST UNSCHEDULED MAINTENANCE

   INSTRUCTIONS:    <MODE  1 >
      ..........................................................
      CHECK THE FOLLOWING LIST OF ITEMS AND INDICATE THOSE THAT HAVE
      BEEN COMPLETED. MAKE SURE THAT ITEMS 1 AND 2 HAVE BEEN DONE
      BEFORE PROCEEDING.
      .........................$................................
      1. ..... EMERGENCY BOX
      2. ..... FIRST AID SUPPLIES
      ..........................................................
      ..... SIGNS ATTACHED AND IN PLACE
      ..... COIN LOCKERS REPAIRED AND OPERATIVE
      ..... POOL DRAINED AND CLEANED
      ..... POOL PAINTED
      ..... FILTRATION SYSTEM CHECKED AND OPERATING
      ..... CHLORINE IN USE
      ..... POOL DECK CHECKED AND CRACKS REPAIRED
      ..... POOL BENCHES CHECKED
      ..... POOL BENCHES PAINTED
      ..... DIVING BOARDS INSTALLED
      ..... GUARD CHAIRS CHECKED AND REPAIRED
      ..... SHOWER AREA CLEANED AND REPAIRED
      ..... CHECK "DEPTH AND NO DIVING" MARKING
      ..... POOL CHEMICALS IN STORAGE ROOM
      ..... VACUUM POOL UNTIL CLEAN
      ..... CHECK POOL SAFETY EQUIPMENT
            ..... TWO PAIRS OF STEEL TOED BOOTS (POOL OFFICE)
            ..... SAFETY MASK, SAFETY GOGGLES   (EQUIP ROOM)
            ..... RUBBER APRON               ( "      " )
            ..... PAIR RUBBER GLOVES
            ..... ONE BUCKET (RAND CHLORINE ROOM)
```

FIGURE 3–12 Sample work order, no. 2.

```
            WORK  ORDER  —  308
                    REPRINT


BLUETT/ON POLE BY RINK
======================

MAJOR CODE        BLU18      ELECTRICAL PANEL 1, BOX 1
EQUIPMENT CODE    001        ELECT. PANEL 1, BOX 1
PART NUMBER       XX
JOB NUMBER        01         ELECTRICAL PANEL S&I

SCHEDULED DATE   09/15/91           FREQUENCY  Y01    USER CODE
LAST SCHEDULED MAINTENANCE          LAST UNSCHEDULED MAINTENANCE

INSTRUCTIONS:     < MODE  1 >
        ********   PERFORM THE FOLLOWING SERVICES AND   ***************
        ***************   CHECK OFF WHEN COMPLETE    ********************
        *******************************************************************
        1. CHECK FOR BURNED WIRES
        2. CHECK WIRE NUTS
        3. TIGHTEN LOOSE CONDDUIT AND BX CONNECTORS
        4. INSTALL SLOT CAPS ON EMPTY BREAKER SLOTS
        5. TIGHTEN SERVICE BAR SCREWS
        6. TIGHTEN ALL BREAKER SCREWS
        7. TIGHTEN ALL NEUTRAL BARS & SCREWS
        8. TIGHTEN DOOR
        9. TIGHTEN PANEL FACE
        DATE OF INSPECTION
        NAME OF INSPECTOR
        INSTRUCTIONS NO  (YES/NO)
        ADDITIONAL NOTES
        *
        *
        *
        *
```

Vehicle and Equipment Replacement Schedules

Replacement schedules for vehicles and equipment may be generated by a fleet management program or can be developed on a spreadsheet. Figure 3–15 illustrates a simple vehicle and equipment replacement schedule.

Vehicle and Equipment Inventories and Histories

If not part of a fleet management package, a database that lists important data for each vehicle and major piece of equipment is relatively easy to develop. Figure 3–16 shows a sample inventory. One way in which vehicle and equipment histories can be maintained on the computer is shown in Figure 3–17.

Building and Facility Maintenance

Many of the computer applications previously described, including preventive maintenance scheduling, energy management, replacement schedules, and inventories and histories, also function for buildings and facilities.

FIGURE 3–13 Preventive maintenance standard and schedule.

PREVENTIVE VEHICLE MAINTENANCE STANDARDS

VEH NO	VEHICLE OR EQUIPMENT	TYPE OF REPAIR	MH NEEDED	FREQUENCY	1990 STANDARD	1990 ACTUAL	1991 STANDARD
01	1973 Ford 2000 Tractor	PM	4	2/year	8 MH	9 MH	8 MH
02	1989 Chevrolet Cavalier	PM	2	4/year	8 MH	13 MH	8 MH
03	1990 Ford Dump Truck	PM	6	4/year	24 MH	21 MH	24 MH
04	1986 Toro Parkmaster	PM	6	7/year	42 MH	48 MH	42 MH
05	1991 Ford Pickup	PM	4	4/year	16 MH	15 MH	16 MH

PREVENTIVE VEHICLE MAINTENANCE SCHEDULE

VEHICLE OR EQUIPMENT	JAN	FEB	MAR	APR	MAY	JUN	JUL	AUG	SEP	OCT	NOV	DEC	TOTAL
1973 Ford 2000 Tractor			4								4		8
1989 Chevrolet Cavalier	2			2			2			2			8
1990 Ford Dump Truck	6				6			6			6		24
1986 Toro Parkmaster				6	6	6	6	6	6	6			42
1991 Ford Pickup			4			4			4			4	16

FIGURE 3–14 Gasoline monitoring spreadsheet.

Preventive Maintenance Scheduling

Major buildings and facilities present maintenance managers with the same types of problems, albeit on a smaller scale, as those encountered in the entire park system. Because the problems are similar, the approach to maintaining a major building or facility should be the same as well.

FIGURE 3–15 Vehicle and equipment replacement schedule.

EQUIPMENT AND REPLACEMENT
COST PROJECTIONS

PREPARED 1991

EQUIPMENT DESCRIPTION	YEAR PURCHASED	AGE AT REPLACMT	1992/1993	1993/1994	1994/1995	1995/1996	1996/1997	1997/1998	1998/1999	1999/2000	2000/2001	2001/2002	2002/2003	LINE ITEM TOTALS
FORD 3000 TRACTOR W/LOADER	1963	27 YRS	20,000										35,000	83,000
10' BACKHOE (PURCHASE)			10,000										18,000	28,000
FORD VAN	1981	11 YRS	25,000					35,000					49,000	109,000
FORD RANGER	1985	7 YRS	18,000					25,000					35,000	78,000
CHEVY STAKE BED TRUCK	1987	6 YRS		21,000					29,500					50,500
CHEVY 4X4 TRUCK	1988	5 YRS		23,000					32,000					55,000
DETACHABLE HIGH LIFT (PURCHASE)				16,500										16,500
PARK POLICE CAR	1991	3 YRS			14,000			17,000			20,000			51,000
PARKS CAR (1988 CAPRICE)*													20,000	0.00
AIR COMPRESSER (PURCHASE)						16,000								16,000
WELDER GENERATOR (PURCHASE)						10,000								10,000
TURF SPRAYER						8,500								8,500
FORD 300 TRACTOR	1960	34 YRS				26,500								26,500
CHEVY UTILITY TRUCK	1974	21 YRS				19,500					27,500			47,000
FORD TAURUS WAGON	1990	4 YRS				17,200				22,500				39,700
CHEVY DUMP TRUCK	1991	4 YRS					41,000							41,000
FORD 445 TRACTOR W/LOADER	1987	10 YRS						37,000						37,000
72 " TORO MOWER	1987	10 YRS							19,500					19,500
10' MOWING TRAILER	1991	7 YRS							5,000					5,000
CHIPPER	1990	10 YRS									12,500			12,500
			81,000	60,500	48,500	63,200	41,000	114,000	86,000	22,500	60,000	0.00	157,000	733,700
														0.00
FORD BUS	1991	3 YRS					62,000					87,000		145,000
TOTAL			81,000	60,500	48,500	63,200	103,000	114,000	86,000	22,500	60,000	87,000	157,000	882,700

* NOTE PARKS CAR TO BE REPLACED BY POLICE CAR

FIGURE 3–16 Vehicle and equipment inventory.

PAGE: 2   EQUIPMENT LIST   91-08-08

CONTROL #	DESCRIPTION	SYSTEM	MANUFACTURER	MAKE\MODEL	SERIAL NO.	FACILITY	FLR/ROOM
42905745	Line Trimmer	Sm. equipment	Echo			Parks	Open area
43005763	Roto Tiller	Sm. equipment	Toro			Parks	Open area
43105753	Water Pump	Sm. equipment		1 1\2"		Parks	Open area
43205762	2 Gas powered Edgers	Sm. equipment				Parks	Open area
43305760	Line Marker (old)	Sm. equipment		1 cyl		Parks	Open area
43405748	Hydraulic Auger	Sm. equipment		3pt Hitch		Parks	Open area
43501435	Centrifugal gas pump	Sm. equipment		3" 8hp		Parks	Open area
43605758	Pressure Washer	Sm. equipment	Hotsy			Parks	Open area
43701409	Blower	Sm. equipment	Echo	backpack		Parks	Open area
43805600	Gas Trash Pump	Sm. equipment				Parks	Open area
43906959	PeecoVac gas powered	Sm. equipment				Parks	Open area
44005755	3 gang Mower	Sm. equipment	Roseman	3pt hitch		Parks	Open space
44105719	300 gal. Sprayer	Sm. equipment	Clark			Parks	Open space
44205759	36" mower	Sm. equipment	Bobcat	walk behind		Parks	Open space
443	7' sweepster Broom	Sm. equipment		HF		Parks	Open space
50106932	Rotary mower	Lg. equipment	Alamo			Parks	Open space
50201690	Parkmaster Mower	Lg. equipment	Toro			Parks	Open space
50305741	Backhoe Tractor	Lg. equipment	John Deere	310C		Parks	Open space
50405747	Bucket Tractor	Lg. equipment	John Deere	401B		Parks	Open space
50505739	Lowboy Tractor	Lg. equipment	John Deere	301		Parks	Open space
50605742	Kubota w\gill	Lg. equipment	Kubota	6200		Parks	Open space
50805736	Air Compressor	Lg. equipment	Sullair	185		Parks	Open space
50905737	Crawler Tractor	Lg. equipment	John Deere			Parks	Open space
51005731	Ice Resurfacer	Lg. equipment	Zamboni			Parks	Open space
51105733	Utility Trailer	Lg. equipment		Single Axle		Parks	Open space
51205734	Utility Trailer	Lg. equipment		Tandem Axle		Parks	Open space
51305735	Equip. Trailer med.	Lg. equipment		Tandem Axle		Parks	Open space
51405730	Float Trailer	Lg. equipment				Parks	Open space
516	Eq. trailer\water Hv	Lg. equipment		Tandem Axle		Parks	Open space
517	Sm. Lt. duty trailer	Lg. equipment		Field Lining		Parks	Open space
51806928	Enclosed Trailer	Lg. equipment	Pace			Parks	Open space
60106861	89 Chev Wagon	Car	Chevrolet	Caprice Wagon	1G1BN81Y8KA1277	Golf	Open area
60206885	89 Chev. Pick up	Truck	Chevrolet	Pick Up 2wd	1GCGC24K9KE2081	Golf	Open area
60306882	89 GMC Pickup	Truck	GMC	Pick up 4wd	1GTGK24K6KE5325	Golf	Open area

FIGURE 3–17   Vehicle and equipment history.

```
1981 FORD VAN

Date        Mileage      Type of Service

09/11/85                 Replaced tires.
10/10/85    18,569       Oil and lube, air filter.
10/22/85                 Replaced front brakes, drum and front
                         shocks, set front pads, set rear shoes,
                         replaced wiper blades.
05/01/86    20,361       Oil and lube, air filter.
06/05/86                 Replaced master cylinder, bumper bolt.
12/18/86    22,706       New tires.
01/23/87                 Tune up.
02/10/87                 Oil and lube, air filter, checked
                         cooling system.
09/06/88                 Oil and lube, air filter, tune up,
                         checked cooling system, fixed oil leak.
10/28/88                 Flushed radiator, added antifreeze,
                         checked brakes.
02/23/89    30,000       Oil and lube, checked cooling system.
04/12/89    30,130       Welded exhaust pipe into exhaust to fix
                         leak.
10/17/89    32,078       All fluids checked out o.k., anti-freeze
                         needs, drain, flushed and filled.
12/14/89    32,305
03/01/90    32,680       Replaced choke unloader and vacuum line
                         from carburetor to vacuum advance on
                         distributor.  Tire repair-right rear.
03/03/90    32,701       Oil change, Oil filter and lube.
                         Checked air filter.  Left kingpin needs
                         rebuilding.
04/10/90    32,903       Mileage check.
05/04/90    33,089       Mileage check.
07/18/90    34,032       Mileage check, replaced master cylinder.
```

The city of Evanston, Illinois, has developed a comprehensive, easy-to-use, preventive maintenance program for buildings and, in particular, for equipment such as HVAC systems, pumps, and motors. The program runs on an Apple IIe and uses DB Master software.[13]

Evanston's program enables a manager to schedule preventive maintenance and print work orders. It can also print equipment labels to be placed on each piece of equipment so that maintenance personnel know that they are working on the right piece of equipment. The program also generates a combined work history report for each piece of equipment. Figure 3–18 is an example of the type of work order that can be produced by the Evanston program.

Energy Management

Several computerized energy management programs on the market enable a maintenance manager to control HVAC, lighting, and other electrical systems within a major building or facility.

Most of these systems are extremely complex and difficult and costly to install and use. For this reason, energy management systems are primarily effective in large buildings (community center, maintenance center) or major facilities (ice rink, tennis/racquetball complex) which contain many HVAC, lighting, and electrical systems that require management.

Programs can be designed to turn on and off electrical systems, pumps, and motors; cycle systems to make the most efficient use of energy; operate HVAC systems when temperatures are appropriate; and monitor energy usage in all systems.

Plant Management

Another interesting specialized computer application available to maintenance managers involves the management of large numbers of trees and other plant materials. Agencies that have responsibility for street trees, manage a nursery, or operate a greenhouse and conservatory may find these types of programs useful.

The Maryland National Capital Parks and Planning Commission has developed a computerized plant management program with a wide range of capabilities. The program uses a database that enables managers to organize and monitor the inventory in an eighty-five-acre nursery.[14]

FIGURE 3–18   **Preventive equipment maintenance work order.**

```
              CITY OF EVANSTON    PREVENTIVE MAINTENANCE PROGRAM

    SERVICE CENTER       REF.#:07-A027  HVAC            WORK TO BE DONE
    A/C FLT SRVCS OFFICE LOWER ROOF N SIDE        1.CHECK PROPER OPERATION
    MANF:TRANE CO.             PRT#:RAUC-504-B.   2.CLEAN UNIT    5
    SER#:C81-G-23855     FIL:                     3.CHECK OIL LEVEL IN COMP.
    REM:PART # 169-834-IC COMPRES LUB:            4.CHECK TEMP. DIFF. AT COIL
                               BELT:              5.FREON LEVEL, SIGHT GAUGE
    DATE:_____TIME:_____COST:_____       6.


    SERVICE CENTER       REF.#:07-B024  HVAC            WORK TO BE DONE
    A.C.                 N SIDE ON UPPER ROOF     1.CHECK PROPER OPERATION
    MANF:TRANE               PRT#:RAUA-4004-RD.   2.CLEAN UNIT   17
    SER#:J81-H24339      FIL:NONE                 3.CHECK COMP. OIL LEVEL
    REM:FOR AHUB5             LUB:NONE            4.CHECK TEMP.DIFF AT COIL
    40 TON                   BELT:               5.FREON LEVEL, SIGHT GAUGE
    DATE:_____TIME:_____COST:_____       6.


    SERVICE CENTER       REF.#:07-C043  HVAC            WORK TO BE DONE
    A.C.FOR APT.E SIDE   APARTMENT ROOF           1.CHECK PROPER OPERATION
    MANF:TRANE               PRT#:RAUC-202-A      2.CLEAN UNIT   17
    SER#:C 81G-23492     FIL:NONE                 3.CHECK FREON LEVEL
    REM:TYPE #169-717-1C.    LUB:NONE            4.CHECK TEMP. DIFF. AT COIL
                             BELT:               5.
    DATE:_____TIME:_____COST:_____       6.


    SERVICE CENTER       REF.#:07-C044  HVAC            WORK TO BE DONE
    EXHAUST FAN          APARTMENT ROOF           1.CHECK PROPER OPERATION
    MANF:GREEN-HECK          PRT#:G 60DX          2.CLEAN UNIT   17
    SER#:EFC-1           FIL:NONE                 3.
    REM:                     LUB:NONE            4.
                             BELT:               5.
    DATE:_____TIME:_____COST:_____       6.
```

Other organizations have developed database programs that enable a manager to monitor and track information about park and street trees. These programs can manage tree inventory data; record work conducted on trees; track service requests; numerically summarize tree inventory data, work history data, and service requests data; and generate listings of trees (hazardous trees, diseased trees, pest trees), and sometimes computer map tree locations.[15]

Computer-Aided Design

Computer-aided design (CAD) programs may be particularly beneficial to designers and draftsmen. Packaged software programs with a wide range of capabilities are currently on the market. In general, CAD programs permit a designer to create consistent, accurate, easy-to-read drawings. Some of the more interesting applications enable a maintenance manager to create and revise drawings; store drawings and plans for later use; scale and dimension all or part of any drawing; copy all or part of a drawing quickly; annotate drawings with a variety of text styles; plot drawings in any size or scale; and create, revise, and plot in layers.

For the most part, CAD programs are complex and expensive. The need for special hardware components, including enhanced memory, math co-processor, digitizers, and plotters, also add to the cost.

NETWORKS AND COMPUTER INFORMATION SERVICES

In addition to basic applications and specific software programs, another excellent source of information and assistance for the maintenance manager is a number of specialized computer networks and information services.

One of the more applicable computer networks for recreation professionals is NRPA/SCHOLE, developed by the National Recreation and Park Association in cooperation with Boston University. NRPA/SCHOLE is an interactive information network that links people and information by computer. The network is designed specifically for the park, recreation, and leisure service community and includes features such as electronic mail, updates on legislation and public policy, national employment bulletins, and the ability to choose and order appropriate items. LOGIN or Local Government Information Network is another information network with applications for public agencies.

An example of an information service is the Turfgrass Information File, compiled and maintained by Michigan State University in cooperation with the Golf Course Superintendents Association of America. This service provides computer-based bibliographical access to published materials on turfgrass research and management.

Another example of an information service is a microcomputer software clearinghouse developed by the University of Maryland's Institute for Governmental Service with a grant from the W. K. Kellogg Foundation. The institute surveys, reviews, and distributes information about microcomputer application software developed by vendors, governmental agencies, and individuals, as well as programs in the public domain.[16]

Finally, the Natural Resources Computer Newsletter (NARCON) is another source of specialized information about a wide range of natural resource-oriented topics. NARCON is available to subscribers for a nominal fee.

CONCLUSIONS

The computer applications described in this chapter represent only the tip of the iceberg. There are literally thousands of computer-related programs and services that can benefit maintenance managers and recreation professionals.

It is hoped that this brief exposure to some of these applications will encourage maintenance managers to consider their needs and circumstances, resources and capabilities, and the ways in which computers might benefit their departments and agencies.

REVIEW QUESTIONS

1. What is the practical value of computers for the maintenance manager?
2. What is the major justification for the belief that in establishing a computerized maintenance system, software should be selected first and hardware second?
3. For what purposes can word processing be used in maintenance operations?
4. What are the names of some of the more common word processing software packages?
5. For what purposes can the spreadsheet be used in maintenance operations?
6. For what purposes can database software programs be used in maintenance operations?
7. Identify and briefly describe some of the more notable computerized applications available to maintenance managers for vehicle and equipment maintenance.
8. Briefly describe the benefits of Computer-Aided Design (CAD) programs and what they accomplish for the park and recreation planner.

NOTES

1. Paul W. Chan, "The Advantages of Microcomputer Database Management," *Public Works* 117 (February 1986): 46–47.

2. A. J. Klawitter, "Benefits of Computer Information Systems." Paper presented at the Illinois Park and Recreation Conference, Rosemont, Illinois, November 1986.

3. Marilyn Ballas, "Spreadsheets: The Simple to the Sublime," *Shareware* 4, no. 2 (April/May 1989): 6–7, 38–43.

4. Chan, "Microcomputer Database Management."

5. Ibid.

6. Ibid.

7. Ibid.

8. American Public Works Association Research Foundation, "Making Full Use of Microcomputers in Public Works," *Public Works* (February 1987): 52–54.

9. Ibid.

10. Stephen Gonzalez, "Let Your Computer Simplify Project Management Tasks," *Illinois Parks and Recreation* (September/October 1988): 47–51.

11. Mike Heck, "Project Management Programs for Executives," *Info World* (May 23, 1988): 47–59.

12. "Software Selection," *Fleet Equipment* 14, no. 10 (October 1988): 53–61.

13. Ibid.

14. Carl Hahn, et al., "Automated Plant Management Systems: Plant Material, Nursery, and Botanical Garden Management," *Proceedings of the National Workshop on Computers in Recreation and Parks* (Alexandria, VA: National Recreation and Park Association, 1982): 153–154.

15. Nancy Michaelson, "Urban Tree Management Programs," *Natural Resources Computer Newsletter* 3, no. 4 (May 1988): 10–11.

16. American Public Works Association Survey, "Microcomputer Software Clearinghouse," *Public Works* (November 1986): 70.

CHAPTER 4

MANAGING MAINTENANCE PERSONNEL

P eople are the most important element in any service operation, including effective maintenance management. The finest equipment, supplies, and facilities will mean little if competent personnel in sufficient numbers are not available. Not only must personnel be competent and positively motivated to do the jobs that have to be done, but in addition, they must understand fully and thoroughly the scope of their duties and responsibilities and the general operation of the entire system. Moreover, maintenance personnel must know, without question, to whom they are responsible and who is responsible to them. Capable supervision must be available to provide guidance for those who need direction and to provide training assistance designed to make workers self-sufficient and eligible for more responsible, better-paying jobs when these become available.

MAINTENANCE PERSONNEL MANUALS

A separate personnel manual or a section of the overall maintenance manual should be devoted to personnel policies that apply to the maintenance personnel of an organization. Such a document should include an outline of the duties of each staff position, the minimum requirements for appointment to these positions, the rules of employee conduct, and other information that clearly defines what management expects of each employee.

JOB DESCRIPTIONS

Job descriptions should be developed for managers, supervisors, foremen, warehouse personnel, equipment operators, mechanics, tradespeople, manual workers, tree trimmers, heavy equipment operators, storekeepers, and all other maintenance personnel positions included in the overall organization. Figures

4–1 and 4–2 are examples of job descriptions written for various kinds of positions in the maintenance field.

RECRUITING MAINTENANCE PERSONNEL

Recruiting skilled trades personnel who are reliable is often difficult. The following are suggestions that may be helpful in recruiting capable skilled tradespeople:

1. *Promote from within, whenever possible.* This tactic ensures that the organization and the applicant know the other's strengths and weaknesses in advance of the promotion, thus minimizing the possibility of negative "surprises."

2. *Ask staff personnel for assistance in recruiting candidates.* Staff tradespeople are likely to be acquainted with, and thus able to recommend, qualified tradespeople in the area. Furthermore, staff members are not likely to recommend people whose performance would reflect poorly on them.

METROPOLITAN PARK/RECREATION SYSTEM
JOB DESCRIPTION

POSITION TITLE: RECREATION MAINTENANCE AND REPAIRS FOREMAN

Distinguishing Features of Work

This is skilled and supervisory work in the repair and maintenance of the Recreation and Parks System. Direction and supervision over a group or groups of men performing a variety of tasks is required. Effective planning of work, considerable technical knowledge, and ability to apply independent judgment in carrying out assignments are required.

Illustrative Examples of Work

Supervises and directs subordinates in the performance of their duties.

Maintains time and work records, prepares reports.

Plans, organizes, schedules work crews engaged in various tasks.

Determines need for repair of equipment.

Performs related work as required.

Qualification Requirements

Graduation from an accredited high school or vocational school. Experience in the supervision of recreation and parks facilities, construction, maintenance and repair; or any equivalent combination of training and experience.

Ability to deal efficiently and tactfully with employees and the general public.

Versatility and initiative in dealing constantly with changing assignments.

Ability to supervise and coordinate the activities of a large group of workers engaged in recreation and park repairs and construction activities.

Must have a minimum of one year's experience in a supervisory capacity.

FIGURE 4–1 Sample job description, no. 1.

METROPOLITAN PARK/RECREATION SYSTEM
JOB DESCRIPTION

POSITION TITLE: MAINTENANCE MAN I

Distinguishing Features of Work

    This is semi-skilled work in the maintenance of park and recreation facilities.

    Work involves the performance of semi-skilled manual duties in the maintenance of parks, ball diamonds, indoor facilities, and playground areas. The maintenance man works under the direction of the Maintenance Manager.

Illustrative Examples of Work

    General clean-up (pick-up of litter and debris) of playground areas.

    Minor repairs to playground apparatus.

    Janitorial work in buildings used by the Recreation Department.

    General lawn care as may be required.

    Minor repairs to buildings such as replacing broken glass.

    Assistance in the preparation of equipment and facilities used in the summer recreation program.

Qualification Requirements

    Eighteen years of age. High school or vocational school graduate preferred. Experience in maintaining grounds and buildings highly desirable. Ability to follow simple oral and written directions. Skill in operation and care of tools and equipment.

Special Requirement

    Must possess a valid state driver's license.

FIGURE 4–2   Sample job description, no. 2.

3. *Recruit from the armed services.* Armed services tradespeople are usually well trained in one skill area and familiar with several others.

4. *Recruit trades personnel from the construction industry.* Government-sponsored recreation systems can seldom match private industry salaries paid to tradespeople in areas of rapid growth. However, park and recreation organizations can offer certain compensating benefits such as year-round employment, indoor work, and a pleasant environment. Such benefits are often attractive to older experienced tradespeople weary of working outdoors during inclement weather and subject to the uncertainty of periods of unemployment.

5. *Recruit personnel for grounds maintenance from those with a farming or agricultural background.* Farmers usually have learned plant propagation and care techniques. In addition, most farmers are acquainted with motorized equipment operation, maintenance, and repair.

6. *Secure qualified maintenance personnel through the establishment and operation of apprenticeship training programs.*

7. *Hire graduates from four-year university park and recreation professional training programs where "Maintenance Practice and Management" is a required course for graduation.*

8. *Hire park maintenance specialist graduates from two-year technical institutes or possibly trade high school graduates.*

UNDERSTANDING PERSONNEL

A supervisor gets work done with and through people; it is essential that he or she be concerned with selection, training, placement, motivation, and evaluation of employees. Employee productivity determines supervisory success or failure, and therefore guesses and trial-and-error supervisory methods are not good enough. Employees must be persuaded to work toward the goals and objectives of the maintenance division. Supervisors are responsible for selecting the best employees from those available and carefully placing them in positions where they can function best. Employees then need to be trained, using the best training methods available, and motivated toward outstanding performance. Supervisors must be able to evaluate worker performance and recommend those who will succeed when promoted to the positions of greater responsibility.

In summary, the effective supervisor must get extraordinary performance from ordinary people—a challenging task for a professional.

MOTIVATING EMPLOYEES

Worker performance is regulated by two factors: competence and commitment. Experience, skill, and knowledge applied to a job result in competence. Motivation produces commitment, and committed employees are always in demand because supervisors can depend upon them to do their best. Workers who are competent and committed are rare, so we settle for competent workers who can be motivated to outstanding performance.

It is important to understand that motivation is always present. Everyone is motivated all of the time, but not always in the direction that a supervisor or management wants. Motivation is not something that a supervisor does to employees. Rather, motivation is the feeling, attitude, or outlook of the individual about his or her self and the environment. Generally, people conduct themselves according to their self-perceptions and how they view and interpret their environment.

Motivation or outlook is individualistic. If we accept the basic premise that all individuals are different and that each person has his or her own needs and drives, then we must recognize that attempts at group motivation will always come up short of the desired result.

If supervisors are to be reasonably effective in motivating individual workers to achieve organizational objectives, they must develop an individual approach to motivation, that is, they must know their workers as individuals.

They must understand their drives, needs, and expectations. Supervisors must learn their workers' achievement objectives and their capabilities. In summary, supervisors must know their people so thoroughly as individuals that they will never have to resort to threats, fear, or rank as devices for motivation or control.

Basic Supervisory Motivational Techniques

While no reputable behavioral scientist would deny the importance of money as a temporary motivator, research evidence indicates that money is not as important as a permanent motivating device as we might believe. Several other motivational approaches promise more permanent results, such as employee participation, management by objectives, and "stretching."

Employee participation in the decision-making process. Employee participation supports the time-honored adage "Shared decisions equal coadvocates," and helps to guarantee that each employee gets a "piece of the action" and thereby enjoys power and achievement, which McClelland[1] and Ghiselli[2] believe are the two main sources of motivation.

An important consideration here is that going through the motions, or tokenism, will not work. The manager must develop a willingness to accept and put employee ideas and suggestions into organization operations, at least initially, on a limited experimental basis.

Management by objectives. Job standardization, in which each job detail is engineered down to the finest details and demands rote performance on the part of the worker, is one of the major reasons why workers become bored and lose interest in their jobs. In a management by objectives system, a supervisor explains the objectives of an operation and allows the worker to decide the specific manner, within reasonable limits, in which the job will be done.

Stretching. One of the greatest shortcomings of managers and instructors in all types of situations is underestimating the capabilities and capacities of other people. Stretching, as a motivational device, is simply a matter of challenging workers slightly beyond the normal estimate of their capabilities.

The Individualized Approach to Motivation

The individual approach to motivation means utilizing a leadership style and motivating factors that fit an individual worker, the job, the times, and the supervisor's objectives.

Behavioral science research tells us that it is acceptable, but only temporarily, to motivate employees through appropriate leadership styles or by monetary rewards or incentives. For lasting results, managers must ultimately motivate employees according to their basic human needs and interests, or by the satisfaction and challenge of their work.

SUPERVISORY COMMUNICATION

Developing and Maintaining Cooperation

Cooperation is the key to a successful park and recreation operation, but its achievement is never automatic. Supervisors are in a strategic position to resolve or control conflicts that threaten effective cooperation as they interact with their workers.

If supervisors are to be successful in bringing about cooperation, they must be effective communicators.

Communication and Acceptance of Change

Adequate communication is essential, particularly to an individual's sense of security and to his or her ability to adapt to conditions of stress and uncertainty. All of us are interested in developments that may affect our lives. Developments connected with a job are particularly threatening to our economic and psychological security. Moreover, being informed is important and related to the need for recognition. We cannot shut off job-connected information and still expect employees to adapt to conditions of stress or to perform mightily without motivation.

Interpersonal Communication

As effective as organizational communication might be, it is by its nature impersonal and represents a "shotgun" approach in communicating with employees. Bulletin boards and employee newsletters serve a useful purpose, but they will never take the place of interpersonal communication between the supervisor and worker. Direct person-to-person communication is the critical link that must be preserved. Otherwise, organizational operation will suffer.

Communication and Job Instruction

Often supervisors do not recognize that job instruction is a critical form of communication. Through job instruction, supervisors communicate with their workers about standards of work performance. They are literally showing the workers what they regard as acceptable performance in terms of quality, quantity, time, and safety in the work process.

Command of the art of listening is essential in effective supervision—the supervisor must be a patient and active listener. If a supervisor is to be successful in correcting a situation, he or she must listen carefully to the gripes and complaints that come from workers when something is wrong. To listen understandingly is not passive, but a vigorous activity. It involves three distinct active steps: (1) keep out of it—do not intrude physically, verbally, or mentally—shut up and listen! (2) do not plan what you are going to say in response—don't think, listen. (3) understand what is being felt as well as what is said—listen to *intent* as well as *content.*

Is Your Communication Understood?

We communicate to gain cooperation through behavioral and attitudinal changes. However, our best efforts at communication may be wasted if we do not attempt to determine whether or not our message has been understood by the receiver. A supervisor can do this by asking questions that force the message recipient to reveal what he or she understands. The question "Do you understand?" is unacceptable because it will be inevitably answered with the socially acceptable answer "yes," which gives you, the message sender, no idea as to what is understood. Only by encouraging the receiver to express reactions, by follow-up contacts, and by subsequent review of performance, can a supervisor obtain adequate "feedback" and accurately judge whether or not the message has been understood properly.

PERSONNEL TRAINING

Generally, the volume of park and recreation maintenance work varies greatly from season to season. This variation obviously has a direct effect on the number of maintenance employees required to do the work at a particular time of the year. It is neither practical nor economically feasible to employ a constant number of maintenance personnel on a year-round basis when there is insufficient work during certain seasons to justify a full staff. Many park and recreation organizations, therefore, are able to retain only key individuals around which to build their maintenance force during peak visitor-load seasons.

The seasonal nature of certain types of maintenance work results in the necessity to shift maintenance employees from one job to another according to varying demands.

Because of the need for flexibility among the year-round maintenance employees and the annual need for temporary, full-time seasonal employees, there is a constant need to train new employees and to retrain permanent employees who serve on a year-round basis.

There are two parts of maintenance employee training programs. The first part is employee orientation, which includes familiarizing new employees with the maintenance manager; immediate supervisors; fellow workers; the work of the division; job responsibilities; job performance standards; the work schedule; policies regarding visitor use, pay periods, personal appearance and grooming, vacation, sick leave, injury, absence, and tardy notification.

A checklist is a practical device to help guarantee that each employee receives complete and uniform information during orientation.

The second part of employee training is designed to improve employee knowledge, skills, and attitudes related to job performance.

The maintenance manager is responsible for maintenance personnel training programs, but may delegate training authority to members of the supervisory staff.

Certain fundamental questions arise with respect to personnel training:

1. How are the training needs of employees determined?
2. What are some of the basic principles of learning?
3. What are the most effective sensory avenues of receiving and retaining information?
4. What is the best method for a trainer to use in instructing an employee to do a job?

Each of these questions are considered below.

Identifying Employee Training Needs

Detailed training can be developed after fact finding, which may be segregated into the following two categories:

- What the job requires in the way of skills and abilities.
- What skills and abilities the worker now possesses.

To obtain information about the skill and knowledge demands of a job, a trainer should first review the maintenance objectives and standards for the area, facility, or equipment that a worker is responsible for maintaining. In addition, the trainer should study job descriptions that indicate the kinds of work and skills demanded by that position. If job descriptions are not available, the trainer must proceed to prepare his or her own analysis of job requirements.

To discover what the workers can do or are doing, the trainer should consult various records of production, training backgrounds, and experience of individuals within the work group. The trainer might also proceed to arrange for trials or tryouts of performance on various kinds of equipment to determine the skills and abilities of employees. Finally, the trainer should observe the workers' methods and work habits on the job.

Basic Principles of Learning

A basic understanding of the trainee learning process is important to the success of any training endeavor. The following principles, while not comprehensive, provide a reasonable foundation upon which trainers can launch their efforts:

- *Learning progresses from the simple to the complex.* The training program must be planned to progress naturally from the simple skills, either physical or mental, to the more difficult or complex knowledge required.

- *Learning is based upon what is already known.* The trainee must be able to relate new knowledge and skills to what is already known. The skilled instructor will develop a store of comparisons and analogies which will help the trainee understand what is being presented.

- *Repetition is necessary.* In many cases, the learner will not understand all the new material completely when it is first presented. The trainer must develop the habit of repeating it and presenting it in different ways to be sure it is thoroughly understood.

- *Learning must be used.* Everyone tends to forget those items of knowledge and those skills that are not used regularly. The training program must provide opportunities to use what is gained.

- *Success is important.* Knowledge not only must be used but must be used successfully to become permanent. The instructor should be careful to see that the trainee is successful in the application of new knowledge.

- *Incorrect habits must be changed.* Where incorrect responses have been learned, the trainer must first show the learner why they are wrong or undesirable and then help build up a new pattern of response.

- *Learning can be transferred.* A pattern of response or a fund of knowledge that has been developed to meet one situation can be used to solve a new problem or meet a new need. The training program should provide opportunities to develop this ability.

- *Learning does not always progress steadily.* The instructor must be prepared to meet situations as when learning slows down for a period of time and then shows an upward trend. Individual trainees may have different patterns of progress, and the trainer must adjust to these.

- *Learning depends upon experience.* The workplace training program should provide a variety of experiences in order to give the student the greatest possible number of opportunities to learn.

- *Individuals learn at different rates.* Training programs must be flexible enough to allow each trainee to progress at the rate that is best for the individual's own development.

Receiving and Retaining Information

To a considerable extent, learning depends on communication—communication from the trainer to the trainee in conveying information and ideas as well as communication from the learner to the trainer indicating the learner's understanding. The reception of information is largely dependent upon the sensory capacities of the individual. Of the five basic human senses, two of these, seeing and hearing, in most situations are the most effective. When conveying ideas and information, we tend to rely too much on the learner hearing what we have to say rather than relying on the capacity to see, which in combination with hearing is far more effective in the retention of information. Table 4–1 was developed as the result of a study done by the Industrial Extension Service of the School of Engineering at North Carolina State University.

TABLE 4–1   Relative recall according to sensory avenues of receiving information.

Method of Instruction	Recall After 3 Hours	Recall After 3 Days
A. Telling Alone	70%	10%
B. Showing Alone	72%	20%
C. Telling & Showing	85%	65%

The implications then for effective instruction would be to de-emphasize the lecturing and telling, emphasize the showing and demonstrating, and also encourage the trainee to do the job.

Pattern for Instruction

A highly successful four-step method of instruction was developed for industrial purposes during World War II. This pattern of instruction provides a simple and practical approach to the trainer's task. The four-step pattern is based upon the principles of learning that were outlined earlier, and it emphasizes two-way communication between the trainer and the learner, both in the telling and in the doing.

Any trainer who is interested in improving instructional skills should follow the pattern for instruction outlined below:

1. Prepare the trainee.
   Ensure a learning situation by:
      Putting the trainee at ease.
      Finding out what the trainee knows.
      Arousing the trainee's interest.

Placing the trainee correctly.

2. Present the training.
   Stress key points by:
   Telling.
   Showing.
   Explaining.
   Demonstrating.

3. Try out the trainee's performance.
   Be sure the trainee knows by:
   Having the trainee perform the operation.
   Having the trainee explain key points.
   Correcting the trainee's errors.
   Reinstructing the trainee.

4. Follow up on the trainee.
   Practice is the key to good performance; therefore:
   Allow the trainee to work independently.
   Encourage questions from the trainee.
   Frequently check the trainee's performance.
   Taper off on viewing the trainee's performance.

In summary, the trainer must:

1. Prepare the learner.

2. Present the job or idea by telling, showing, and illustrating, one step at a time.

3. Help the trainee apply the instruction until the habit is formed.

4. Follow through to guarantee the success of the training.

Such instructional steps have application to all instructional situations whether the trainer is attempting to communicate an idea or to develop employee skills to do a particular job.

An extensive index of audio-visual aids for all aspects of maintenance instruction is available from the Environmental Management Association.[3]

Opportunities Outside the Organization

To further assist employees toward career development, the park and recreation organization should encourage employee participation in relevant courses offered by trade schools, technical institutes, and institutions of higher learning that are close at hand and offer evening classes or correspondence courses. Maintenance equipment manufacturers periodically provide short training courses covering maintenance, operation, and repair of their products and will, in response to requests, provide such courses locally.

The highly successful Park and Recreation Maintenance Management School is conducted annually by North Carolina State University. This school stresses the management of maintenance operations and utilizes the instructional services of outstanding practitioners in the field of park and recreation maintenance.

Employee participation in maintenance training programs away from the job can be best encouraged by paying the tuition and travel expenses and to continue salaries or wages during absences. Not only should employee attendance be stipulated prior to granting permission to attend, but the employee also should be required to share newly acquired knowledge, skills, and understandings with fellow employees and the manager upon return to the job. The responsibility here is two-fold: the employee must be willing to share what has been learned and the maintenance manager must schedule sufficient time for the employee to share this information.

One last step in the process is necessary if the maintenance manager is to show employees that he or she is committed to the importance of employee training and career development. The maintenance manager should attempt to introduce the new ideas or methods brought back by the employee into organization operations on at least a limited basis until their value can be tested.

The building maintenance division should emphasize the importance of awareness of new maintenance methods and materials. Building maintenance trade publications should be made available to employees, with articles of particular significance routed either directly to employees or to supervisory personnel for presentation to employees by the supervisor.

Custodian Training

Since many custodians have received little formal training for their work, maintenance managers must place high priority on effective continuing training. Complicating the problem are the usual high turnover and frequent improvements in cleaning technology requiring revisions of methods and introduction of new materials. This means the custodial section must devote time to orientation, classroom instruction, on-the-job training and retraining, preparation and revision of cleaning manuals, and careful record keeping.

Good training starts even before the employee reports for work. It includes an orientation period during which a supervisor personally assists a new worker in the following ways:

1. Explain appropriate dress for the job assignment (preferably by phone before the first day of work).
2. Introduce the person to the other workers.
3. Define duties clearly so that the employee knows exactly what is expected of him or her.

4. Explain basic rules and regulations governing employment, such as those dealing with safety, accidents, smoking, drinking, and absenteeism.

5. Explain the length and nature of the probationary period, if one is in effect.

6. Show the employee where tools are located and the location of the work area, locker room, cafeteria, and time clock.

7. Encourage him or her to seek help if need be, and explain where to find it.

8. Explain when and where paychecks are given out.

9. Answer any questions he or she may have.

The purpose of this kind of orientation is not to teach all required job skills; that comes later. The purpose, at this point, is to create an impression of a friendly, well-organized, and efficient operation. Such first impressions can be surprisingly effective in encouraging receptive, cooperative attitudes among new employees. In many cases, trial and error is unavoidable because the new custodian must be put to work immediately.

Detailed instruction should come in two forms, on-the-job training and formalized classroom sessions. Because most cleaning jobs require a certain amount of manual dexterity and muscular coordination, actual supervised trials provide the most productive learning experiences for the novice. On-the-job training naturally consists of such supervised trials and errors, and classroom instruction should also include these experiences. In most cases, trial and error starts early because the new custodian starts working immediately. Therefore, a new employee must be given some instruction at the start to prevent the development of bad work habits and methods. More detailed instruction should be given as soon as possible to help develop the most efficient approaches to various tasks.

For training sessions, choose employees who, through practice or talent, have become the best cleaners and ask them to demonstrate those operations that they have mastered. These sessions can be scheduled in the appropriate work areas with small groups of new workers. To get the message across, the supervisor should have novices attempt the operation on the spot under the scrutiny of the expert. This is the optimum teaching method for such information.

Because of the variety of tasks and materials the custodian must master, formal training sessions are also necessary in a well-developed training program. These meetings, when well managed, serve to instruct custodians in basic topics, such as the most efficient way to clean an activity room and in such esoteric matters as how various cleaning chemicals react with different surfaces. Through these sessions administrators and supervisors disseminate what they have learned about recent improvements in cleaning methods and technology. Such sessions can serve, therefore, to instruct new employees and to retrain experienced workers.

For new employees, custodial managers should provide some instruction in as many cleaning techniques and procedures as possible. Though few employees will thoroughly master all methods and custodial tasks, each should be familiar with all and expert in several. This familiarity improves cooperation among custodians, since each understands the problems his or her colleagues have to handle. Limited versatility creates flexibility that is essential if a custodial operation is to function successfully in the event of unexpected absences.

Since there is one most efficient way to handle each job and many less efficient methods, good training that effectively teaches custodians the right way will cut labor costs. To realize this potential saving, instructors must thoroughly cover each step of the major custodial jobs.

Maintenance Operations Manual

To supplement training, managers should prepare maintenance job description manuals. While a manual can never replace on-the-job and classroom instruction, it can serve other important needs. It is a readily available reference for the worker who cannot remember all the details of more complicated or less frequently performed jobs. A good manual will present for each task a numbered *sequence of operations,* which explains, in order, each step to be followed. Regular employees will not carry such manuals on their routine rounds, but new workers may need them, and supervisors can use such a complete inventory of operations to instruct new workers and to advise experienced ones.

Records of Employee Training Performance

All administrators should keep records of the instruction every member of the custodia. staff receives. In addition, they should award certificates every time an employee satisfactorily completes another training course. Perhaps insignia, to be worn on uniforms, could be designed signifying the expertise acquired. Such touches stress the importance of training to employees and can even motivate them to perform at higher levels.

EMPLOYEE SAFETY

The relationship between employee training and safety is a close one. Reducing accidents is largely a problem of creating a safety-consciousness, which in turn is dependent upon educational and training efforts.

The development of this consciousness has become an increasing interest to both government and industry in recent years. Accidents are expensive, and they benefit no one. When accidents are frequent, insurance rates increase and valuable people are lost for extended periods of time. Employees may find their physical well-being seriously impaired. Thus, there is rather unanimous agreement that safety-consciousness is most desirable.

The increasing need to develop a safety-consciousness means another responsibility for the supervisor. The supervisor is the one who must make such a program "click." Indeed, he or she must also be sold on safety. It is not enough to give safety lip service at meetings, and then let matters take their natural course. Employees are quick to sense this.

To put over safety, supervisors must believe in it and work at it so the employees cannot mistake where they stand. Safety must be regarded this way: Efficient production is impossible without safe production. The supervisors must force themselves for a time to look at production and service problems with an eye toward safety, and it will become second nature.

Employee Accidents

The most meaningful information on the extent of the occupational accident problem in parks was gathered several years ago in a cooperative survey made by the National Recreation and Park Association and the National Safety Council. This survey of injury frequency ranked park and recreation employees as receiving more than three times the average number of injuries of all industries reporting to the council.[4]

The survey also revealed that in one year 1 out of every 35 park and recreation employees receives a disabling injury and that approximately two-thirds of the park and recreation occupational injuries involve maintenance personnel.[5] See Figure 4–3.

THE OCCUPATIONAL SAFETY AND HEALTH ACT

With the passage of the Occupational Safety and Health Act (OSHA) of 1970, public park and recreation maintenance managers began to discover what some

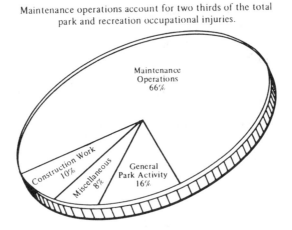

FIGURE 4–3   Park and recreation occupational injuries.

industrial managers realized decades ago, that good safety is good business; it not only saves lives and limbs, it also saves time.

Although public employees are exempted by the act, Executive Order No. 11612 requires federal agencies, including the National Park Service, to develop effective and comprehensive occupational safety and health programs. Administration of the act by the various states also requires that comprehensive occupational safety and health programs applicable to all employees of the state and its political subdivisions be established. State, county, and municipal employers and employees would, therefore, be subject to virtually the same degree of official control as those in the private sector. However, such public employee protection is contingent upon each state submitting a plan to conduct its own Occupational Safety and Health Program and having that plan approved by the Secretary of Labor. See Table 4–2 for the status of state OSHA plans.

Approval by the secretary of labor of any state OSHA plan requires the inclusion of a provision covering all state and local government employees. Park and recreation maintenance employees employed by private enterprises are automatically covered by the federal OSHA act whether the act is administered by the federal government or if a state-approved OSHA plan is in force. Any state that has federal approval for their OSHA plan is eligible for 50 percent federal funding to implement its program.

Since 1973, the year California's OSHA program began, workplace fatalities have dropped 8.75 percent, amputations are down 40 percent, fractures 6 percent, explosive-related injuries 28 percent, and construction injuries 30 percent in that state.[6]

OSHA COVERAGE AND OBLIGATIONS OF FEDERAL AGENCIES AND THEIR EMPLOYEES

Section 19 of OSHA applies to all federal agencies and requires the heads of these agencies to conduct occupational safety and health programs consistent with standards developed under the act, including the maintenance of adequate records of occupational injuries and illnesses and the preparation of periodic reports for submittal to the secretary of labor. On July 26, 1971, the president signed Executive Order No. 11612 that further details the responsibilities and duties of heads of federal agencies and the secretary of labor in the administration of the act. Federal employees, in addition, have the responsibility to comply with safety and health standards, including rules, regulations, and orders promulgated under the act.

Duties

The law enumerates certain duties for both employers and employees. The employer has the general duty to furnish to each employee employment and a place of employment free from recognized hazards that are known, or likely, to cause death or serious physical harm.

The employer also has the duty to comply with occupational safety and health standards promulgated under the act and to obey other regulations

TABLE 4-2   States with approved OSHA plans, as of June 1991.

States	Operational Status Agreement[2]	Different Standards[3]	7(c)(1) On-Site Consultation Agreement[4]	On-Shore Maritime Coverage	Date of Initial Approval	Date Certified[5]	Date of 18(e) Final Approval[6]
Alaska		•	•		07/31/73	09/09/77	09/28/84
Arizona					10/29/74	09/18/81	06/20/85
California	•	•	•	•	04/24/73	08/12/77	
Connecticut[1]			•		10/02/73	08/19/86	
Hawaii		•	•		12/28/73	04/26/78	04/30/84
Indiana					02/25/74	09/24/81	09/26/86
Iowa			•		07/12/73	09/14/73	07/02/85
Kentucky					07/23/73	02/08/80	06/13/85
Maryland			•		06/28/73	02/15/80	07/18/85
Michigan	•	•			09/24/73	01/16/81	
Minnesota			•	•	05/29/73	09/28/75	07/30/85
Nevada	•				12/04/73	08/13/81	
New Mexico	•				12/04/75	12/04/84	
New York[1]			•		06/01/84		
North Carolina	•		•		01/26/73	09/29/76	
Oregon	•	•	•	•	12/22/72	09/15/82	
Puerto Rico	•				08/15/77	09/07/82	
South Carolina			•		11/30/72	07/28/76	12/15/87
Tennessee			•		06/28/73	05/03/78	07/22/85
Utah			•		01/04/73	11/11/75	07/16/85
Vermont	•		•	•	10/01/73	03/04/77	
Virginia			•		09/23/76	08/15/84	11/30/88
Virgin Islands					08/31/73	09/22/81	04/17/84
Washington	•	•		•	01/19/73	01/26/82	
Wyoming			•		04/25/74	12/18/80	06/27/85
Total - 25	9	6	17	5		24	14

[1] Plan covers only state and local government employees
[2] Concurrent federal jurisdiction suspended
[3] Standards frequently not identical to the federal
[4] On-site consultation is available in all states either through a 7(c)(1) Agreement or under a state plan
[5] Developmental steps satisfactorily completed
[6] Concurrent federal jurisdiction relinquished (superseded Operational Status Agreement)

Source: OSHA, Office of State Programs.

adopted in administration of the act.

The duty of the employee is to comply with occupational safety and health standards and all rules, regulations, and orders issued pursuant to this act which are applicable to his or her own actions and standards.

Though both employer and employee have duties, prescribed penalties are invoked only against the employer. No legal penalties can be assessed against the employee.

As a practical matter, few employers are being charged with violations of the general-duty provision cited here. This means that the heart of the enforcement activity focuses on the safety and health standards promulgated by the secretary of labor.

Employee Rights Under OSHA

OSHA spells out a number of rights held by employees. These fall under three main headings:

- Rights with respect to standards.
- Rights with respect to access to information.
- Rights with respect to enforcement.

1. The employee can participate in the standards-development process.
2. The employee must be kept informed of significant safety and health information, specifically of the law itself, of the summary of accident experience in the establishment, and of any safety violations alleged to exist in the establishment.
3. The employee must file complaints of violations with the Department of Labor or with compliance officers during inspections.
4. An employee or a representative of employees may accompany the compliance officer during an inspection.

If asked to do so, the Department of Labor is required to keep confidential the name of a complaining employee. Employers must not discriminate against employees exercising their rights under OSHA.

OSHA Standards

Standards are at the heart of the safety process established by OSHA. The safety and health standards promulgated by the Secretary of Labor are designed to protect working people from occupational injury and illness. These standards are the principal criteria used by OSHA compliance officers when inspecting establishments. Safety and health standards are not an invention of the federal government. On the contrary, most of the OSHA standards are developed by nationally recognized standards-producing organizations established mainly by and for industrial management.

OSHA Injury/Illness Records

Three types of injury/illness records must be maintained at each establishment:

- A log of occupational injuries and illnesses.
- A supplementary record of occupational injuries and illnesses.
- An annual summary of occupational injuries and illnesses.

The log may be maintained on Form OSHA-100 or on any privately prepared equivalent.

OSHA Inspections

One of the key sections of the Occupational Safety and Health Act ensures OSHA compliance officers free entry into work establishments and access to certain records, which may provide information on working conditions related to occupational safety and health.

Section 8(a) of OSHA provides that the compliance officer, upon presenting appropriate credentials to the owner, operator, or agent in charge, is authorized to:

- Enter without delay and at reasonable times any factory, plant, establishment, construction site, or other area, workplace, or environment where work is performed by an employee of an employer.
- Inspect and investigate during regular working hours and at other reasonable times, and within reasonable limits and in a reasonable manner, any such place of employment and all pertinent conditions, structures, machines, apparatus, devices, equipment, and materials therein, and to question privately any such employer, owner, operator, agent, or employee.

Refusal to admit the compliance officer and any interference with his investigations can result in legal action and possible penalties.

The Opening Inspection Conference

After the compliance officer has been identified, a senior executive should meet the officer. Certain records that will assist in the investigation may be asked for and given. The officer will, in this conference, seek to evaluate the establishment's safety and health programs. An employer's representative should be chosen to accompany the compliance officer on the inspection.

An authorized representative of the employees must also be given the opportunity to accompany the compliance officer during the course of an actual inspection. In a unionized establishment, arrangements for the selection of such a representative by the union should be made in advance to avoid delays. If there is no authorized employee representative, the compliance officer will interview employees from time to time on the inspection tour and the production schedule must not interfere with the employee interviews. Neither may the employer discriminate, in any way, against an employee for anything said or shown to the compliance officer.

The Inspection

The route and duration of the inspection will be determined by the compliance officer who can go where he or she chooses, talk to whom he or she wishes, take photos, record instrument readings, and examine records.

A point of controversy in connection with the inspection has been the matter of pay for employees who represent the employees during the inspection. In general, the law does not require the employer to pay the employee for the time spent accompanying a compliance officer. However, there may be cases when nonpayment would be considered discriminatory, as, for example, when an establishment that has previously compensated employees for making safety inspections suspends the practice for a particular employee.

The Closing Inspection Conference

After the inspection (and/or review of records), the compliance officer closes the visit by conferring with the employer or a representative. During this conference, the compliance officer will discuss any apparent violations noted and may discuss with the employer the nature and implementation of corrective measures. The employer will be notified of any alleged violations for which any citations have been issued.

OSHA Violations

Alleged violations fall under one or more of the following three headings:

- General duty.
- Safety and health standards.
- Regulations.

Few citations for violation of the general duty clause in OSHA are currently being issued. For the most part, OSHA limits citations to alleged violations of standards or regulations. However, the general duty clause is part of the law, and any employer may be charged with its violation.

Citations may allege violations of any of the following types:

- *Imminent danger.* The act defines imminent danger as, "Any conditions or practices in any place of employment which are such that a danger exists which could reasonably be expected to cause death or serious physical harm immediately or before the imminence of such danger can be eliminated through the enforcement procedures otherwise provided by this act."

- *Non-serious violation.* If a condition exists, which the compliance officer believes is likely to cause injury but not death or serious physical harm, or if the employer did not know of the hazard, the violation will be considered nonserious. A tripping hazard on a level surface would be an example.

- *De minimix violation.* This term is used for a violation that has no immediate or direct relationship to safety or health. An example would be the lack of partitions for individual toilet facilities.

- *Willful violation.* A violation is willful if the employer either intentionally or knowingly violated the act or, even though he or she did not realize the violation, he or she was aware that a hazardous condition existed and made no reasonable effort to eliminate the condition.

- *Repeated violation.* A repeated violation is one for which a second citation is issued for violation of the same standard or the general duty clause. This differs from a failure-to-abate violation in that the repeated violation occurs after the original violation was abated.

A citation may be issued to the employer for violations of safety and health standards by employees. The employer is considered responsible for requiring employees to comply with standards. An example would be the failure of employees to wear personal protective equipment required by the standards. Employers must take all necessary steps to ensure employee safety compliance.

Unfortunately, OSHA does not go far enough. Based on standards primarily developed by and for the private sector of industry, OSHA does not relate to many of the special problems of park and recreation employee safety. In addition, OSHA standards relate to physical conditions of an industrial nature. More development is needed in the areas of work procedures and employee safety instruction.

EMPLOYEE SAFETY TRAINING

Unsafe acts along with unsafe conditions are the two major sources of accidents. One of the major causes of unsafe acts is lack of knowledge or skill. The remedy is training. It is the supervisor's job to see that employees within a work group are properly trained to perform their jobs in a safe manner. This obviously presupposes the supervisor's ability to teach. In brief, there are two widely used techniques for training workers to perform their jobs in a safe and efficient manner: Job Safety Analysis (JSA) and Job Instruction Training (JIT). When these two techniques are combined and properly utilized, employees learn to perform their jobs safely.

JSA is a procedure for breaking a job down into steps, determining the hazards involved and the recommended safe procedures for performing each step of the job. In its final form, it is a written guide for how to do a job safely.

JIT is a highly successful four-step method for teaching job skills. Supervisors should be capable in the use of this procedure. (See "Pattern for Instruction" in the "Personnel Instruction" section of this chapter.) When JIT is used in connection with the steps in the JSA, it becomes an effective technique for safety training.

Courses offered through correspondence are often utilized in connection with individual or home study. The advantages to individual study are that the trainee can set his or her own pace and set a study schedule that is most convenient.

SEVEN STEPS TO SAFETY

Before any effective employee safety hazard control program can be developed, a maintenance manager must be genuinely committed to the importance of employee safety. Maintenance managers must realize that:

- Accidents can be prevented.
- Accident prevention costs less than the costs of accidents.
- Safety is just good management and efficient operation.

While the humanitarian aspects of safety cannot be disregarded, the economic aspects of insurance costs, medical expenses, efficiency, and public and employee relations demand attention in the accident control program. Accident prevention requires no complicated or unwieldy organization; it can and should be integrated into all phases of recreation maintenance operations and management.

If a maintenance manager follows the hazard control measures outlined in the following "Seven Steps to Safety," an excellent start will have been made in a program of employee safety:

1. *Initiate a safety program with enthusiasm.* A maintenance manager must want to stop accidents and be willing to exert the energy necessary to accomplish this.

2. *Assign someone to help with the details.* Assign a good supervisor to become informed on applicable safety standards established by OSHA, training, accident reporting, and program activities.

3. *Locate the hazards.* Watch for things that cause accidents. Accident statistics will assist in locating safety hazards. Encourage employees to suggest

safer ways of doing maintenance work.

4. *Make the job safe.* Remove hazards. Make machines, equipment, and operations as foolproof as possible. Examples of safety equipment are guards for saws, goggles for grinding equipment, and welding masks.

5. *Control employee work habits.* Teach the safe ways of doing the job. Enforce compliance with safety regulations and make new rules when necessary.

6. *Keep simple safety records.* Uncover accident causes, check progress, and compare experience with others. Simple records consist of an accident report form and an accident analysis chart. Finally, recognize that records will help reveal injury hazard areas.

7. *Get employees into the act.* Involve first-line supervisors and grass-roots employees. Make them safety conscious. Solicit their suggestions and utilize their ideas. Devote staff meeting time to safety. Brainstorm and develop innovative approaches to the employee safety program.[7]

SPECIAL EMPLOYEE SAFETY PROBLEMS

A broad spectrum of safety problems and hazards are to be found in the park and recreation maintenance field.[8] While all problems and hazards will not pertain to a given operation, alert managers will analyze their situations and direct the staff to institute the safety control measures that are appropriate. Special safety problems and hazards of park and recreation situations include the following.

Temporary and Seasonal Employees

Park and recreation organizations have many seasonal and part-time employees according to peak visitor seasons. The temporary employee group is largely made up of students with little work experience and safety training and older retired or semiretired workers who are often in a state of poor health. When orientation and training time for the inexperienced temporary employee is limited, a concise safety training packet should be developed and mailed to the worker prior to reporting to work, with the admonition to study the material in preparation for a test on the material when he or she reports. With an older temporary employee, for correct job placement, double check for physical limitations and the health status of the individual either by a health examination or a check into previous work performance.

Language Barriers to Safety

Some temporary or seasonal employees may be functionally illiterate and, therefore, unable to read or write. Others may communicate in a foreign language and be handicapped by their inability to understand English. Under such circumstances, prepare employee job safety instructions in both English and the foreign language(s) in question.

Workers in Isolated Locations

Because of the size of many recreation areas, maintenance and construction workers must often work alone or in small groups at locations isolated from emergency medical aid. Such employees should be trained in proper use and care of safety equipment for their job assignment. Employees who must work alone, particularly in isolated areas, should be self-reliant, trained in first aid, and capable of recognizing potential hazards to themselves and to the public. A hazard reporting system should be established as well as an accident reporting procedure.

Vehicles and Traffic Hazards

Employees doing maintenance and construction on roads and in parking lots are exposed to the hazards of moving vehicles in addition to the normal accident exposure from operating vehicles. Whenever possible, advance warning signs, barricades, and flaggers should be used. Tool carts and vehicles may be placed between oncoming or passing traffic and the work point, in addition to but not in lieu of, barricades and flaggers. Flasher units, signs, and traffic cones should be used to warn and channel traffic for worker protection. Trucks and other maintenance and construction vehicles that may have to stop or impede traffic should be equipped with special rotating or blinking lights. Advance warning lights placed well ahead of the work site are imperative so that motorists can anticipate the operation. Flaggers who are used to direct traffic should wear high visibility (orange) vests and safety hats. Vests must be reflectorized for night use.

Tools and Equipment

Park and recreation maintenance and construction require the use of a wide variety of hand and portable power tools, most of which are potentially dangerous when used by inexperienced employees. Tools range from a pair of common hand pliers to power saws and powerful hydraulic equipment. Special training and supervision are required for the safe use of tools. The National Safety Council indicates that the following minimum requirements for the use of tools should be observed:

1. *Provide and use the right tool for the job.* Quality tools should be pro-

vided, and employees should be trained and instructed to use the right tool for a given job. Electrical tools should bear the listings of the Underwriters Laboratories (UL) label and should either be double insulated or electrically grounded through three wires and grounded circuits.

2. *Tools should be well maintained and kept in safe condition.* Procedures should be established for employees to report and turn in defective, unsafe tools, electrical equipment, and extension cords. A record system for regular tool and equipment inspection and maintenance should be established. Centralized tool control is desirable and will help ensure uniform inspection and maintenance.

3. *Supervisors should train and supervise employees in the correct use of tools for each job.* Such training is especially important for electrical equipment and power tools because of the danger of fatal shock and permanently disabling injuries. Hand cutting tools, such as axes, saws, chisels, and knives, must be kept sharp for proper functioning, and the user must be trained in the proper use of these to avoid accidents.

4. *Tools should be stored in a safe place.* Serious accidents occur because tools have fallen from overhead places or individuals are injured as a result of carrying sharp or pointed tools in pockets or leaving them where sharp points or cutting edges are exposed.

Protective Equipment

Safety glasses should be provided and worn by employees using any hand or power tool when there is a danger of flying chips, sparks, or other hazards to the eyes.

Steel-toed safety shoes protect the feet from heavy objects that might fall or roll over a worker's toes. Additional protection to the instep is provided by metatarsal guards. Safety hats should be worn to protect workers' heads from falling objects. Heavy gloves should be worn to protect hands and wrists when handling sharp or rough material, but gloves should not be worn around moving machinery where rotating parts might catch the glove and pull the hand into danger. Rubber gloves, aprons, and splash-resistant goggles should be worn when handling corrosive chemicals and toxic pesticides and herbicides. In addition to other protective equipment, air-filtering respirators should be worn by all personnel involved in paint, herbicide, and pesticide spraying operations.

Rubbish Removal

Collection and removal of garbage and refuse in parks usually does not involve use of heavy duty compactor trucks with the dangerous shearing action of the compactor blade. However, a variety of injuries, such as strains and overexertion, are constant hazards to the unwary park refuse collector. An additional danger to the refuse collector is the possibility of cuts or punctures from injection syringe needles sometimes found in loose debris, with the possibility of infection from HIV virus and subsequent AIDS infection. Heavy duty gloves will minimize such danger. For this reason it is necessary to establish lifting, loading, and lowering procedures and train workers on the safety size and weight range of materials to be handled. Whenever possible, mechanical loading equipment should be used to handle refuse containers that cannot be safely handled by two people.

Refuse containers should be no larger than the thirty-two to thirty-three-gallon size (preferably of open mesh) or twenty-gallon size if they are to be handled by one person only. Fifty-five-gallon steel drums are still used by some park systems as refuse containers. Because of their heavier weight and bulk, at least two persons should handle them. Holes for water drainage purposes should be punched or drilled in the bottom of solid containers.

Supervisors should train employees in proper lifting methods by means of posters, motion pictures, and printed material. Refuse collection truck drivers should be trained in safety procedures to protect members of their crews and the public. Well-understood signals between the driver and the crew must be developed for proper teamwork in stopping, backing up, and picking up containers. A guide should stand near the rear of the truck to direct the driver.

If trucks must stop on roads and at driveways, they should be equipped with warning lights and caution signs. Local and state vehicle codes for lighting and signals should be followed.

Mowing Operations

Safety requirements for walk-behind and riding mowers, both rotary and reel type, are given in OSHA Standards (29 CFR, Section 1910.243). According to the National Safety Council's public employee guide, *Street and Highway Maintenance,* the main safety points to consider in mowing operations are:

1. Keep both hands on the handlebars or steering wheel.
2. Two or more mowers working in tandem should: (a) stay at least 15 feet apart, and (b) refrain from side-by-side mowing.
3. Always look out for "blind" spots.
4. Operators should wear head, eye, and foot protection.
5. On large tractor-mower combinations, (a) units must have heavy rollover bars; (b) operators must wear safety belts; (c) operators should mow as far as possible from people to minimize the danger of the mower striking and throwing objects hidden in the turf; and (d) chain or other types of curtain guards should be installed around rotary mowers as further protection from objects thrown by the mower blades.

6. Because of the danger of amputation, operators should be instructed never to unclog or adjust a mower until the power is turned off.
7. To avoid fire and explosion, the motor should be turned off and allowed to cool before refueling.
8. Tractor-mowers that travel on roads or highways should conform to all local and state regulations and should be equipped with flasher lights, high visibility flags, and slow-moving vehicle signs.

Landscaping

Landscaping can involve a variety of power and hand tools ranging from shovels to portable chain saws. Power equipment such as a chain saw is exceptionally dangerous to the inexperienced or untrained users. Hedge trimmers, axes, machetes, and hand saws can also cause painful injury and can be used safely only if employees are thoroughly trained and the tools are kept in safe condition and good repair. For anything but the lightest landscaping, safety hats, safety shoes, and safety glasses should be worn. Safety belts and ropes used in tree trimming should be inspected daily for wear. Trees should be felled, and heavy timber should be cut only by trained foresters or others thoroughly familiar with the hazards of the equipment and heavy work involved. All of the precautions for tractor mowing are even more critical in the operation of a "bush hog" for cleaning brush, especially in rocky and rough terrain.

EVALUATING EMPLOYEE PERFORMANCE

Supervisors tend to handle personnel selection, indoctrination, and training fairly well, but then shirk their responsibility to the new worker once on the job. The excuse often given by the supervisor is that satisfactory workers are capable of caring for themselves so "I spend my time with the marginal-problem cases."

Enlightened supervisors recognize that there are dividends to working with all employees, particularly the good workers. They realize that it is important to build on the strengths of their work groups, rather than on the weaknesses. Therefore, it is imperative that supervisors avoid the armchair approach to reviewing employee performance. Rather, they should spend maximum time on the job site personally observing employee performance and getting direct feedback on irritations that affect good performance. By operating in this manner, supervisors do not have to depend upon periodic spot ratings that tend to produce a distorted picture of employee performance. Instead, employee appraisal is continuous, informal, and routine rather than "snoopervision," which is resented. In reality, the seemingly informal appraisal of employee performance must be carried on in a more precise, systematic manner than it might outwardly appear.

Employee evaluation is time consuming and, thus, expensive. However, its potential value as a basis for permanent assignment, promotions, pay adjustments, employee training, validation of recruiting, and other personnel selection procedures justifies the cost if the information recorded is objective and valid.

Why Evaluate?

A written record of employee performance is essential if supervisors are to make objective, defensible recommendations regarding training, transfer, dismissal, promotion, or permanent appointments for each employee. Literally, supervisors must rate each employee, and this is not an easy task. The accuracy of a given rating depends upon many things, including the rating skills and immediate disposition of each rater, the range of contact with the individual being rated, and the tangibility of the traits under consideration. On the last point, word meanings play a part. The level of abstraction influences the range of possible differences in opinion.

Ratings are by nature ambiguous, awkward, and imprecise. Perhaps it would be convenient if production records, examination results, and seniority rules were adequate to relieve supervisors from the necessity of using ratings. But they cannot, and there is no evidence that they ever will. A great many decisions and actions in the course of human relationships depend upon a matter of opinion. Instead of decrying this fact, time and attention should be given to finding a means of putting such opinion on a more systematic and factual basis.

Rating Application

Ratings can be applied to two areas in a relationship between supervisors and workers: (1) organization control, which is the traditional emphasis, and (2) individual worker guidance. Assuming that there is a formal rating system calling for evaluations at several specified times, a probationary worker might serve as a hypothetical case in point. Does this worker turn out a reasonable quantity of work? Does this person waste too much material or damage equipment excessively? Does this person get to work on time, have a number of questionable absences, cooperate with others, ask for advice when needed?

The answers to these questions serve organization control purposes directly. They also provide guidance for managerial actions that affect the central aspirations of the probationary worker—training, transfer, dismissal, permanent appointment, and promotion. It would be unrealistic to deny their frustrating potentials to the employee. However, it would be equally unrealistic to ignore the importance of systematic answers to such questions for the advancement of legitimate organizational goals. But, the answer in each case has equal potential as a basis for praise of the individual where the facts warrant it. Each answer can provide constructive guidance to the individual and the supervisor as well.

Guarding Against Bias and Error

If there is a formal worker evaluation system in a given situation, it may be unsuited to what the supervisor sees as appropriate, but it is unlikely that anything can be done about it. Whether or not there is an official personnel rating system, the supervisor should not forget that he or she has to make judgments and recommendations. One thing the supervisor can do, regardless of rating system conditions, is to guard against bias and error in ratings.

The first step is to learn what these hazards are. Bias is an inclination toward a conclusion as one approaches the problem. Sometimes it may be based upon reason, but when it is completely unreasonable, it is called prejudice. Prejudice ignores facts or applies irrelevant facts to the situation at hand in order to support an emotionally satisfying conclusion. Prejudice obviously has an unfair influence upon rating results, but rational bias may be equally harmful. Moreover, there is sometimes a fine line between rational bias and rationalization of prejudice.

The danger in rational bias is that it may cause a supervisor to rate a person based on past behavior. For example, a worker might be absent three times without good cause. After the fourth absence, the supervisor may assume the worker was "goofing off" again. Yet, the fourth time this person might have a valid reason for absence. Thus, even when bias seems reasonable, it is important to check the case by fact finding and situational thinking.

Even as bias may cause discrimination of individuals on rational but insufficient grounds, prejudice causes irrational discrimination. Its basis may be conscious or unconscious. While it is unlikely that supervisors can do much about the latter, they can control conscious prejudice by checking their ratings against these questions: "Am I making this judgment on the basis of the real individual or on the basis of race, religion, or ethnic background?" "Do I make the judgment because the individual is a man, or a woman?" It is important to recognize that positive and negative discrimination is unjust. Individuals do not deserve special favors any more than they deserve unfair condemnation.

Generalized Rating Errors

Apart from the specific influence of bias upon ratings given to individuals or groups, many raters commonly make generalized errors in their rating efforts. The most common rating errors can be grouped in these classifications: (1) leniency, (2) the halo effect, (3) central tendency, (4) contrast, and (5) association.[9]

Leniency is the most common rating error and gives a highly overrated picture of the employee's performance, thus destroying any potential the rating might have for constructive employee guidance.

The halo rating effect occurs when the rater is particularly impressed (negatively or positively) by one particular trait, characteristic, or area of employee performance and tends to allow this impression to overinfluence rating the individual in other areas of performance.

Central tendency often results when the rater is not familiar with a particular trait, characteristic, or area of performance on a particular employee-rating form or scale. The rater often covers ignorance by giving the employee an average or central rating.

Contrast occurs when a rater compares an employee with himself or herself. To avoid contrast error, the rater must become circumspect and realize that he or she is not rating employees objectively.

Association takes many forms including: (1) failure on the part of the rater to distinguish semantically among terms that describe different rating traits or characteristics, (2) the tendency for a rater to rate adjacent traits on a scale more consistently than those that are separated by a greater distance on the form, and (3) rater fatigue or irritation associated with leniency or severity in rating. To minimize association error related to fatigue, particularly when forced to use a complex time-consuming rating form, the rater should rate all employees on the same trait before going on to the next item.

Systematic Rating

How can a supervisor become more systematic? More systematic rating depends upon the development or reinforcement of two attitudes by the supervisor: (1) that evaluation is a continuous responsibility, and (2) that conscious effort is necessary to improve the evaluation. Without these attitudes, forms and procedures have little value.

The Employee Performance Record

The Employee Performance Record devised by Flanagan and Burns is an approach with great potential for increasing the supervisor's systematic attention to the evaluation problem.[10] This technique does not require the supervisor to make the traditional overall judgments required by a twenty- or thirty-item rating scale of ambiguous or imprecise characteristics or traits. Instead, the supervisor needs only to record day-to-day observations of *exceptional* (not routine) worker performance in specific on-the-job incidents. These continuing factual records of outstandingly effective or outstandingly ineffective specific performance provide the basis for whatever opinions or recommendations the supervisor may have to express periodically, or on special occasions, regarding the employee.

The Employee Performance Record form, which the supervisor uses to record the exceptional incidents of worker performance, provides equal space for recording effective behavioral incidents on one half of the form and incidents of ineffective behavior on the other half. See Figure 4–4. Recording incidents of effective as well as ineffective behavior provides a constructive basis for postappraisal interviewing.

The remainder of the form is developed by the supervisor according to the categories and subcategories of responsibility for the employee's particular job. For example, a broad category of job responsibility might be called "Physical and Mental Qualifications." This category might then be broken down into (1) physical condition, (2) coordination, (3) checking and inspecting, (4) arithmetic computation, (5) learning and remembering procedures and instructions, (6) judgment and comprehension, (7) understanding and repairing mechanical devices, and (8) improving equipment and showing inventiveness. Another broad category of job responsibility might be "Work Habits and Attitudes" with a further breakdown of (1) productivity, (2) dependability, (3) accepting supervision and organizational procedures, (4) accuracy of reporting, (5) response to departmental needs, (6) getting along with others, (7) demonstrations of initiative, and (8) assuming responsibility. Space must be provided on the form for the brief recording of incidents (both commendable and undesirable) that occurred within a particular category of job responsibility. The supervisor then classifies the incidents according to the category guidelines that the form provides.

Using the Flanagan and Burns rating system will give a supervisor daily records of actual employee behavior. This, however, definitely should not be perceived by the workers as a "black book" routine. Positive as well as negative incidents must be recorded to get the true picture.

Ideally, a supervisor should consider the events of each day at its close, then record the exceptional, nonroutine incidents. The supervisor should not put off recording until next week or even tomorrow because of the danger that bad behavior will predominate over the good, or that the supervisor will forget the bad work done by the worker who is already favored and the good work by the worker with whom there is little acquaintance or who is disliked.

The Trait-Oriented Employee Rating Form

A trait- or characteristic-oriented employee rating form is presented in Figure 4–5. This rating system is different from the Employee Performance Record because it rates employees on the basis of general traits or characteristics rather than specific situational behavior. Several difficulties are connected with the use of this form.

First, the form encourages the recording of general perceptions in pre-established categories rather than specific instances of behavioral performance. This often results in the inability of the rater to identify specific instances of performance that were the basis of a "low" rating. Obviously, mutual respect, trust, and confidence suffer in such situations. Second, the form does not provide the opportunity for the rater to indicate "insufficient opportunity to observe" and thus not evaluate an individual in one or more categories. Supervisors are forced to guess and probably give an "average" rating because they

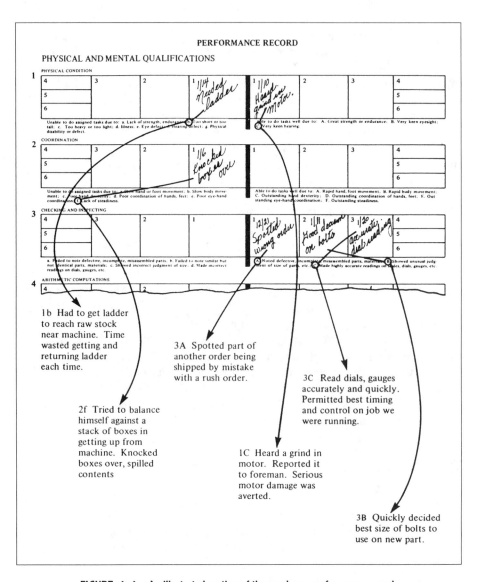

FIGURE 4-4   An illustrated section of the employee performance record.

are not sure. Third, employee evaluations should be continuous, not sporadic. Customarily, employee evaluations must be completed and turned in once or twice a year. With pre-established trait or characteristic rating categories, a supervisor has the tendency to wait until just before the deadline to complete the form and turn it in. Consequently, the supervisor must recall incidents that may have occurred months previously and that are only dim recollections that invite rating bias and encourage other types of generalized rating errors.

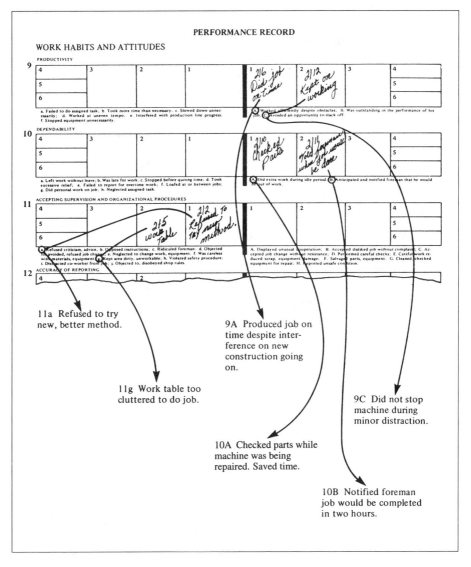

FIGURE 4–4   *(Continued)*.

The Flanagan-Burns Employee Performance Record tends to minimize the rating problems mentioned. However, the Trait-Oriented Employee Rating Form does have some advantages that undoubtedly account for its popularity and high incidence of use. First, the Trait-Oriented Employee Rating Form does not require the manager or supervisor to develop job rating categories that are specific to the worker's job. Initially, this makes it easier for a supervisor, but certainly not easier when called upon to provide information of employee performance that is specific to the job in question. Second, the Trait-Oriented Employee Rating Form requires only that the rater "check" the appropriate level (i.e., unsatisfactory, average, excellent) of a characteristic. It is not required first to identify the category of work responsibility within which the exceptional behavior occurred and then briefly record what the employee did

METROPOLITAN RECREATION DISTRICT
Employee Performance Rating Report

NAME _____ DEPARTMENT _____ POSITION _____

SECTION A   DATE OF REPORT _____

PERFORMANCE FACTORS	UNSATISFACTORY	BELOW STANDARD	STANDARD	GOOD	EXCEPTIONAL
RELIABILITY	Frequently reports late, is absent or leaves early, lacks proper attention to duty.	Occasionally tardy without reason, attendance irregular which hinders performance.	Usually on time, average attendance and work performance.	Always on time. Diligent in duties.	Always on time and spends extra time on job to improve himself. Very diligent in duties.
KNOWING THE JOB AND WORK QUANTITY	Displays inadequate ability despite constant and proper instruction.	Limited knowledge of job. Does not work to capacity.	Average knowledge of job and work habits.	Knows all phases of job. Works to capacity.	Knows all phases of job and strives to improve. Far above expectations.
INTEREST AND WORK ATTITUDE	Dislikes work, no enthusiasm, needs constant direction and watching.	Interest spasmodic, rarely enthusiastic. Needs considerable supervision.	Normal amount of interest in work. Some enthusiasm. Conscientious but needs regular supervision.	Interested in work. Usually enthusiastic. Only occasional supervision required.	High interest in work, very enthusiastic, always dependable in highest degree. Minimum supervision.
COOPERATION AND RELATIONSHIP WITH PEOPLE	Does not work well with or assist others in department. Antagonistic.	Seldom works with others. Occasionally will assist them if required to do so.	Generally works well with others. Frequently offers assistance.	Quick to volunteer in department projects, assignments; works well with and assists others.	Always inspires good teamwork. Exceptional in projects and assignments.
JUDGMENT	Poor sense of values, makes poor, impractical decisions.	Jumps to conclusions, makes decisions which should be referred to supervisor.	Decisions and judgment dependable on routine matters.	Uses common sense. Most decisions acceptable.	Sound judgment and decisions always based on thorough analysis.
QUALITY OF WORK	Makes constant mistakes. Inaccurate and makes errors. Cannot work under pressure.	Work not neat, or not consistently up to required standard.	Generally up to minimum standards in work. Works normally under pressure.	Work generally neat and well arranged. Makes accurate and adequate decisions when required to do so.	Work constantly neat and very well arranged. At best during pressure periods. Very accurate in all phases.
INITIATIVE	Needs much attention. Lacks self reliance and drive. Needs too much prodding.	Rarely suggests; good follower. Relies heavily on others.	Progressive. With encouragement often offers sound suggestions to improve job.	Resourceful. Develops assignments ably; makes new or original contributions.	Looks for and takes on additional tasks. Highly ingenious. Improves standards. Self starter with sound ideas.

COMMENTS   This space to be used for additional remarks for any above or below standard performance. If below standard, remarks should state what specific action is being taken to improve rating.

FIGURE 4-5   A trait-oriented employee rating form.

and the result of the behavior. In short, registering a check mark is immediately easier for the rater. However, the check mark is often a marginal basis for a promotion or discharge recommendation.

The Diagnostic Post-Appraisal Interview

Rating results must be communicated back from the supervisor-rater to the worker-ratee if employee resistance to rating is ever to be overcome. Keeping rating results from employees can only cause suspicion and distrust, which

SECTION B		SECTION B TO BE COMPLETED FOR SUPERVISORY EMPLOYEES ONLY		
PERFORMANCE FACTORS	UNSATISFACTORY	BELOW STANDARD	STANDARD	GOOD	EXCEPTIONAL
LEADERSHIP	Lacks full support and cooperation of subordinates. Easily prejudiced and maintains poor discipline.	Enjoys only passive support and cooperation. Not sufficiently objective or impersonal in business relations.	Obtains good support and cooperation. May encounter occasional difficulties in relationships with subordinates; not of serious nature, however.	Strong leader who has willing support and cooperation. Rarely experiences even minor difficulties.	Outstanding example of leadership. Always has enthusiastic support and cooperation of subordinates.
PERFORMANCE OF DEPARTMENT	Requires close supervision. Often has problems and is behind schedule.	Work occasionally lags. Requires more than normal supervision.	Performs well with reasonable promptness under normal supervision.	Consistently reliable under normal conditions. Department does special as well as required work with minimum supervision.	Work always on schedule even under most difficult circumstances. Little or no supervision needed.
ORGANIZATION AND PLANNING OF WORK	Frequently unable to assemble data for sequence of work.	Can only follow existing procedures involving routine details.	Capable of good planning of normal work, but needs guidance on major changes or projects.	Needs little guidance in any assignment. Well organized.	Clearly sees objectives. Planning and organization always outstanding.
DELEGATION OF RESPONSIBILITY	Over burdens self with unnecessary detail giving rise to conflicts between subordinates as to responsibilities.	Does not delegate wisely. Subordinates have too much or too little authority. Sometimes lacking a clear understanding of what is expected of him.	Generally does an adequate job of delegating. Subordinates know in most cases just what their responsibilities are.	Subordinates have better than average knowledge of their functions and relationships.	Excellent judgment in delegating responsibility. Subordinates know what is expected of them at all times.

COMMENTS: This space to be used for additional remarks for any above or below standard performance. If below standard, remarks should state what specific action is being taken to improve rating.

SECTION C

1. In your opinion is employee properly placed in right job? Yes ___ No___ If "No," what type of work do you feel he is best suited for?_____

2. Has employee expressed a desire for any other type of work with the Park District? Yes___ No___ If so, what position or in what department?_____

3. Do you consider the employee a candidate for promotion at this time? Yes___ No___ If "No," in the near future? Yes___ No___ To what job do you feel he could be advanced? _____

4. Has employee expressed dissatisfaction with his rate of promotion? Yes___ No___

5. What steps are presently being taken or are planned to prepare employee for promotion? (If "None" also state reason.) _____

OVERALL RATING ☐   ☐ ☐   ☐ ☐   ☐ ☐   ☐ ☐   ☐

UNSATISFACTORY   BELOW STANDARD   STANDARD   GOOD   EXCEPTIONAL

Employee's Signature _____ Date _____ Supervisor's Signature _____ Date _____

FIGURE 4-5 (Continued).

shatters mutual understanding and respect. The postappraisal interview should be approached from the standpoint of a private positive review of the worker's job performance with emphasis on correction and assistance to the worker rather than criticism and censure. Potentially, the diagnostic postappraisal interview is that time when the supervisor-rater can demonstrate the value of personnel rating to the employee by accentuating the positive.

Data provided by the Flanagan-Burns Employee Performance Record provides excellent postappraisal discussion information for both effective and ineffective employee job behavior and serves both worker guidance and job control requirements.

Maier points out that postappraisal interviews can be approached by the supervisor in three different ways: (1) the tell-and-sell approach, (2) the tell-and-listen style, or (3) the problem-solving approach.[11] Unless a supervisor is dealing with an uncooperative surly employee, he or she should use the tell-and-listen or problem-solving approaches, which stress the supervisor's role as a listener. This encourages an employee to explain and work out solutions to his or her own problems. Such an outcome develops employee self-confidence and a feeling of trust and mutual respect between worker and supervisor.

One of the problems that must be overcome is a supervisor's tendency not to discuss an employee's work performance at any time other than at the end of a performance rating period. In most cases a performance rating report is completed on an employee twice a year, but sometimes only once a year. A supervisor should not make the mistake of letting an employee go for that period of time without a discussion of those items that should be discussed at the time of occurrence. For instance, if an employee has been late to work three or four times, a supervisor should immediately talk with the employee rather than make a notation of the lateness and identifying it much later during the performance rating report. The performance report is an overall evaluation of the employee during a particular time period and should not hinder the supervisor in performing day-to-day responsibilities.

EMPLOYEE DISCIPLINE

Positive employee self-discipline results from the combination of willingness to carry out supervisory instructions, abide by known work rules, and inhibit personal behavior that might undermine the achievement of organizational objectives. Contributing to positive employee self-discipline are fair and carefully established work rules and regulations that are clearly understood and accepted.

Constructive work-group discipline generally rests upon a foundation of well-established policies executed through consistent supervisory practices. Consistent practice is helped by a clear listing of reasonable work-group rules, and the penalties for their violation are clearly understood by all employees. A systematic method for instructing employees as to work rules and job performance standards must be established.

There must also be a well-established procedure for fact finding as a basis for prompt disciplinary decision making prior to any disciplinary action. Supervisors may be involved with a great many disciplinary actions, ranging from a minor reprimand to legal prosecution for illegal job-associated activity. While other personnel in the organizational hierarchy may also be involved in decisions regarding cases of severe breaches of discipline, the supervisor must have documented detailed records of employee behavior as a basis for the action taken. With regard to positive motivation, supervisory warnings that prevent more serious breaches of discipline are preferable to more punitive measures. This is particularly true when the penalty causes hardship on the employee's family through economic deprivation.

Reprimands

In any reprimand situation, according to Sherwood, "The emphasis should be placed upon cooperative effort to avoid repetition of the incident rather than upon 'bawling out.' "[12] An employee should be given the opportunity to discuss the problem with the supervisor personally so that the employee has the chance to clear up any supervisory misunderstanding. In the majority of cases, the supervisor's method of reprimand is more important than what is done. The supervisor must handle the situation with extreme caution or run the risk of terminating any future mutual trust, respect, or two-way communication with the employee.

When approaching an employee, a supervisor must clearly establish which rules or regulations were broken. The supervisor should also interpret the consequences of the employee's act or failure to act. The reprimand should be given by the supervisor in private, allowing the employee ample opportunity to make a positive response.

Transfers

Unfortunately, the military game of "shape up or ship out" has also been played in civilian governmental service and in private industry. While there are several legitimate uses for transfer, such as meeting fluctuating workloads or increasing worker versatility, "there is little that can be said for the quality of supervision which 'passes on' its problem cases."[13]

LABOR RELATIONS

A maintenance supervisor is rarely involved in making final decisions relating to union contracts and policies. However, the importance of a maintenance supervisor's day-to-day relationship with the union should not be underestimated. A maintenance supervisor is on the firing line when it comes to handling grievances, taking disciplinary action, and adhering to other terms of the union agreement. Mistakes made at this point can be costly, which is why supervisors and group leaders must carry out management's policies and abide by the union contract to the letter.

Management Actions to Assist Supervisors in Labor Relations

Job descriptions should be developed by the park and recreation organization before entering into a collective bargaining agreement with the union. It is important that these job descriptions include the proviso that the employee may perform other tasks assigned. Such a provision in job descriptions, when included in the union agreement, guards against the inability of management to utilize services of employees when needed for emergency or nonemergency jobs not included in the job description.

A grievance procedure, which is simply a means for settling worker dissatisfactions through established channels, should be developed by a park and recreation organization even if an employee union does not exist.

Supervisory training for functional union understanding should be provided by the park and recreation organization if supervisors are expected to handle union complaints and grievances. Such a training program should include the following elements:

1. Familiarize the supervisor with collective bargaining laws of the state and local jurisdiction and keep supervisory personnel aware of new legislation.
2. Develop detailed supervisory understanding of the local collective bargaining agreement so as to avoid mistakes in abiding by the terms of the union contract.
3. Familiarize the supervisor with the local employee grievance procedure.
4. Train the supervisor to handle an employee grievance. Grievances are important managerial problems, and they demand prompt action, regardless of how trivial the complaint may appear. A grievance is a sign that something is irritating a person. Low morale, lack of job satisfaction, and complaining are contagious. The first line supervisor is the key to locating symptoms of employee dissatisfaction. This person must learn to be a good listener and to spot nonverbal complaints. Skill in interviewing and counseling will aid in finding the underlying causes of employee dissatisfaction. Recognize that behavior patterns may be symptoms of other problems unrelated to employment. Also, grievances, as expressed by an individual, often do not point to the heart of the problem. Management and union practices and employees' personality differences all have some effects on grievances.

Although grievances occur wherever people are employed, competent managers can do the following to prevent situations that precipitate grievances: anticipate grievances, have a well-defined procedure for handling them, and take care of them promptly.

A four-step approach for the proper handling of grievances utilized by the Aluminum Company of America[14] includes the following:

- *Receive the grievance properly.* This includes listening intently, taking notes, and generally impressing the complainant with your concern, and, finally, either making a decision then or advising the worker when to expect an answer from you.
- *Get the facts.* Gather all facts on the assumption that the case will have to be defended before an appeals board. Systematically check records that might dispute or support the facts as reported. Check personnel regulations. Verify the facts with other workers. Review the complaining employee's record. Reconcile any conflicting facts before making a decision.
- *Take action.* Any action that would make "right" any "wrong" situation caused by the supervisor or any other member of management might be included here, such as "going to bat" for a wronged employee if the facts warrant it or explaining to the worker what was wrong if the facts indicate this. Remain calm and advise the worker how to proceed with the next step of the grievance procedure if there is a threat to appeal. The supervisor should do nothing that would be detrimental to himself or herself at the hearing of the case. The supervisor should communicate in a dated written memorandum to his or her supervisor all facts in the situation.
- *Follow up.* Involved here is the supervisor making certain that the decision or planned action resulting from the grievance has been carried out, thus minimizing the possibility of other grievances coming from the same source.

5. Familiarize supervisors with the employee appeal procedure. Appeals arise from supervisory decisions, particularly those involving disciplinary penalties. When the employee does appeal a supervisory grievance decision, it is important for the supervisor to recognize that appeal boards usually require two types of proof. These are identified by Pfiffner[15] as (1) specific evidence of offenses or work rule infractions at particular times, dates, and places, and (2) assurance via facts and systematic records that the supervisor has exercised consistent efforts to warn, caution, help, and rehabilitate the worker.

In an appeals situation, the strength of the supervisor's case, in addition to the handling of the grievance, often rests upon a range of supervisory skills that include communication, counselling, training, and evaluation habits. Inconsistencies in employee evaluation, sarcastic communications, prejudicial treatment, and failure to inform employees of appeal rights work against the supervisor and invite the appeal board to reverse the supervisor's decision or reprimand the action.

REVIEW QUESTIONS

1. What approaches might be helpful for recruiting capable skilled maintenance workers for the recreation maintenance organization?
2. What is motivation?
3. Money has been identified as a temporary motivator. Identify and describe sound techniques or methods that have potential as permanent motivators.
4. As a supervisor, how would you attempt to motivate each employee in your work group?
5. What single leadership style is best for motivating all employees?
6. Identify the advantages of interpersonal communication between supervisor and employee compared to written organizational communication from management to employee.
7. Employee orientation should include certain elements. What are these elements?
8. What are the basic principles of learning upon which a job trainer can rely?
9. Describe the relative effectiveness of "telling" and "showing" and the "combination of telling and showing" on the human reception and retention of information.
10. Describe the four-step pattern of instruction developed by industry during World War II.
11. As a supplement to training, explain the utility of maintenance operations manuals.
12. Reducing employee accidents rests largely upon what major factor?
13. Describe the scope of park and recreation occupational injuries as compared with the average of all industries.
14. What is the extent of injuries to park and recreational maintenance operations personnel as compared with total park/recreation occupational injuries?
15. What is OSHA? How does it influence local governmental public park and recreation maintenance employees?
16. Describe the problem of employee safety with temporary and seasonal employees. Indicate what steps can be taken to minimize the problem.
17. Describe the minimum safety requirements recommended by the National Safety Council for the use of tools by maintenance personnel.
18. Personal protection equipment for maintenance personnel should include what equipment?
19. What is the purpose(s) of employee ratings?
20. Describe rater bias and prejudice. Indicate what a rater might do to avoid bias and prejudice.
21. The most common employee rating errors are leniency, the halo effect, central tendency, and contrast and association errors. Describe the cause and influence of each and indicate what the rater might do to minimize their effects.

22. Outline the advantages of using the Flanagan-Burns Employee Performance Record rather than the Trait-Oriented Employee Rating Form.
23. Describe the purpose and proper procedure of the diagnostic postappraisal interview.
24. Outline the four-step approach that a supervisor may use in properly handling an employee grievance.
25. Describe the two basic requirements necessary for constructive work group discipline.
26. Describe the proper supervisory steps to be taken when reprimanding an employee and the criteria to determine whether or not to transfer the reprimanded worker.

CHAPTER BIBLIOGRAPHY

Adam, Everette, and Ebert, Ronald J. *Production and Operations Management—Concepts, Models, and Behavior.* Englewood Cliffs, NJ: Prentice-Hall, 1978.

Brademas, D. James; Lowen, George A.; and Beaman, John. *Personnel Performance Appraisal Practices in Leisure Services Agencies.* Champaign-Urbana, IL: University of Illinois, 1981.

Buechner, Robert D. *Public Employee Unions—Organizations—A Manual for Park and Recreation Officials.* Management Aid Bulletin no. 81. Arlington, VA: National Recreation and Park Association, 1969.

Calvert, Robert. *Affirmative Action: A Comprehensive Recruitment Manual.* Garrett Park, MD: Garrett Park Press, 1979.

Culkin, David, and Howard, Dennis. "Collective Bargaining and Recreation and Park Operation." *Parks and Recreation* 17 (October 1982): 60.

Dessler, Gary. *Personnel Management—Modern Concepts and Techniques.* Reston, VA: Reston Publishing, 1978.

Fazio, James R., and Gilbert, Douglas L. *Public Relations and Communications for Natural Resource Managers.* Dubuque, IA: Kendall/Hunt, 1981.

Halloran, Jack. *Supervision: The Act of Management.* Englewood Cliffs, NJ: Prentice-Hall, 1981.

Horney, Robert L. *Administrative Development Series, Part I and Part II.* National Recreation and Park Association Management Aid Bulletins Nos. 91 and 92. Arlington, VA, 1972.

Imundo, Louis. "Employee Discipline: How To Do It Right." Managers and Supervisors Seminar, Oakland County, Michigan, September 1983.

International City Managers Association. *Effective Supervisory Practices.* Chicago: International City Managers Association, 1965.

Monday, Wayne R., and Noe, Robert M., III. *Personnel: The Management of Human Resources.* Boston: Allyn and Bacon, 1981.

National Foremans Institute. *The Supervisor's Workshop.* Waterford, CT: American Park and Recreation Society, 1968.

Pankon, Peter. "How to Keep a Firing from Backfiring," *Nations Business* 71 (June 1983): 74.

Paul, William; Robinson, Keith; and Herzbert, Fredrick. "Job Enrichment Pay-Off." *Harvard Business Review* 31 (March/April 1969): 95.

Schuler, Randall L. *Personnel and Human Resource Management.* St. Paul, MN: West Publishing Co., 1981.

Sterle, David E., and Duncan, Mary E. *Supervision of Leisure Services.* San Diego, CA: San Diego State University Press, 1973.

Sternloff, Robert E. "Conducting Education Programs for Leisure Services Personnel." A position paper prepared for and adopted by the National Council of the National Recreation and Park Association, Arlington, Virginia, 1973.

Strauss, George, and Sayles, Leonard R. *Personnel: The Human Problems of Management.* 4th ed. Englewood Cliffs, NJ: Prentice-Hall, 1980.

Weber, George O., ed., and Fincham, Michael W. *A Basic Manual for Physical Plant Administration.* Washington, DC: The Association of Physical Plant Administrators of Universities and Colleges, 1974.

NOTES

1. David McClelland, *Studies in Motivation* (New York: Appleton, Century, Crofts, 1955).
2. E. Ghiselli, M. Haire, and E. Lawler, *Managerial Thinking: An International Study* (New York: Wiley, 1966).
3. Environmental Management Association, *Index to Visual Aids for Environmental Sanitation and Maintenance Management Education and Training,* 1710 Drew Street, Clearwater, Florida.
4. National Safety Council, *Public Employee Safety Guide—Parks and Recreation* (Chicago: National Safety Council, 1974), 4–5.
5. Ibid.
6. Leonard Wilcox, "You Can Survive an OSHA Inspection," *INC.* (February 1981): 49–51.
7. National Safety Council, *Public Employee Safety Guide,* 16–17.
8. Ibid., pp. 6–13.
9. David E. Sterle and Mary R. Duncan, *Supervision of Leisure Services* (San Diego, CA: San Diego State University Press, 1973), 87.
10. John C. Flanagan and Robert K. Burns, "The Employee Performance Record: A New Appraisal and Development Tool," *Harvard Business Review* 33 (September/October 1955): 95–102.
11. R. R. Maier, *Principles of Human Relations,* 6th ed. (New York: Wiley, 1959), pp. 403–09.
12. Frank P. Sherwood and Wallace H. Best, *Supervisory Methods in Municipal Administration* (Chicago: International City Managers Association, 1958), 223.
13. Ibid.
14. Aluminum Company of America, "A Four-Step Approach to Handling Grievances," in *Effective Communication on the Job,* eds. Joseph M. Dooher and Vivienne Marquis (New York: American Management Association, 1956), 207.
15. John M. Pfiffner, *The Supervision of Personnel,* 2d ed. (Englewood Cliffs, NJ: Prentice-Hall, 1958), 368.

CHAPTER 5

MAINTENANCE OF BUILDINGS AND STRUCTURES

P ark and recreation buildings and structures represent millions of dollars in initial construction with replacement costs estimated annually at a growing 10 percent over and above original construction costs. Consequently, park and recreation building and structure maintenance is very important. This chapter is organized into the three major aspects of building and structure maintenance: (1) building structure and systems maintenance, (2) preventive maintenance, and (3) custodial or housekeeping maintenance. The building maintenance organizational chart presented in Figure 5–1 illustrates this organizational arrangement for a large park and recreation program.

The principles of building maintenance presented here apply not only to large building structures but also to smaller buildings and structures, such as picnic shelters; campground washhouses; swimming pool locker, shower, and toilet areas; vacation cabins; snack bars; and to certain aspects of outdoor partial structures, such as amphitheaters and campfire seating circles.

If a building maintenance division can hire only two people, exclusive of custodial personnel, one of them should be a general purpose maintenance person capable of working on several building structural components. The other person should be capable of providing general care to the systems within the building.

ORGANIZATION AND STAFFING

In a small park and recreation system, the maintenance staff often consists of a handful of generalists—personnel who are multiskilled. Their supervisor is often the overall maintenance manager. To develop a building maintenance staff to serve a small recreation system, the maintenance manager should hire the following basic corps of trades personnel:

129

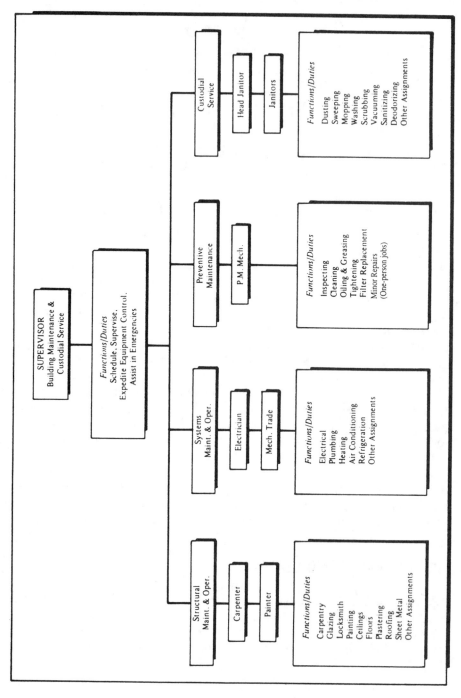

FIGURE 5–1 An organizational chart for the building maintenance of a large park and recreation system.

- *Carpenter,* competent to handle cabinet making, furniture repair, glazing, screening, puttying, caulking, latches, and locks.
- *Electrician,* trained in and capable of handling both lighting and power.
- *Mechanic,* capable also to work as a plumber and steamfitter.
- *Painter,* capable also to glaze, putty, caulk, spackle, and lay asphalt and vinyl asbestos floors; install insulation around pipes; and is familiar and reasonably capable in handling most kinds of surface coatings and coverings.

The staff should be augmented as additional personnel are required. A carpenter's helper and a second mechanic would be of great benefit. (The second mechanic will allow the department to divide pipe work into heating and cooling—for technical reasons, one person is seldom strong enough in both fields.)

STRUCTURAL AND SYSTEMS MAINTENANCE

Significant improvements continue to be made in almost every category of building structures and systems materials, and the maintenance materials and methods necessary for these. Building maintenance requires an organization capable of emergency, preventive, and corrective work on a wide variety of structures and systems. Building structural work is highly diversified in that it includes roofs, walls, windows, doors, floors, and foundations. Structural maintenance work requires personnel skilled in handling lumber, masonry, concrete, mortar, flashings, wall and floor coverings, and a variety of other structural maintenance and repair materials.

Systems to be maintained include wiring, ducts, pipes, elevators, and escalators built into a structure. Maintenance of such systems requires personnel skilled in heating and ventilating, air conditioning, plumbing, electrical lighting, gas, compressed air, fire alarms, and sprinklers. Other specialists needed, in order of descending importance, are a combination of roof and sheet metal mechanic, a mason, a machinist, and a welder.

Building maintenance staff organization in small recreation systems is usually quite simple, with individual trades people reporting directly to the maintenance manager, a building superintendent, or possibly a shop supervisor.

MAINTENANCE STANDARDS FOR BUILDINGS

Building maintenance standards are the established level at which the structure should be maintained to ensure maximum, overall economy consistent with its functional requirement. For example, a warehouse scheduled for removal within five years should not be maintained at the same standard or level of maintenance as a warehouse scheduled for retention for twenty-five years. Consequently, more than one level or standard of building maintenance may be developed and approved for use by the recreation system policy-making authority. Multiple-level building maintenance standards developed by the National Park Service are presented in the appendix to this chapter.

BASIC APPROACHES TO STRUCTURE AND SYSTEM MAINTENANCE

The two basic philosophies that prevail in the general maintenance field, corrective maintenance and preventive maintenance, often clash regarding building maintenance. Corrective maintenance emphasizes reacting to maintenance problems after they occur rather than anticipating them. Although reaction to a problem is an important part of any complete maintenance program, it should never compromise an organization's total program as is sometimes the case when maintenance funds are inadequate. Inevitably, this leads to crisis maintenance, which, ultimately, is the most expensive kind of program. Preventive maintenance emphasizes the identification and elimination of potential problems before they disrupt building operations. An effective preventive maintenance program does require an initial outlay of time and money for proper organization. However, it normally repays the original cost many times over by minimizing potential damage, reducing emergency overtime work, and eliminating expensive rush purchasing.

PREVENTIVE MAINTENANCE

To establish a preventive maintenance program, the key to minimizing emergency repair work, a procedure must be established for identifying potential breakdowns and making adjustments or small repairs, thus avoiding the costs of major repairs and unscheduled shutdowns. Identification of the need for preventive maintenance is not established by gazing into a crystal ball but, rather, through the development and institution of systematic inspection procedures. Reduced to its basic elements, preventive maintenance consists of identification of maintenance needs through inspecting and proceeding to clean, lubricate, tighten, adjust, and replace worn or damaged parts when necessary. Preventive maintenance includes such items as the following:

building surfaces, exterior and interior
door closers
door hinges
drains
exhaust fans
fan belts
faucets
filters

light bulbs
light fixtures
mechanical rooms
motors
pumps
shower valves
toilets

Preventive Maintenance Job Inventory

Preventive maintenance job assignments for each park and recreation organization must be tailored according to buildings and equipment and their number, types, and ages. To develop accurate job assignments and instructions, a building maintenance supervisor or delegate—possibly a preventive maintenance mechanic—must develop a complete list of all preventive maintenance tasks. This inventory should include instructions to the mechanic as to how to proceed. The following list is an example of such tasks:

- Inspect buildings in area and report all deficiencies you cannot correct to the work control desk.
- Keep mechanical rooms clean and orderly at all times.
- Tighten or adjust door closers and window locks and hinges.
- Replace burned-out light bulbs and fluorescent tubes.
- Open clogged toilets and drains with plunger or hand auger. If fixture requires power auger or must be disassembled, report it to the work control desk.
- Repair leaking water faucets and shower heads.

Such jobs are not assigned according to a regular schedule, but are done whenever a preventive maintenance mechanic discovers them during rounds, or whenever a building occupant reports them. After inspecting the reported problem, the preventive maintenance mechanic should either correct the condition alone or report it to the work control desk. To guide the mechanic, the preventive maintenance supervisor should stress the importance of not attempting jobs requiring considerable time, a high level of expertise, or additional personnel.

Scheduling Preventive Maintenance Work

Organizing various maintenance jobs into a work schedule is one of the most difficult aspects of establishing a preventive maintenance program. Once the work inventory for equipment maintenance has been compiled, the main problem is integrating tasks into the daily and weekly maintenance work routines. While most preventive maintenance personnel can remember their normal daily and weekly tasks, few can be expected to remember such infrequent tasks as monthly valve testings, semiannual greasings, and even annual cleaning or replacement of parts.

Once routine or preventive jobs have been defined from equipment manuals, they should be filed for easy reference. Two filing techniques have proven quite effective as reminders of infrequent maintenance tasks.

1. *Reminder tab file.* This procedure utilizes a card file consisting of one card for each piece of equipment needing preventive maintenance. Each card

identifies a piece of equipment according to its location and lists each type of maintenance required, indicating recommended frequency, replacement parts, lubrications, and supplies needed. Space is provided opposite each preventive maintenance job to record performance dates. Colored code tabs are attached to cards to identify daily, weekly, monthly, semiannual, and annual jobs. By checking this file regularly, the preventive maintenance mechanic can find when each job was done last and quickly determine when the next one is due. See Figure 5–2.

   2. *Frequency code cards.* This alternative procedure requires a different card for each preventive maintenance task. Different card colors indicate task frequency (weekly, monthly, semiannual, etc.). Each card includes cross-references to all other work needed. More cards are required under this system but this allows more room for listing important data, parts, and supplies, and for recording dates when work is accomplished.

   To supplement information from card files, the preventive maintenance mechanic can use floor space diagrams and community and park maps to further organize the work routine. Maps and diagrams of the work area will allow the preventive maintenance mechanic to locate all major equipment maintenance jobs and mark the diagrams and maps, using a color code that complements the card file system. The preventive maintenance mechanic can then plan

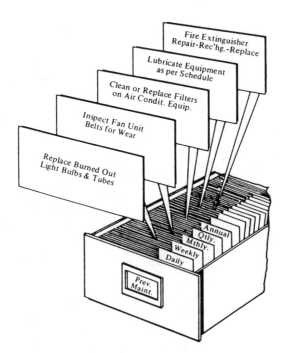

FIGURE 5–2   Reminder tab file for preventive maintenance.

to take the most time-saving routes to follow on different days. Since many jobs are not done daily, several routes are necessary. Even though the routes vary frequently, time spent mapping the best route is still time well spent. Such planning saves wasted steps and reminds the preventive maintenance mechanic to carry appropriate tools and supplies.

Preventive Maintenance Personnel

An effective preventive maintenance mechanic is a troubleshooter who possesses a variety of skills. Ideally, preventive maintenance mechanics will come from a broad, multitrade background and bring with them expertise for analyzing equipment breakdowns, estimating work, coping with emergencies, and understanding operating instructions for complex electrical and mechanical equipment. Of equal importance, they should have initiative and the ability to work independently and perform competently. They must also recognize their own limitations and not attempt jobs requiring excessive time, greater skill than they possess, or additional personnel.

Locating personnel with these qualities is not easy, training them is difficult, and keeping them is even more difficult, especially since skilled specialists generally command higher salaries and greater esteem. Some organizations, therefore, have tried to upgrade the job by establishing a separate higher job classification for preventive maintenance mechanics and paying good people what they deserve.

Preventive Maintenance Work Assignments

Area maintenance and crew maintenance are two widely used methods for accomplishing preventive maintenance work. Many organizations combine these two approaches to benefit from the advantages of each.

Area Maintenance

Using the area maintenance method, a preventive maintenance mechanic is responsible for a clearly defined area. One system, for instance, may assign each preventive maintenance mechanic a specific number of buildings. Another system may assign a maximum number of gross square feet of specific building floor space per preventive maintenance mechanic. The appropriate assignment depends upon the conditions in each system. Preventive maintenance mechanics may set up small shops for their area where building plans, manuals, records, tools, and regularly used parts and supplies are kept. Major tasks include inspecting, cleaning, lubricating, adjusting, and making small repairs—tasks which are closely related and generally accomplished on the job site.

The equipment job inventory establishes the limits of the mechanic's work responsibility.

The advantages of the area maintenance method include more thorough coverage, resulting in early discovery of developing problems, and on-the-spot repairs that save paperwork and travel time. Area maintenance personnel become familiar with local problems and peculiarities of the area, its equipment, and its occupants. The area method allows for flexibility in scheduling, which averts schedule conflicts with special recreation programs and events. Area maintenance also establishes the basis upon which personal job commitment grows. When workers are solely responsible for an area, they usually develop considerable pride in its condition.

The greatest limitation to area maintenance is the individual working alone. Unless a job is within easy reach and can be handled by one person without need for additional personnel or special tools, a crew or contractor must be called in. A preventive maintenance mechanic can replace most light bulbs but must call in a contractor or special crew with tall ladders for bulb replacement in high ceilings. When the hand auger or plunger will not work to clear a toilet drain, a plumber with a special power tool must be summoned. Door hinges can be tightened by the preventive maintenance mechanic, but repairs to locks require a locksmith.

Crew Maintenance

The crew approach to maintenance tends to overcome the limitations inherent in the single-person area method. Using this approach, a crew combines to cover a larger zone. In a small system, the area might include all recreation buildings. The crew supervisor organizes the maintenance work: inspecting, making job lists, ordering parts and supplies, assigning workers, and reviewing their work. Ability as an organizer spells the difference between effective and ineffective crew maintenance.

A crew has flexibility and can complete more jobs than a single worker. Assuming good supervision, only the necessary number of workers would be assigned to handle each job; in some instances, everyone on the crew might work alone to accomplish individual assignments. In other situations, the entire crew might be assigned to a single project. Further flexibility comes from the relative ease with which a crew compensates for absences.

Certain disadvantages and complications are associated with crew maintenance. Crew members do not become as familiar with the larger territory and its troubles as would the single mechanic. Team coverage makes the fixing of responsibility for unsatisfactory performance more difficult. A major complication with crew maintenance is the difficulty in assigning proper numbers of crew personnel. There is a tendency to assign two or more people even if a job does not warrant them, resulting in featherbedding and economic loss to the organization.

Preventive Maintenance Shop

Both area and crew maintenance are best served when a small shop serving as a base of operations is established for each major area of the park and recreation system. The preventive maintenance shop should contain the following:

- Maintenance and operating equipment manuals provided by manufacturers.
- Technical drawings, including the "as-built" architectural, structural, electrical, and mechanical prints for each building in the area.
- Records, inventories of equipment and preventive work to be done, and logs of work completed.
- Supplies, a small stock of repair parts, and maintenance materials most frequently used.
- Tools—those usually found in a maintenance mechanic's kit include such items as wrenches, a bulb extractor, an electric drill, a flashlight, a set of screwdrivers, pliers, a water key, toilet plunger and auger, fuse puller, a grease gun, and a hammer.

Preventive Maintenance Records

In addition to keeping equipment and work inventories and work schedules, a maintenance mechanic should maintain concise daily records of all work completed for each piece of equipment. Major equipment jobs should be noted in two places—on a dated tag attached to the equipment and on the inventory record kept in the maintenance shop. These records, if properly kept, complete a work history for all equipment in the area.

Maintenance personnel also should record all work for the department's work control system. Figure 5–3 shows a form for reporting work time expended and materials used. In the time consumption charged to each job, a mechanic includes time allowed for planning, ordering supplies, travel, cleanup, and recordkeeping. Since maintenance workers also use time for planning, tool care, recordkeeping, coffee breaks, and such things as resupply, a shop time allowance of perhaps 15 percent of the workday is generally acceptable.

EQUIPMENT AND SUPPLIES
FOR BUILDING MAINTENANCE

The use and availability of proper maintenance equipment and maintenance supplies greatly influence the adequacy of a building and structure maintenance program. New and improved maintenance equipment and supplies are continuously available. A common-sense approach would be to test the many new products offered on the market today on a limited basis prior to accepting any one of them as a total replacement. With changes in cleaning technology developing so rapidly, a recreation maintenance manager should assign one person to review current maintenance publications and to investigate new developments that might prove economical in future operations. Manufacturers of maintenance supplies readily provide information and assistance regarding the proper use of their products and the development of justifications for new purchases.

Criteria for Purchasing Equipment

Personnel. Prior to purchasing a particular piece of maintenance equipment, competent operating personnel must be available to operate the equipment. Should operating personnel not be available, the possibility of having the maintenance service provided on a contractual basis should be investigated.

Work Categories	Bldg. No.		Bldg. No.		Bldg. No.		Bldg. No.	
	Time Hrs.	Material Cost	Time Hrs.	Material Cost	Time Hrs.	Material Cost	Time Hrs.	Material Cost
Air Conditioning								
Carpentry								
Electrical								
Heating								
Painting								
Plumbing								
Roofing								
Ventilation								
Other Specify*								
TOTAL								

RECREATION/PARK SYSTEM

PM AREA _____ DATE _____

Signed _____

*Refers to vacations, sick leave, shop time, etc.

FIGURE 5-3   Preventive maintenance daily work report.

Frequency of use. Should the maintenance equipment item under consideration be required only on an occasional basis, then it would be well to investigate the possibility of renting such equipment when it is needed.

Replacement parts and repair service. A major consideration in the selection of maintenance equipment would be the immediate availability of parts and repair service so as to minimize the "down" time of the equipment in question.

Equipment storage space. Proper storage for maintenance equipment is essential to minimize deterioration and accelerated repairs due to improper storage. Adequate storage space should be available before acquiring maintenance equipment.

Equipment versatility. In appraising expensive equipment, maintenance managers in park and recreation systems should make special note of the machine's versatility. Some floor cleaning pieces, for example, can clean, scrub, buff, and even vacuum. Every additional job that a tool can handle bolsters the economic justification for purchasing it. Some of the greatest savings can come in the area of floor maintenance, a job that consumes 30 to 40 percent of the custodial budget.

Equipment size. Before selecting a particular brush, broom, or machine, analyze each size available. A nineteen-inch disk floor machine, for instance, may cost 15 percent more, but it will cover 25 percent more area. The size of the equipment must also be correlated with characteristics of the area. A forty-eight-inch broom will obviously cover twice as much space as a twenty-four-inch broom, but it may prove too cumbersome for cramped hallways and stairs.

Equipment standardization. Standardization is important because it simplifies repair and replacement of key parts. It also reduces stock room costs and confusion, since parts for only one type of each machine need to be stored. According to one expert, standardization is valuable enough to justify giving those companies featuring it a 5 to 10 percent advantage in a competitive bidding situation.

Custodial Maintenance Equipment

The following list of custodial maintenance equipment is recommended for building custodial care in a small park and recreation system:

1. Floor machines, 18 in.
2. Vacuum cleaner, domestic type.
3. Vacuum cleaner, industrial type with attachments.
4. Floor machine, large, capable of scrubbing large areas (gymnasiums).
5. Wall washing machine.
6. Carpet-pile-lifter machine.

Evaluation of Supplies

Maintenance supplies, because of their regular use, usually represent costly budget items. It is most important, therefore, that the various kinds of supply items available to accomplish a particular task be evaluated as to their efficiency and appropriateness for the type and location of the building or facility being maintained.

Standardization

The benefits of standardization in the use of supplies may be experienced in standardized personnel training and in financial saving because of ordering greater quantities at lesser costs. Standardization has practical application to maintenance equipment in that replacement parts and repair service for multiple pieces of equipment of the same brand greatly simplifies the repair process.

Stockpiling of Maintenance Supplies

Stockpiling supplies, as well as some building and construction materials, can prove to be economical. Certainly time can be saved by immediately scheduling work without waiting for parts and materials to be ordered and delivered. However, adequate storage must be available, together with personnel who are responsible for a system of inventory control to ensure availability and to prevent overstocking of particular items. In addition, control over environmental factors such as heat, cold, ventilation, light, and dampness is essential in any successful stockpiling effort.

Stockpiling can result in lower prices by the use of contracyclical purchasing, that is, to purchase items during periods of depressed prices. The proximity to a supplier is another important consideration as to whether or not one should stockpile. If a supplier is close at hand, in most instances, it would be wise to use their storage facilities if the maintenance department's storage is limited or nonexistent. The type and amount of equipment and supplies will vary with each building and structure and its pattern of use. Careful analysis and sound planning will result in the saving of substantial costs.

CUSTODIAL OR HOUSEKEEPING SERVICES

Today's building custodial work is, by necessity, the responsibility of a specialist knowledgeable in the use of the latest maintenance equipment, materials, and techniques. No longer is the building custodian a manual laborer who sells the services of muscles. An effective building custodian is now a specialist who understands the chemistry of cleaning agents and the synthetics and plastics involved in building and furniture construction; an engineer who understands the proper use and care of power equipment; and a businessperson who wisely and economically spends the maintenance dollar for top quality results. Modern day maintenance custodians also must serve effectively as public relations persons, police officers, trainers of other employees, and guardians of public health and safety in and around the building or structure for which they are responsible.

Custodial Cleaning Standards

Ideally, a housekeeping manager would begin a cleaning operation by first establishing standards or levels of cleanliness and then deducing what finances, personnel, equipment, and supplies are necessary to achieve them. Unfortunately, housekeeping managers rarely enjoy the opportunity to start from scratch. Instead, they usually inherit an ongoing operation in which standards are determined by past funding levels. It is also unfortunate that a housekeeping manager rarely finds logically developed and widely accepted standards to apply.

Most authorities recommend that every recreation system develop its own building cleaning standards without explaining what these standards should be or how they should be discovered. The discussion of cleaning standards is usually concluded with the statement that each agency establish standards according to "organizational or community preference."

In practice, there are two kinds of cleaning standards: general and specific. General standards usually apply to the whole park and recreation system or to individual recreation buildings, and it is usually the members of the recreation system governing board who decide which level of cleanliness—fair, good, or excellent—will be met under current budgetary restrictions. Specific cleaning standards apply to the frequencies and methods used for specific cleaning tasks. To accomplish a change in general standards, the custodial division alters the specific standards. For example, as part of a program to upgrade a recreation system from fair to good, a custodial manager might require all hallways to be damp-mopped three times weekly instead of once weekly and all rugs and carpets to be vacuumed daily rather than weekly.

General and specific cleaning standards require the establishment of performance categories such as fair, good, or excellent. Each category should be clearly defined in specific, although arbitrary, performance levels by the custodial manager. Note the multilevel housekeeping standards that appear in the appendix to this chapter.

The manager of a well-organized custodial division will be able to show the recreation system governing board how much time (and therefore how much money) will be needed to provide each level of cleaning for every kind of building area. Table 5–1 illustrates how such an area cleaning time list might be developed for recreation center buildings. Methods utilized for determining

TABLE 5–1   Achievement levels of cleaning for major areas in a hypothetical recreation center building.

	Excellent	Good	Fair
Center Office	12 min.	10 min.	8 min.
Center Gymnasium	25	20	15
Center Shower & Locker Room	30	25	20
Center Lounge	20	15	10
Center Meeting Room	17	15	10
Small Library	21	15	10
Bathroom Fixtures	23	20	20
Equipment & Supply Room (150 sq. ft.)	7	5	3

cleaning performance times are discussed later in this chapter.

When a custodial manager inherits an ongoing cleaning service with implicit standards based on past funding, the manager should avoid altering the operation and defining explicit standards until he or she knows how well the current service is operating. To evaluate the current service, the manager should determine how both the building custodians and the building occupants appraise the existing program.

Such an evaluation can be conducted on the basis of two prepared questionnaires. The first questionnaire would require custodial personnel to describe the tasks for which they believe they are responsible, noting the frequency of execution and self-evaluation of the effectiveness of their job performance. A second questionnaire would then be prepared and distributed to recreation building occupants requesting that they describe the cleaners' work and rate the results as good, fair, or poor.

From an analysis of the information provided by this evaluation, the custodial manager can get a fairly accurate indication of the work being done as well as a fairly reliable estimate of the actual cleaning standards being achieved. This information then should provide an initial basis for recommendations to the system administrator and the system policy-making body for service expansion or reduction and a policy statement establishing cleaning standards.

Custodial Staffing

A policy statement from the policy-making body that establishes general cleaning standards will greatly simplify the practical problems of determining custodial staff needs. A cleaning standards policy will provide a goal for cleaning frequencies and methods that a custodial manager can convert into numbers of custodians and types of cleaning equipment. However, the cleaning standards policy statement is only the starting point in solving staffing problems.

Following the establishment of cleaning standards, the building maintenance manager should develop a custodial task inventory that consists of all the building housekeeping jobs for which the division is responsible during one complete year. The evaluation questionnaire suggested earlier can be of considerable help as a start in developing the custodial task inventory. The task inventory will allow the housekeeping manager to determine what the annual worker-hour load for his or her section should be. With hour deductions for vacations, holidays, and estimated sick leave, the total work force needs cannot be justified in terms of high personnel costs. Therefore, the custodial task inventory must be refined in order to more accurately determine custodial needs.

Three basic approaches to determine proper staffing levels are used with no widespread agreement as to which method is the most effective except the general agreement that the more complex methods will probably increase custodial efficiency and will require more time and energy to put into practice.

The following staffing determination methods are presented in order of complexity, from simple to complex.

1. *Staffing by square footage.* This approach simply uses a crude rule-of-thumb guide, such as one person-year per 15,000 general square feet (arbitrary figure). The manager simply divides the recreation system's total building floor area by the arbitrarily selected figure to identify the number of persons needed to handle the annual workload. Because of its simplicity, it is probably the most popular staffing method. Because it fails to distinguish among the different kinds of space to be cleaned (e.g., gym floors versus office space), it is definitely the least accurate method unless carefully modified on the basis of experience and results.

2. *Staffing by typical area measurement.* This system is a modification of the traditional time and motion study and requires custodial managers to follow six basic steps.

- Catalog each building in the system for the different spaces to be cleaned: office, meeting, activity room, and so forth.
- Time the work of several custodians in each kind of area and observe the different cleaning methods employed.
- Average all times for like areas. This number will be important for calculating total work force and for estimating future workload changes resulting from new buildings.
- Divide each building into floors. Calculate workload for each floor by multiplying the number of each kind of area by its average cleaning time. For example, 6 offices at 10 minutes per office means 60 minutes cleaning time is required.
- Add all the times together. Divide by the number of minutes each custodian works per day to get the number of people required to perform the duties at the specified cleaning level.
- To establish the budget request, classify the positions and multiply the number of positions by the proposed wage.

3. *Staffing by time and motion study.* This method requires a total inventory of each task a custodial division must perform.

- Supervisors must go into every room of every building in the system and count the number of desks, chairs, file cabinets, trash baskets, light fixtures, air registers, window shades, and blinds, and then record the different types of cleaning surfaces on these fixtures, floors, walls, and ceilings.
- With such an inventory, supervisors look up what the average cleaning time should be for each task. A source might be the average cleaning times as estimated and published by the Environmental Management Association, 1710 Drew Street, Clearwater, Florida, or as modified to experience. (See Figure 5–4 and Figure 5–5.)
- Using the cleaning standards utilized by the organization, custodial managers then multiply the frequencies for each job by the average cleaning time.
- By adding the results, managers will find the total number of worker hours required annually. From this sum, the number of workers needed for the custodial staff can be determined.

Since these calculations use national averages, the important variable to watch for is local differences in worker productivity, which can be significant. Custodial managers can develop a more accurate variant of this method by measuring and averaging actual work times of employees and comparing them with the time standards of the Environmental Management Association. This kind of inventory is time-consuming to compile, but it will provide several potential benefits:

1. It will help the manager establish staffing requirements with greater accuracy than other methods.
2. It will enable the manager to develop realistic and equitable job assignments.
3. It will provide the manager with comprehensive job descriptions.
4. It will allow the manager to exercise daily quality control by use of complete task check lists.
5. It will permit the manager to exercise effective job correction procedures.

Following the selection and use of one of the methods mentioned above to determine annual workload, the custodial manager should proceed with several additional calculations. The number of hours per work week (assuming 40) are multiplied by the number of weeks per year (52), which results in 2,080 potential work hours per year. However, the custodial manager must correct the 2,080 hours to allow for vacation time, holidays, and average sick leave, which usually reduces the number of productive work hours to approximately 1,800. By using this figure, the manager can divide the annual worker-hour workload to get the number of custodial personnel needed. The manager can then estimate the number of supervisors necessary to provide a proper span of control over the custodians. The proper span of control is the number of subordinates a particular

Building _____ Room _____ Square Feet _____

Operation	Weekly Fre-quency	Quantity	Unit Measure	Unit Time	Weekly Time
Ash Tray, clean			Each	0.25	
Ash Urn, empty			Each	1.00	
Bookcase, dust			Each	0.36	
Bulletin Boards, change			Each	1.80	
Chairs, Medium, dust			Each	0.58	
Chairs, Small, dust			Each	0.37	
Chalk Boards, clean			100 Lin Ft	17.70	
Desk, Large, dust			Each	0.80	
Desk, Small, dust			Each	0.63	
Doors, clean			Each	0.67	
Drinking Fountain, wash			Each	2.00	
Filing Cabinets, dust			Each	0.37	
Floor, dry clean (Heavily Obstructed)			M Sq Ft	16.00	
Floor, dry clean (Slightly Obstructed)			M Sq Ft	10.00	
Floor, dry clean (Unobstructed)			M Sq Ft	5.00	
Furniture, vacuum			Each	2.16	
Hospital Unit, clean			Each	15.00	
Hospital Unit, Check Out, clean			Each	30.00	
Lamps, dust			Each	0.25	
Lecturn, dust			Each	0.25	
Lockers, dust			100 Lin Ft	5.00	
Mirror, wash and polish			Sq Ft	0.10	
Pencil Sharpener, empty			Each	0.25	
Piano, dust & wash keys			Each	2.50	
Radiator, dust			Each	0.60	
Rugs, vacuum			M Sq Ft	22.20	
Shelves, dust			100 Lin Ft	2.00	
Sink, Soap Dispenser, clean and refill			Each	2.00	
Stairs, dust			Flight	4.00	
Telephone, dust			Each	0.15	
Toilet, clean, private			Each	1.00	
Towel Disp, clean/refill			Each	0.25	
Venetian Blind, dust			Each	3.50	
Waste Basket, empty			Each	0.25	
Window Sill, dust			Each	0.20	
Windows, wash, inside			Sq Ft	0.168	

FIGURE 5–4   Sample inventory of light duty custodial tasks.
Reproduced with permission of the Environmental Management Association.

supervisor can supervise effectively and is influenced by such factors as the managerial skill of the supervisor, the level of competence of the subordinates being supervised, availability of training, and so forth. The number of supervisors added to the number of custodians should give the total work force needed.

Custodian Work Assignments

Two methods are widely used for assigning regularly scheduled custodial work. The first, individual cleaning, assigns one person the responsibility for all custodial work in a designated area such as one floor of a large building. The second method, crew cleaning, assigns a group of custodians to handle all the cleaning jobs in a larger area, such as a whole building. The following are potential advantages of each method.

Building _____ Room _____ Square Feet _____

Operation	Weekly Fre-quency	Quantity	Unit Measure	Unit Time	Weekly Time
Airvents, clean			Each	2.00	
Drapes, remove & replace			Pair	20.00	
Elevator, clean			Each	3.25	
Floor, mop, damp (Heavily Obstructed)			M Sq Ft	32.00	
Floor, mop, damp (Slightly Obstructed)			M Sq Ft	23.00	
Floor, mop, damp (Unobstructed)			M Sq Ft	16.00	
Floor, scrub (Heavily Obstructed)			M Sq Ft	55.00	
Floor, scrub (Slightiy Obstructed)			M Sq Ft	45.00	
Floor, scrub (Unobstructed)			M Sq Ft	35.00	
Floors, auto scrub			M Sq Ft	12.00	
Floors, refinish (Heavily Obstructed)			M Sq Ft	180.00	
Floors, spray buff			M Sq Ft	100.00	
Light Fixture, relamp & clean			Ea/Sec/	10.00	
Mats, wash & replace			Each	10.00	
Rugs, shampoo			M Sq Ft	210.00	
Stairs, mop			Flight	10.00	
Toilet & Partition, clean			Each	3.00	
Urinal, clean			Each	2.00	
Venetian Blind, wash			Each	20.00	
Walls, wash			Sq Ft	0.30	
Windows, wash, outside			Sq Ft	0.168	

FIGURE 5–5 Sample inventory of heavy-duty custodial tasks.

Individual Cleaning

1. Pride of achievement is generally stronger when an employee knows he or she has sole responsibility for an area.
2. Less monotony results when an employee has a variety of different tasks to handle each working day.
3. The improved morale due to pride of achievement and less monotony helps reduce turnover, which is always a problem with custodial workers.
4. Responsibility for poor work, breakage, and even petty thievery is established when each area is assigned to one employee.
5. It is relatively easy for one custodian to arrange a work sequence around the use needs of the occupants.

Crew Cleaning

1. The primary advantage is greater specialization. Instead of one person performing all the tasks in a certain area, crews specialize in a limited number of tasks and, theoretically, complete them more efficiently. Because of specialization, proponents claim that more work is accomplished by fewer workers.
2. Morale is improved because employees have company while working.
3. Less custodial equipment is needed than with area assignments.
4. Custodial workloads are more equitably distributed.
5. Unexpected absences cause less disruption, since several workers cover every area and can fill in.

Many organizations find it advantageous to combine individual and crew cleaning. For many simple, daily tasks, individual area assignments seems to be most efficient. For many of the heavier, more complicated and less frequent jobs, crew assignments are more appropriate. Damp mopping, dusting, trash collecting, and similar simple jobs require only one person; two or more would be wasteful.

On the other hand, refinishing floors, cleaning high areas with scaffolds, and cleaning and reinstalling venetian blinds inevitably require more than one person. Such infrequent jobs could be assigned to specialized crews that would perform them in all buildings according to a regular schedule. This approach eliminates the problem of teaching every individual specialized skills that would only be used occasionally.

LABOR-SAVING DESIGNS AND PRACTICES

Building Design and Cleanability

Few architects seem to have a reasonable conception of how cleaning will be accomplished in a building they design and build for an unsuspecting client.

Building cleanability is important because custodial labor costs have more than doubled in the last twenty years, while numerous innovations in methods, equipment, building design, and materials have occurred. Few of these changes in design reflect greater cleanability without the vigorous prompting of alert custodial managers during the design stage of building development.

If a custodial manager is to succeed in a program of greater building cleanability, a two-step process must be followed. First, the manager must impress upon the architect the necessity of certain essential custodial facilities and design features that will guarantee economical cleaning service. This is best accomplished by providing the architect with a check list. Second, the custodial manager must insist on the opportunity for plan review at every important phase of the design process. When developing a check list of materials, design features, and custodial facilities, the custodial manager should take into systematic consideration the following possibilities.

Floors

- Avoid floors requiring hand maintenance or care by other than average custodians.
- Avoid recesses and projections along corridors.
- Insist that concrete subfloors be machine trowelled and properly cured with all depressions and high points corrected before the application of resilient tile. Such irregularities wear more quickly and increase maintenance costs.
- Install floor drains in all washrooms.
- Avoid floors that meet at different levels. Flush joints are preferred; if a difference of elevation is unavoidable, then choose ramps with nonskid surfaces instead of steps.
- For wall bases, use scrub-free material, cove design, and rounded joints.

Walls

- Use glazed materials on walls of abuse-prone hallways, stairways, washrooms, kitchens, and custodial closets.
- Require paints that are durable, washable, light reflective, and light in color. Where decorative effects are needed, try plastic wall coverings with proper flame-spread ratings.
- In general, select materials that can be dusted as well as wet-cleaned.

Ceilings

- Gypsum base acoustical tile is better than softer materials. Hard plastered ceilings covered by high quality enamel are best for food service and washroom areas. Health departments usually prohibit acoustical treatments for these ceilings.

Openings

- Walkways leading to doors should be of hard material and properly drained to prevent tracking.
- Use matting or walk-off rugs at entrances to trap soil.
- Choose flush rather than panelled doors to prevent collection of dust.
- Remember that translucent or tinted glass is easier to maintain than transparent glass.
- Caulking should be smooth and continuous.
- To eliminate painting, select aluminum window framing instead of wood or steel.
- In multistory structures, consider a permanent device for window washing. At the very least, provide lugs for window washers' safety belts.
- For minimum maintenance, use marble or slate window sills.

Furnishings and Equipment

- Dispensers and cabinets should be large enough to provide at least a full day's requirements; double dispensers for holding a reserve supply are most effective and reduce waste.
- To permit rapid cleaning and prevent damage to equipment, hang fixtures such as urinals, ash trays, and water fountains on the wall.
- Use soap dispensers with metal or plastic containers that may be refilled without spilling.
- Metal, plastic, and composition materials are more easily cleaned than wood furniture.
- Lockers should be placed on concrete or ceramic base so soil cannot be trapped underneath, and their tops should be slanted for easy cleaning.
- Place waste receptacles immediately adjacent to areas where waste is created, using liners and covers for odorous or edible material.

Custodial Facilities

- Provide adequate sources of hot and cold water throughout the building as well as sufficient electrical outlets in halls and stairways for custodial use.
- Be sure custodial closets and lockers are adequate in number and size and are properly located.

• Devise a standard layout to provide storage for all reserve supplies and to facilitate laundering, treating, and hanging tools, such as dust cloths, dust mops, and wet mops.

Figure 5–6 enumerates and illustrates criteria for custodian closets as recommended by the University of New Mexico Physical Plant Department.

CONTRACT CLEANING

Most custodial managers consider contractual cleaning at some point—often when faced with a major expansion or revamping of their operations. Private firms are sometimes able to provide better service than an in-house operation and

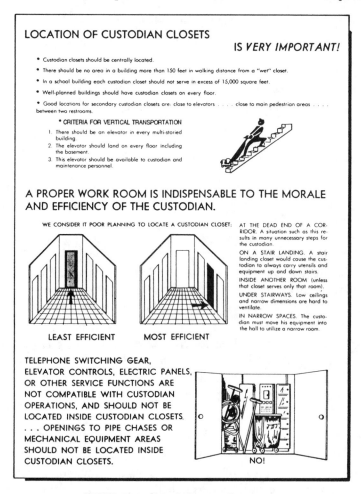

FIGURE 5–6 Criteria for custodian closets.

Reproduced with permission of the University of New Mexico Physical Plant Department.

at a lower cost. Through extensive studies, specialized cleaning firms are able to engineer carefully planned housekeeping programs that eliminate much of the waste that can develop in an in-house cleaning operation. However, before deciding whether or not to employ a contractor, a manager should analyze existing operations and evaluate the following advantages and disadvantages.

A primary advantage is that a contractor will take over administrative tasks, such as staffing, scheduling, supervising, and training. A good firm can manage these tasks more efficiently than a small park and recreation organization with a cleaning staff of less than ten employees. Such a service can also prove economical for the large park and recreation system with widely scattered buildings and for those systems that have difficulty finding enough employees.

A distinct disadvantage, under certain conditions, can be a deterioration in cleaning quality. The inescapable fact about contract cleaning is that making a

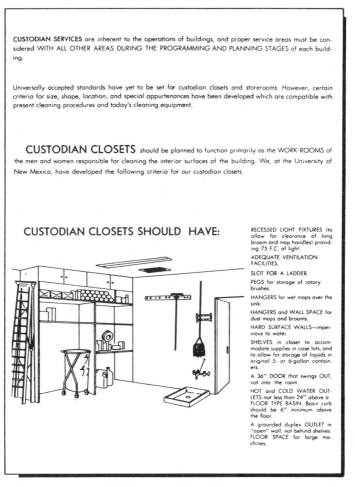

CUSTODIAN SERVICES are inherent to the operations of buildings, and proper service areas must be considered WITH ALL OTHER AREAS DURING THE PROGRAMMING AND PLANNING STAGES of each building.

Universally accepted standards have yet to be set for custodian closets and storerooms. However, certain criteria for size, shape, location, and special appurtenances have been developed which are compatible with present cleaning procedures and today's cleaning equipment.

CUSTODIAN CLOSETS should be planned to function primarily as the WORK ROOMS of the men and women responsible for cleaning the interior surfaces of the building. We, at the University of New Mexico, have developed the following criteria for our custodian closets:

CUSTODIAN CLOSETS SHOULD HAVE:

RECESSED LIGHT FIXTURES (to allow for clearance of long broom and mop handles) providing 75 F.C. of light.
ADEQUATE VENTILATION FACILITIES.
SLOT FOR A LADDER.
PEGS for storage of rotary brushes.
HANGERS for wet mops over the sink.
HANGERS and WALL SPACE for dust mops and brooms.
HARD SURFACE WALLS—impervious to water.
SHELVES in closet to accommodate supplies in case lots, and to allow for storage of liquids in original 5- or 6-gallon containers.
A 36" DOOR that swings OUT, not into the room.
HOT and COLD WATER OUTLETS not less than 24" above a FLOOR TYPE BASIN. Basin curb should be 6" minimum above the floor.
A grounded duplex OUTLET in "open" wall, not behind shelves.
FLOOR SPACE for large machines.

FIGURE 5-6 *(Continued)*.

profit is the primary goal of all commercial firms. Maintaining the best environment for recreation will always be secondary to this end. In order to maximize profits, such firms face a constant temptation to cut services as much as they possibly can and still hold the job.

Additional disadvantages of contract cleaning include less flexibility, delays in service for unusual or emergency jobs, charges for "extras," less control over the type of individuals hired for the work, and additional security problems.

Large recreation systems are less likely to benefit from contract services than small systems, but even they may find it profitable to supplement their ongoing, in-house service with some contract work. Many systems contract out dangerous jobs, such as washing upper story windows, as well as the more specialized tasks of tree trimming and athletic field luminaire replacement. This kind of arrangement allows the system to bring highly trained personnel to their location for difficult projects and simultaneously retain an in-house staff for regular and emergency cleaning.

Contract Cleaning Specifications

Before employing a contractor, a set of detailed specifications should be prepared, covering all facets of the job, including how, when, and by whom the work is to be done. To prepare these specifications, a custodial manager should first compile a complete inventory of areas to be cleaned and specify cleaning standards to be achieved for each. Such a survey can also provide a realistic price estimate to use in evaluating all bids submitted. See the *Specifications for Contract Janitorial Services* in the appendix to this chapter.

The maintenance manager should also evaluate the contractor's integrity and competence as carefully as the price. This can be accomplished by investigating the contractor's references, previous work, personnel, working methods, and financial status. Any bid that is considerably lower than all others should be investigated. If the low bid cannot be traced to some economy in methods, do not award the contract to that bidder. Otherwise, the contractor will probably be forced to cut services in order to make a profit. It would be wiser to hire a firm with a reputation for responsible performance. After the contract is awarded, some member of the maintenance division staff should be assigned the task of systematically inspecting the contractor's work to ensure that it is in compliance with all provisions of the contract.

REVIEW QUESTIONS

1. Describe the basic corps of workers necessary for structural and system building maintenance.
2. Indicate the basic elements involved in a preventive building maintenance program.

3. Describe a satisfactory method for scheduling the infrequent but routine preventive maintenance jobs.

4. What criteria should be considered when determining the feasibility of purchasing various building maintenance equipment?

5. Describe building custodial cleaning standards and how they are developed.

6. Outline the three methods of determining building custodian staffing requirements.

7. Discuss the advantages and disadvantages of individual and crew custodial cleaning.

8. In what ways does building design relate to building "cleanability?"

9. Describe the recommended features that should be included in a building custodian closet.

10. Cite the advantages and disadvantages of contract building cleaning.

11. What investigative steps should a maintenance manager take in the event that an unusually low bid for janitorial work is received from an unfamiliar contractor?

12. What should be included in written contract specifications for contract janitorial services?

CHAPTER BIBLIOGRAPHY

Books and Manuals

ASHRAE Guide and Data Book. New York: American Society of Heating, Refrigerating and Air Conditioning Engineers, 1972.

Do-It-Yourself Encyclopedia. Indianapolis, IN: T. Audel, 1968.

Environmental Management Association. *Sample Inventory of Light and Heavy Custodial Tasks.* 1710 Drew Street, Clearwater, Florida 33515. n.d.

Feldman, Edwin B. *Building Design for Maintainability.* New York: McGraw-Hill, 1975.

Housekeeping Handbook for Institutions, Business and Industry. New York: Frederick Fell, 1978.

Magee, Gregory H. *Facilities Maintenance Management.* Kingston, MA: R. S. Means Co., 1988.

A Manual of Roofing Practice. Oak Park, IL: The National Roofing Contractors' Association, 1976.

Matulionis, Raymond C., and Fretag, Joan C. *Preventive Maintenance of Buildings.* New York: Van Nostrand Reinhold, 1991.

Roofing and Waterproofing Manual. Oak Park, IL: The National Roofing Contractors' Association, 1981.

Sack, Thomas F. *A Complete Guide to Building and Plant Maintenance.* 2nd ed. Englewood Cliffs, NJ: Prentice-Hall, 1971.

Seeley, Ivor H. *Building Maintenance.* London: Macmillan, 1976.

Shear, Mel A. *Handbook of Building Maintenance Management.* Reston, VA: Reston Publishing Co., 1983.

Sweezey, Kenneth M. *Formulas, Methods, Tips and Data for Home and Workshop.* New York: Popular Science Publishing Co., 1969.

U.S. Department of Interior, Park and Recreation Technical Service. *Energy Planning and Management for Parks and Recreation.* Washington, DC: U.S. Government Printing Office, 1981.

Weber, George O., ed., and Fincham, Michael W. *A Basic Manual for Physical Plant Administration.* Washington, DC: The Association of Physical Plant Administrators of Universities and Colleges, 1974.

Wenger, Karl F., ed., *Forestry Handbook.* Section 15, Outdoor Recreation Management. New York: Wiley, 1984.

Magazines

Building Operating Management. Trade Press Publishing Company, 470 E. Michigan Street, Milwaukee, Wisconsin 53202.

Building Research, Journal of the BRAB. Building Research Institute, BRAB Building, National Research Council, 2101 Constitution Avenue, NW, Washington, DC 20418.

Buildings: The Facilities Construction and Management Magazine. Stamats Communications, Inc., c/o Wayne Bayliss, 427 Sixth Avenue, SE, Cedar Rapids, Iowa 52406.

The Buildings Magazine. American School and University, Educational Communications Division of North America Publishing Company, 134 North 13 Street, Philadelphia, Pennsylvania 19107.

Campground Management. Woodall Publishing Co., 28167 N. Keith Dr., Lake Forest, Illinois 60045.

Engineer's Digest. Intertec Publishing Corp., 9221 Quivira Road, Overland Park, Kansas 66215.

Government Product News and Publishing Digest. Industrial Publishing Company and Lakewood Publications, Inc., Cleveland, Ohio.

Grist, Trends, Design. Park Practice Program. National Recreation and Parks Association, 2775 S. Quincy Street, Arlington, Virginia 22206.

Leisure Manager. Institute of Leisure and Amenity Management. John S. Turner and Associates, Ltd., Victoria House, 25 High Street, Over, Cambridge CB45NB, England.

Park and Grounds Maintenance. Madisen Publishing Division, Appleton, Wisconsin.

Plant Engineering. Technical Publishing Company, 1301 S. Grove Avenue, Barrington, Illinois 60010.

Recreation Resources. Lakewood Publications, Inc., 50 S. Ninth Street, Minneapolis, Minnesota 55402.

APPENDIX 5–A

MULTIPLE LEVEL
MAINTENANCE STANDARDS FOR BUILDINGS

FOUNDATIONS

Level I

1. No termites or insect infestations.
2. Concrete free of spalling, leaks, cracks, and exposed reinforcing.
3. No warping, checking, splitting, broken, and damp wooden members.
4. Exposed masonry units have no cracked or open joints, leaks, cracked, or spalling elements.
5. Bolts and fasteners in place and secure.
6. Vents free from rust and corrosion, holes or rotten fabric, clogged or blocked openings, loose or missing hardware, and securely attached.
7. Ground surfaces free of debris and trash and graded.
8. Quarterly inspection to insure conformance.

Level II

1. No termites or insect infestations.
2. Concrete and masonry free of leaks and cracks.
3. No broken or damp wood members.
4. Bolt fasteners secure.
5. Vents free from rust, holes, loose hardware.
6. Ground surface free of debris and trash.
7. Semi-annual inspection to insure conformance.

Level III

1. No termites or insect infestations.
2. Concrete, masonry, and wooden units free of leaks and dampness.
3. Bolts and fasteners secure.
4. Vents free from holes.
5. Annual inspection to insure conformance.

Source: A Basic Manual for Physical Plant Administration (Washington, D.C.: The Association of Physical Plant Administrators of Universities and Colleges, 1974), pp. 191-99. Reproduced with permission of the Association of Physical Plant Administrators of Universities and Colleges.

EXTERIOR WALLS

Level I

1. Masonry units free of cracks and spalling, eroded or sandy joints, cracked units, stains, leaks.
2. Wood has no warping and cracking, rot and termites, stains, loose and missing fastenings, leaks.
3. Metal free of rust and pittings, loose, missing, or broken fastenings, holes, and punctures. Repaint when film is less than 3 mils in thickness.
4. Repainting scheduled on a three-to-five year cyclic basis or as required by climatic conditions.
5. Quarterly inspection to insure conformance.

Level II

1. Masonry units free of cracks, stains, and leaks.
2. Wood free of leaks, termites and insect infestations, missing fastenings.
3. Metal has no rust and pitting. Repaint when film is less than two mils in thickness. Replace missing or broken fastenings.
4. Repainting scheduled on a five-to-seven year cyclic basis.
5. Semi-annual inspection to insure conformance.

Level III

1. Masonry units free from leaks.
2. No termites and insects.
3. Metal painted for protection.
4. Repainting scheduled on a seven-to-ten year cyclic basis.
5. Annual inspection to insure conformance.

INTERIOR WALLS AND CEILINGS

Level I

1. Free from leaks, cracks, decay and insect infestations, stains, and scuff marks, loose fastenings.
2. Paints and coverings free from abrasions, punctures, tears, fading and stains, and adhesive failures.
3. Repainting on a one-to-three year cyclic basis.

4. Metal surfaces polished.
5. Horizontal and vertical surfaces dust and grime free.
6. Quarterly inspection to insure conformance.

Level II

1. Free from leaks, decay and insect infestations, stains.
2. Paints and coverings free from abrasions, punctures, and tears.
3. Repainting on a two-to-four year cyclic basis.
4. Surfaces dust free.
5. Semi-annual inspection to insure conformance.

Level III

1. No leaks, termites and insect infestations.
2. Repaint on a three-to-five year cyclic basis.
3. Annual inspection to insure conformance.

DOORS AND WINDOWS

Level I

1. Wood sash, doors, and trim have no splits, rot, cracks, loose or tight fits.
2. Metal sash and doors free from rust and corrosion, warping, and loose or tight fits.
3. Screens free from loose, broken, or missing hardware; no rust or corrosion; no holes in fabric or wire; no wood rot, stain, or cracks and breaks.
4. No loose, broken, or missing hardware; free from rust and corrosion; movement free and unhampered.
5. Glass clean and free of broken or cracked elements. Glazing compound secure, none missing.
6. Venetian blinds, draperies, and so forth, clean; free of spots and tears; no broken or loose fastenings; cords free of frayed or broken strands.
7. Daily inspection to insure conformance.

Level II

1. No cracks, rust, or corrosion in wood and metal elements.
2. No holes in screens; no broken or missing hardware; no loose or tight fits.

3. Hardware secure; no broken or missing elements.
4. Glass clean and no more than 10 percent broken elements.
5. Venetian blinds, draperies, and so forth, clean and no tears or broken fastenings.
6. Bi-weekly inspection to insure conformance.

Level III

1. No cracks in wood and metal sash, doors, and trim.
2. Screens free of holes and hardware secure.
3. No more than 20 percent broken glass.
4. Venetian blinds, draperies, and so forth, clean.
5. Quarterly inspection to insure conformance.

FLOORS

Level I

1. Carpet and rugs free of ravelling, cuts and tears, fading and discoloration, loose anchorage, insect damage; vacuumed free of dust and dirt.
2. Resilient floors show no evidence of cracking, chipping, breaking, scratches, tears, uneven and loose bonding; free of moisture; waxed and buffed.
3. Wood free from sagging, splintering, loose, warped, rotten or scratched elements, stains, discoloration, and moisture; waxed and buffed. No termites or insect infestations.
4. All areas free of loose, damaged, or missing bases, binding strips and thresholds, projecting nails, bolts or screws, slippery surfaces, loose or missing nosings or treads.
5. Daily inspection to insure conformance.

Level II

1. Carpets and rugs free of cuts and tears, loose anchorage, insects, dust and dirt.
2. Resilient floors show no evidence of cracking, chipping, breaking, scratches, tears, uneven and loose bonding; free of moisture; buffed.
3. Wood free from sagging, splintering, loose, warped, rotten, or scratched elements, stains, discoloration, and moisture; waxed and buffed. No termites or insect infestations.

4. All areas free of loose, damaged, or missing bases; binding strips; and thresholds; projecting nails; bolts or screws; slippery surfaces; loose or missing nosings or treads.
5. Semi-weekly inspection to insure conformance.

Level III

1. Carpets and rugs free of cuts and tears, loose anchorage, dirt and dust.
2. Resilient floors free of uneven and loose bonding; no moisture; buffed.
3. Wood free from rotten and loose elements, moisture, termites. No dirt and dust; buffed.
4. No loose base strips, projecting nails or fastenings; loose nosings or treads.
5. Weekly inspection to insure conformance.

GUTTERS, DOWNSPOUTS, AND ROOF DRAINS

Level I

1. Free of rust and corrosion, breaks or leaks.
2. Aligned and fastened.
3. Open and clear of leaves and dust, dirt accumulation.
4. Wire guards provided and in place.
5. Splash blocks in place, connection to storm sewer secure.
6. Repainting scheduled on a three-to-five year cyclic basis.
7. Quarterly inspection to insure conformance.

Level II

1. Free of rust and corrosion, breaks or leaks.
2. Securely fastened.
3. Clear of obstructions.
4. Splash blocks in place.
5. Repainted on a five-to-seven year cyclic basis.
6. Semi-annual inspection to insure conformance.

Level III

1. Free of breaks and leaks.
2. Securely fastened.

3. Clear of obstructions.
4. Repainted on a seven-to-ten year cyclic basis.
5. Annual inspection to insure conformance.

ROOFS

Level I

1. Metal free of broken seams, rust or corrosion, holes and open joints, loose, broken, or missing fastenings.
2. Wood shingles, tile, or slate free from warped, broken, split, curled, and loose or missing elements.
3. Built-up roofs free from cracks, exposed coatings, blistered, curled, or buckled felts.
4. Watertight and free of water ponding.
5. Flashing free from rust, corrosion, open joints, loose, and missing fastenings.
6. Quarterly inspection to insure conformance.

Level II

1. Metal free of broken seams, rust or corrosion, holes and open joints, loose, broken, or missing fastenings.
2. Wood shingles, tile, or slate free from warped, broken, split, curled, and loose or missing elements.
3. Built-up roofs free from cracks, exposed coatings, blistered, curled, or buckled felts.
4. Watertight and free of water ponding.
5. Flashing free from rust, corrosion, open joints, loose and missing fastenings.
6. Semi-annual inspection to insure conformance.

Level III

1. Metal free of broken seams, rust or corrosion, holes and open joints, loose, broken, or missing fastenings.
2. Wood shingles, tile, or slate free from warped, broken, split, curled, and loose or missing elements.
3. Built-up roofs free from cracks, exposed coatings, blistered, curled, or buckled felts.
4. Watertight and free of water ponding.

5. Flashing free from rust, corrosion, open joints, loose and missing fastenings.
6. Annual inspection to insure conformance.

HEATING, VENTILATING, AND AIR CONDITIONING

Level I

1. Air filter clear of dust, grease, and lint deposits or cleaned and replaced as necessary to maintain maximum efficiency of unit.
2. System mechanical elements free of dust, dirt, soot, grease deposits, lubricant drippings, rust and corrosion, chemical fumes, and loose, broken, or missing parts.
3. Wiring and electrical free of loose connections, frayed or worn braid, improperly sized or defective fuses.
4. Exposed piping has no clogged, rusted, or corroded, leaking parts. Valves, traps, and strainers clear of scale and leaks.
5. Ducts free from soot, dirt, grease, loose connections, joints, and seams.
6. Boiler standards according to *Heating, Ventilating and Air Conditioning Guide,* American Society of Heating and Ventilating Engineers. Annual inspections made by state inspector.
7. Monthly inspection to insure conformance.

Level II

1. Air filter clear of dust, grease, and lint deposits or cleaned and replaced as necessary to maintain maximum efficiency of unit.
2. System mechanical elements free of dust, dirt, soot, grease deposits, lubricant drippings, rust and corrosion, chemical fumes, and loose, broken, or missing parts.
3. Wiring and electrical free of loose connections, frayed or worn braid, improperly sized or defective fuses.
4. Exposed piping has no clogged, rusted, or corroded, leaking parts. Valves, traps, and strainers clear of scale and leaks.
5. Ducts free from soot, dirt, grease, loose connections, joints, and seams.
6. Boiler standards according to *Heating, Ventilating and Air Conditioning Guide,* American Society of Heating and Ventilating Engineers. Annual inspections made by state inspector.
7. Semi-annual inspection to insure conformance, except for Item #1.

Level III

1. Air filter clear of dust, grease, and lint deposits or cleaned and replaced as necessary to maintain maximum efficiency of unit.
2. System mechanical elements free of dust, dirt, soot, grease deposits, lubricant drippings, rust and corrosion, chemical fumes, and loose, broken, or missing parts.
3. Wiring and electrical free of loose connections, frayed or worn braid, improperly sized or defective fuses.
4. Exposed piping has no clogged, rusted, or corroded, leaking parts. Valves, traps, and strainers clear of scale and leaks.
5. Ducts free from soot, dirt, grease, loose connections, joints, and seams.
6. Boiler standards according to *Heating, Ventilating and Air Conditioning Guide,* American Society of Heating and Ventilating Engineers. Annual inspections made by state inspector.
7. Annual inspection to insure conformance, except for Item #1.

INTERIOR PLUMBING

Level I

1. Free of leaks, breaks, corrosion, stoppages, odors, and gases.
2. Insulation sealed and free of moisture.
3. Valves, checks, traps, operational, free of leaks, corrosion, incrustation, and obstructions.
4. Fixtures free of cracks in china, chips in porcelain, odors, stains.
5. Daily inspection to insure conformance.

Level II

1. Free of leaks, breaks, corrosion, stoppages, odors, and gases.
2. Insulation free of moisture.
3. Valves, checks, traps, operational, free of leaks, corrosion, incrustation, and obstructions.
4. Fixtures free of cracks in china, chips in porcelain, odors, stains.
5. Semi-weekly inspection to insure conformance.

Level III

1. Free of leaks, breaks, corrosion, stoppages, odors, and gases.
2. Valves, checks, traps, operational, free of leaks, corrosion, incrustation, and obstructions.

3. Fixtures free of cracks in china, chips in porcelain, odors, stains.
4. Weekly inspection to insure conformance.

INTERIOR ELECTRICAL

Level I

1. According to National Electrical Code 1965, NFPA No. 70, ASA C1-1965 as adopted by the National Park Sevice.
2. Quarterly inspection to insure conformance.
3. Breaker boxes and fuse panels labeled and identified by circuit.

Level II

1. According to National Electrical Code 1965, NFPA No. 70, ASA C1-1965 as adopted by the National Park Sevice.
2. Semi-annual inspection to insure conformance.
3. Breaker boxes and fuse panels labeled and identified by circuit.

Level III

1. According to National Electrical Code 1965, NFPA No. 70, ASA C1-1965 as adopted by the National Park Service.
2. Annual inspection to insure conformance.
3. Breaker boxes and fuse panels labeled and identified by circuit.

LIGHTING

Level I

1. Illumination units free of dirt and dust and secure. No cracked or broken luminaries and fixture parts, exposed wiring, broken or missing pullcords, loose socket connections.
2. Fluorescent units free of flickering and loud humming lamps.
3. No burned out lamps.
4. Daily inspection to insure conformance.

Level II

1. Illumination units free of dirt and dust and secure. No cracked or broken luminaries and fixture parts, exposed wiring, broken or missing pullcords, loose socket connections.
2. Fluorescent units free of flickering and loud humming lamps.

3. No burned out lamps.
4. Semi-weekly inspection to insure conformance.

Level III

1. Illumination units free of exposed wiring, loose socket connections; no broken luminaries or fixture parts.
2. No burned out lamps.
3. Weekly inspection to insure conformance.

HOUSEKEEPING

Level I

1. Furnishings, tools, and equipment located not to hamper circulation and as per design.
2. Free from protrusions from cabinets, desks, racks, bins, benches, aisles, and work areas. Free of boxes, baskets, and clutter. Boxes, containers, supplies, materials in storage bins, shelves.
3. Wastebaskets and ash trays empty and clean. Radiators, desks, cabinets, louvers, exhibit cases, panels, and displays clean and dusted.
4. Metal surfaces polished.
5. Restroom and washroom areas free of odors and clean. Soap, paper, and towel racks filled. Mirrors clear of fingerprints and shelves clean, polished, and free of debris.
6. No clothing, boxes, packages hung or lying on benches, desks, tables, counters, machines.
7. Drinking fountains clean and clear of debris and leaks. Trash receptacles when paper cups provided. Free of spots and water marks. Fully operational.
8. Stock storage areas clean and cleaning equipment near and in place.
9. Washbasins, toilet bowls, and porcelain clean and bright, free of spots and smears.
10. Daily inspection to insure conformance.

Level II

1. Furnishings, tools, and equipment located not to hamper circulation and as per design.
2. Free from protrusions from cabinets, desks, racks, bins, benches, aisles, and work areas. Free of boxes, baskets, and

clutter. Boxes, containers, supplies, materials in storage bins, shelves.

3. Wastebaskets and ash trays empty and clean. Exhibit cases, panels, and displays dusted.
4. Metal surfaces clean.
5. Restroom and washroom areas free of odors and clean. Soap, paper, and towel racks filled. Mirrors clear of fingerprints and shelves clean, polished, and free of debris.
6. No clothing, boxes, packages hung or lying on benches, desks, tables, counters, machines.
7. Drinking fountains clean, clear of debris and leaks. Fully operational.
8. Stock storage areas clean.
9. Washbasins, toilet bowls, and porcelain clean and bright, free of spots and smears.
10. Semi-weekly inspection to insure conformance.

Level III

1. Furnishings, tools, and equipment arranged neatly.
2. Free from protrusions from cabinets, desks, racks, bins, benches, aisles, and work areas. Free of boxes, baskets, and clutter. Boxes, containers, supplies, materials in storage bins, shelves.
3. Wastebaskets and ash trays empty and clean.
4. Metal surfaces clean.
5. Restrooms and washrooms clean and supplies furnished.
6. No clothing, boxes, packages hung or lying on benches, desks, tables, counters, machines.
7. Drinking fountains clear of debris and leaks.
8. Washbasins, toilet bowls, and porcelain free of spots and smears.
9. Weekly inspection to insure conformance.

SAMPLE SPECIFICATIONS FOR CONTRACT JANITORIAL SERVICES

Metropolitan Recreation District

MAINTENANCE DIVISION   DATE _____

SECTION I   INFORMATION FOR BIDDERS

1-01

The Janitorial Services Contractor shall furnish all labor and equipment necessary to perform the janitorial services, including cleaning, dusting, wicking, mopping, stripping, waxing, polishing, washing, removal of trash and waste materials, refilling of dispensers, plus "As Required" services described herein such as minimal access snow removal in the buildings listed, and to be included in any buildings which might be added in an extension of this contract.

1-02

A general map is attached showing the location of each of the below buildings. The contractor must physically inspect each building before submitting a bid. *Space diagrams of each building are attached as part of these specifications.* These show the area to be cleaned in each building and approximate net area of each room. Floor areas may be verified if desired.

1-03

Buildings to be Cleaned	Gross Square Feet	Net Square Feet to be Cleaned

1-04

Bids are requested in two ways, (1) a monthly Lump Sum charge for each of these buildings, (2) a bid based upon a "Time and Material" basis. The system reserves the right to award the contract for any one or any combination of buildings, whichever is in the best interest of the recreation system, on either the "Lump Sum" or "Time and Material" basis.

1-05

The Standard General Conditions of Contract attached hereto shall apply to this work.

1-06

Contractors are required to submit a bid bond for the sum of items in the lump sum prices based on the *total* lump sum contractual cost for a six-month period; or in lieu thereof a certified check in the amount of 5% of the total lump sum bid. Bond or check are forfeitable if bidder is awarded the contract and fails to perform.

1-07

The Contractor should clarify any questions he or she may have prior to submission of a bid by contacting the Buildings Custodial Services Supervisor, located in the _____ Building, phone number _____.
The submission of a bid shall indicate that the Contractor thoroughly understands the scope of the work to be performed.

1-08

While this initial contract is to be awarded for a six (6) month period, it can be extended for an additional six (6) month period, after periodic reviews and mutually agreed upon amendments up to a total of at least three (3) years.

1-09

It shall be the Contractor's responsibility for compliance with all local, county, state, and federal laws.

SECTION II GENERAL INFORMATION

2-01

The right is reserved by the Recreation District to reject any or all proposals, and to waive any formal requirements as the interest of the District may require. No Bidder may withdraw his bid within thirty (30) days after the formal opening thereof. Acceptance of any proposal will be subject to approval of submittal data and engineering equipment.

2-02

Bidders must allow sufficient time for all bids, either mailed or hand-carried, to reach this office by the date and time indicated for the bid opening. Late bids, including those postmarked prior to the bid opening date, will not be considered.

2-03

Forms for Bid Proposals are included in this specification. Bids are requested in triplicate. If you are not in a position to bid on the work at this time, please so state in writing on the Bid Proposal Form in order that the District may retain your name on its listing of preferred bidders for future work.

2-04

Contractors and Subcontractors should include the applicable Sales and Use Tax on all purchases. Contractors will be required to pay the tax on all purchases and can recover it only as a part of their price.

2-05

This contract is to be in force for a period of six months commencing _____ and terminating on _____ .

2-06

The District and the Contractor shall each have the right to terminate the Contract upon thirty days written notice to the other party.

2-07

In view of the policy of the District with respect to endorsement of products, materials, or equipment of any manufacturer, the Contractor shall not permit endorsements by photographs or written statements involving the District without prior written approval of the District through the Building Custodial Services Section.

2-08

All work under this contract shall be inspected by the Supervisor of Building Custodial Services Section, or representative, to insure strict compliance with the specifications.

2-09

Because of the acute shortage of parking space, the Contractor's personnel will be required to park in those parking areas where assigned. Failure of the Contractor's employees to park their personal automobiles where assigned may result in a parking violation citation, with accompanying monetary penalties or in violations of safety regulations the vehicles may be towed away and held until towing charge is paid.

2-10

Since the District cannot be responsible for losses of Contractor's supplies, tools, or equipment, Contractors are hereby notified of their responsibility for providing proper identification and security for such items at their own expense.

2-11

The Contractor will be responsible for all damages to District property caused by any employees. Such damage shall be repaired promptly by the Contractor to the satisfaction of the District, at no expense to the District.

2-12

The Contractor shall be responsible for payment of all of his or her payrolls including withholding taxes, social security, unemployment compensation insurance, and for payment of his or her public liability insurance and employee bonds. Particular attention is called to records required if the contract is awarded on the "Time and Material" basis.

2-13

Payment for services shall be made to the Contractor once a month upon submission of an invoice consisting of an original and two copies, properly certified.

2-14

The District reserves the right to increase or decrease the cleaning of certain areas as circumstances may require. In the event of increased or decreased cleaning requirements, the Contractor shall submit in writing to the Building Custodial Services Section the change in worker-hours of time and the additional cost or credit to the District. The cost or credit will be expected to be reasonably proportionate to the initial bid price compared with square footage of cleaning area. When the proposal is accepted by the District it shall be confirmed in writing.

2-15

The Contractor shall provide all necessary machines, equipment, tools, and labor, and so on, as may be necessary to perform the work outlined herein. The District Building Custodial Services Section, Maintenance Division, shall approve all cleaning material or supplies, such as roll paper towels, toilet tissue, cleaners, liquid wax, liquid floor soap, seals, detergents, disinfectants, and liquid or bar hand soap for the use by the Contractor. The Contractor shall deposit trash in the refuse containers adjacent to the building.

SECTION III PERSONNEL REQUIREMENTS AND WORK PROCEDURES

3-01

The Contractor shall be present on the job at all times during the working hours, along with a competent Superintendent and any necessary assistants. Prior to the commencement of work, the Contractor shall submit in writing to the Building Custodial Services Section, for prior approval the name of the person intended to be employed as Superintendent for the execution of this contract, along with his or her qualifications and past experience. The Superintendent shall be required to report to the Building Custodial Services Section, Maintenance Division, as necessary to review cleaning requirements and deficiencies with the District Supervisor of Building Custodial Services.

3-02

The District reserves the right to execute a background investigation of any employee of this Contractor and to require the Contractor to remove any employee from the campus whose actions are considered detrimental to the best interest of the District. The Contractor shall at all times enforce strict discipline and good order among employees and shall not employ or permit to remain on the work, any person considered unfit. The Contractor shall enforce all regulations relative to the use of water, heat, power, smoking, and the control and use of fires as required by law. Employees shall not be allowed to loiter on the premises either before or after their working hours.

3-03

Due to the existence of valuable equipment and property, strict supervision shall be maintained to prevent petty larcenies and thefts. The District shall reserve the right to search the Contractor's employees prior to their leaving the premises, without any prior notice of such action.

3-04

Contractor's employees may use janitor's closets in each building where they may change clothing and wash up. The Contractor shall insure orderliness and cleanliness of such areas at all times.

3-05

The successful Contractor shall properly identify each employee engaged for this work. Also, the Contractor shall provide each employee with an identification card, approved in form by the Building Custodial Services Section, for entrance and exit from the building. Additionally, the employee shall be required to punch a time clock each working night upon arrival and departure. Contractor shall submit weekly tabulations of all employees who have worked with accrued time, which form must be signed by Contractor's Superintendent and the Building Custodial Services Supervisor assigned.

3-06

The District will periodically inspect all work performed by the Contractor. Normally, at least a weekly joint inspection shall be conducted by the Contractor or representative and a representative of the Building Services Section.

3-07

Keys for buildings are controlled by the District Night Supervisor, Buildings Custodial Services Section, or the assigned assistant at all times. The Night Supervisor or assistant will unlock all doors after cleaning has been accomplished and see that the building has been secured after quitting time and keys returned to the Building Custodial Services Section Office. Every effort shall be exercised by Contractor's employees to conserve electricity by only lighting areas in which work is currently being performed.

3-08
Contractor's employees shall report on forms furnished by the District to the Supervisor, Building Custodial Services, any conditions of leaky faucets, stopped toilets and drains, broken fixtures, and so forth, and any unusual happenings in the building.

3-09
Contractor's employees shall close and lock windows and turn off all lights when night cleaning is finished, except as may be designated to remain lighted for security lighting.

3-10
Contractor's employees shall not disturb papers on desks, open drawers or cabinets, use telephones, televisions, radios, or drink or gamble while on duty on the campus. Violations will be grounds for dismissal.

3-11
Contractor shall not hire any personnel employed by the District regardless of their classification since work beyond forty (40) hours weekly at the same place of employment entitles workers to OVERTIME RATES.

3-12
For the purposes of coordination and control the Contractor must so arrange employees' HOLIDAYS, SICK LEAVE, AND VACATIONS to conform to District schedules. These specifications are not intended to dictate to the Contractor what leave policies will be. However, the Contractor must make proper allowance for the employees' fringe benefits in this building. The District will not pay for any time away from the job.

3-13
Complete cleaning services will be required daily in all buildings, fifty-two (52) weeks per year.

SECTION IV   WORKMANSHIP AND HOURS

4-01
All work shall be performed Monday through Saturday, inclusive, between the hours of midnight and 4:00 A.M. except as described in paragraph 4-02. Also, the Contractor shall schedule and arrange work so it will not interfere with operational functions of the building. At indeterminate times, some areas of the building will be occupied and used by employees

for after-hours work, and such circumstances shall not alleviate responsibility of required cleaning at a later time.

4-02

Special Personnel Requirements: Contractor shall be required to provide the following personnel as indicated in specified buildings.
LIST HERE ANY SPECIAL COVERAGE BY BUILDING AND TIME:

SECTION V WORK STANDARDS

5-01

Definition of various operations:

Buffing: To clean or shine surfaces such as resilient tiles, terrazzo, wood, slate, and so on with a floor machine.

Cleaning: To remove dirt, impurities, and stains from urinals, water closets, sinks, drinking fountains, light fixtures, mirrors, and the like either by hand or with tools.

Dusting: To remove surface dust or dirt from furniture, files, sills, blinds, telephones, vents, grills, or lighting fixtures, with properly treated cloths.

Emptying: To remove accumulation of trash or residue from waste containers, ash trays, or receptacles, and deposit in designated containers on outside of buildings.

Mopping, Damp and Wet: To wash, wipe, and remove from floor and stair surfaces to leave acceptably clean.

Polishing: To smooth and brighten as by rubbing with polishing cloth using proper pastes, as surfaces may require, such as brass, furniture, counters, or mirrors.

Refill: To replace the contents of a container such as soap, toilet tissue, or towel dispensers.

Stripping: A colloquial term for removing built-up waxes, seals, and other floor dressings from the original natural surface before applying a fresh coat of protective cover to surfaces such as resilient tile, wood, terrazzo, and so forth.

Sweeping: To remove or clear away dirt or debris with a broom or brush. Normally all horizontal surfaces subject to foot or wheel usage should be swept.

Vacuum: To clean with a vacuum cleaner. Regular emptying of collector device is important and proper setting of height above surface will improve effectiveness.

Washing: The act or process of making thoroughly clean by moistening, wetting, scrubbing, and rinsing with water and proper quantities of soap, detergents, and disinfectants as furnished for various objects and equipment.

Waxing: To cover or treat with liquid wax or other floor finish in proper quantities over properly prepared surfaces to protect and beautify.

Wicking: A trade term to describe the process of sweeping, dusting, and cleaning floor surfaces with a treated yarn mop.

5-02
Frequency of Operations—The Contractor shall be required to schedule work to insure that the following frequency of operations are adhered to or exceeded in order to insure the District of the cleaning standard it deserves.

Daily:

1. Clean ash trays.
2. Clean elevator tracks and interiors.
3. Clean mirrors and glass surfaces.
4. Clean toilets, urinals, sinks, fixtures, partitions, paper holders.
5. Clean coatracks.
6. Clean erasers of the chalk board type.
7. Dust: Bookcases; Desks; Filing cabinets; also pianos if present; Lamps; Floors; Tables; Telephones; Window sills; Radiators; Convertors and unit; Ventilator cabinets; Refrigerators and Vending Machines.
8. Empty: Pencil sharpeners; Waste baskets.
9. Refill: Soap dispensers; Toilet tissue holders; Paper towel dispensers.
10. Sweep: Stairs; Floors.
11. Vacuum: Carpeting and rugs (particularly walk-off rugs in entrances).
12. Wash: Chalkboards and chalk trays; Drinking fountains (also sanitize); Hand rails.
13. Damp Mop: Lobbies; Hallways; Restrooms; Laboratories, if necessary.
14. Buff: Lobbies; Hallways.

Weekly:

1. Damp mop floors.
2. Dust shelving, including books, library stacks.
3. Damp mop stairs.
4. Dust lockers.
5. Sweep exterior entrances to adjoining sidewalk.

Monthly:

1. Clean air vents and interior doors.
2. Dust tab arm chairs and venetian blinds.
3. Wax and buff floors (resilient).
4. Vacuum upholstered furniture and draperies.

Quarterly:

1. Scrub uncarpeted floors.
2. Wax resilient floors.

Semi-Annually:

1. Strip and wax resilient tile floors.
2. Wash exterior doors.

Annually:

1. Clean lighting fixtures.
2. Shampoo carpeting.
3. Wash venetian blinds and wash windows interior and exterior.

As Required: Remove snow from porticos and steps, down to juncture with grade or sidewalks. Sprinkle sand when necessary. This type of special service is required *at the expense* of interior cleaning to insure safe access by the public and to avoid hard packing and freezing on steps. This is a judgment decision which must be made depending on type and severity of snow. Optimum is clearing of entire steps in light snowfall to a five feet wide access path in heavy snowfall.

CHAPTER 6

GENERAL OUTDOOR MAINTENANCE

Outdoor maintenance makes up most of the work done by park and recreation maintenance departments. This chapter focuses on outdoor maintenance problems, discussing the following topics: solid waste, sewage disposal, outdoor lighting, fencing, signs, outdoor recreation surfaces, and maintenance of roads, parking lots, and trails. Grounds maintenance, dealing with lawn, shrubbery, and tree care, is discussed in Chapter 7.

SOLID WASTE

Solid waste is one of the most serious problems facing the United States today. In recent years Americans have become increasingly concerned with environmental problems associated with the collection of trash, garbage, and other solid wastes. Environmental Protection Agency statistics indicate that household and municipal waste amounts to 180 million tons per year, more than enough to fill the New Orleans superdome from floor to ceiling twice a day every day of the year. It is estimated that our solid waste production will increase to 216 million tons by the year 2000. The annual disposal of solid waste includes 72 million tons of paper, 14.4 million tons of plastic, and over 28 million tons of glass and metal.[1] Packaging in disposable containers has aggravated the problem because many are nonbiodegradable and will not burn.

As we seek permanent solutions to the solid waste problem, the first step is source reduction (eliminating unnecessary solid waste production and reusing products rather than throwing them away). This is by far the best solution. The next best solution is recycling (including composting). Recycling industries have been and are continuing to be developed throughout the United States. Technological improvements allow us to recycle more and more materials. Remaining solid waste must be disposed of by combustion (preferably with energy recovery) or landfilling.

FIGURE 6–1 Litter is unsightly and costly to pick up.

Litter Control

In park and recreation areas, the solid waste problem focuses primarily on litter control; park and recreation agencies spend millions of dollars each year for litter pickup and removal. The following methods of attacking the litter problem are suggested.

Educating the Public

Widespread educational efforts are needed to make people aware of the problem with littering and to develop in park users a sense of pride in park and recreation areas and to accept personal responsibility for helping to keep them clean. Most littering seems to be more a thoughtless rather than an intentional act. It is thought that by repeating the antilittering message over and over, a conditioned response not to litter can be developed. Keep America Beautiful, a nonprofit organization, has pioneered nationwide litter education efforts, and they have a variety of materials available, including an excellent series of films that can be used in efforts to reach school and civic groups. Woodsy Owl, Willie the Worm, and Pitch In! are other recognizable symbols of other educational efforts. These programs have also developed materials that can be used and/or adapted by a park and recreation administrator.

Techniques that can be used by park and recreation administrators to help educate the public include educational displays, talks by staff members to civic and school groups about the solid waste problem in general and in their parks specifically, and the display of antilitter posters and signs at park and recreation facilities. Be careful when displaying antilitter posters and signs—a park covered with them is as aesthetically unattractive as the litter itself.

Keeping Park and Recreation Areas Clean

Park administrators agree that patrons are more careful with trash and litter when the area is kept as clean as possible. Theme parks in the United States are an excellent example of how effective cleaning can make their facilities more attractive to the public.

Promoting Staff Responsibility

If all staff members accept the responsibility for picking up litter in park and recreation areas, the problem is greatly reduced. In addition, their efforts are contagious and will encourage the public to do the same. All park and recreation vehicles should be equipped with a litter container to ease the disposal problem.

Providing Adequate Trash Receptacles

As park and recreation patrons become more litter conscious, through educational efforts, the public will take greater care to properly dispose of trash and litter. Park and recreation agencies should make litter disposal as easy and convenient as possible by providing an adequate number of properly distributed trash receptacles. Recyclable waste containers are now commercially available with receptacles designated for "plastic only," "cans only," "glass only," and "newspapers only."

Selection of an appropriate trash receptacle is an important consideration. Criteria for the selection of trash receptacles should include the following:

1. *Function.* The kind of litter and trash expected to be deposited is an important consideration. In picnic and camping areas where a mixture of organic material and paper products can be anticipated, a traditional type garbage can is an appropriate container. In a refreshment stand area where candy wrappers, paper cups, and other paper products can be anticipated, a wire mesh container may be appropriate.

2. *Aesthetics.* Receptacles should be attractive and blend with the environment, but at the same time they must be conspicuous enough to discourage littering.

3. *Durability.* Because of heavy use the receptacle must be able to withstand frequent handling and patron abuse.

4. *Easy to handle.* A number of smaller trash receptacles are better than a few large ones because they are easier to handle by the maintenance personnel who must empty them and because better distribution is possible. The thirty- to thirty-five-gallon container has proved to be a reasonable

FIGURE 6–2   Trash receptacles that blend into their surroundings are pleasing to the eye.

size. For example, a thirty-two-gallon container holds about .15 cubic yards or about twenty-five pounds of typical solid waste.

5. *Securely fitting lid.* The trash receptacle should be provided with a tight fitting lid to protect waste from rodents, insects, and other disease-carrying vectors. A self-closing device on the lid is a good idea.

6. *Easy to clean.* The receptacle must be easy to clean.

Metal trash receptacles placed on the ground rust very quickly. To avoid this, attach the receptacle to a permanent post or set the receptacle on a concrete pad. In some locations, animals (dogs, raccoons, bears) present a serious problem. Tight-fitting lids, attachment to permanent posts, and specially designed animal-proof tops are possible solutions.

Keeping trash receptacles clean is a vital maintenance consideration. A dirty, smelly garbage can may ruin an individual's recreation experience. Trash receptacles must be cleaned on a regular basis; steam cleaning is an economical and efficient method. In recent years, the use of plastic liners has become widespread. Plastic liners improve sanitation by keeping trash receptacles from accumulating encrusted waste, and they speed up collection by eliminating the need to lift each container to empty it into the collection vehicle. Generally, bags of at least 2.00 mil thickness are recommended—thinner bags often tear, spilling waste.

In areas of intensive use where large volumes of solid waste can be anticipated, the use of bulk containers should be considered. Bulk containers vary in capacity from one to fifty cubic yards. They are best used as a secondary container (smaller trash receptacles are emptied into the bulk container for storage). The obvious advantage is less frequent collection. A number of campgrounds are successfully using a system whereby each family is given plastic bags, and several large bulk containers are spaced throughout the campground or are placed at the campground exit so campers can deposit their trash and garbage as they leave. In this scenario, collections are generally made daily, but the individual trash receptacle is eliminated and collection is simplified.

Supporting Antilitter Legislation and Enforcement

Because the dumping of solid waste in remote park areas can be a serious problem, park and recreation agencies should make sure that adequate legal measures have been taken to prohibit littering and dumping solid waste in areas under their jurisdiction. Then they should be certain these laws are enforced.

Adopting Special Programs and Ideas to Combat the Litter Problem

Trash receptacles using animal heads are attractive to children and have been successfully used by many park and recreation agencies. The occasional use of a public display of trash and litter collected for a period of time can be an effective educational tool. Many agencies have successfully designed and carried out extensive clean-up campaigns and programs using voluntary service agencies in the community. The adopt-a-highway programs have been particularly successful. Volunteer programs have also been successful on large lakes where shoreline accumulations of trash are particularly difficult for an agency with a limited maintenance staff to handle and in areas where extensive trail systems are maintained.

The solid waste problem is a difficult and expensive one to handle. A well-conceived and coordinated effort by a park and recreation agency can help ease the burden. The only incorrect approach is for an agency to give up and claim that the problem is too big to handle and to be satisfied with a park that is clean only at the beginning of the season.

Waste Collection

Even if park and recreation patrons and employees properly dispose of litter, the problem of solid waste is not completely solved because final disposal still needs to be dealt with. Frequency of collection depends on the amount of use a particular area or facility receives and the number and capacity of trash receptacles used. Normally, collections will be made daily; however, three or four times a week may be sufficient for a lightly used facility or one that receives predominantly weekend use. With heavily used facilities, particularly on weekends and holidays, collection two or three times a day may be warranted.

FIGURE 6–3 Automated litter pick-up saves maintenance labor.

Several different types of vehicles can be used for trash and garbage collection. Volume rather than weight usually determines vehicle selection. Where large amounts of trash and garbage must be collected, a conventional compacting garbage truck should be used. Several companies are manufacturing small garbage trucks designed for park and recreation agency use. When the amount of trash and garbage is relatively light, jeep- or tractor-drawn trailers, pickup trucks, or stake body trucks can be used more appropriately. For trash and garbage pickup in areas where no conveniently established service roads exist, for example, a picnic area or athletic field, the jeep- or tractor-drawn trailer may be most practical to use. Several factors should be considered when selecting the type of vehicle to be used for trash and garbage collection:

1. Amount of material to be collected. Many trips with a small vehicle are not economically feasible nor is the use of a large vehicle for a small amount of material.

2. Loading height of the vehicle. Ease of loading the vehicle by maintenance workers should be considered. In view of this, a pickup truck with a high bed is not particularly desirable for collection.

3. Blowing trash. The trash compartment of the vehicle should be covered to prevent trash from blowing out of the vehicle as it moves from place to place. The use of plastic liners eliminates the hazard of wind-blown loose trash.

4. Durability of the vehicle. Trash and garbage collection vehicles are subject to rough treatment and must be constructed durably. Trailers, when used,

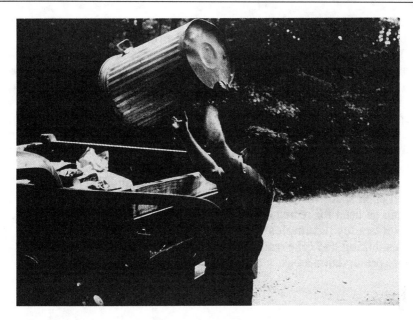

FIGURE 6–4   Loading height is an important feature to consider when selecting a vehicle for trash collection.

should have metal rather than wood bed and side construction.

5. Ease of unloading. Using a vehicle that has a dumping mechanism or a low bed will ease the problem of unloading.

Waste Disposal

Historically, a common method of solid waste disposal in park and recreation areas has been an open pit that is periodically burned off. In 1976, Congress passed the Resource Conservation and Recovery Act to protect human health and the environment from improper waste management. Three acceptable disposal methods for park and recreation agencies are the sanitary landfill, incineration, and recycling.

Sanitary Landfill

Landfilling continues to be the predominant method of waste disposal in the United States—73 percent of waste generated is disposed in this way. A sanitary landfill is an engineering method of disposing solid waste on land by spreading it in thin layers, compacting it to the smallest possible volume, and covering it with soil each working day. During off-season use when the landfill is infrequently used, a one-foot cover should be provided. The final cover should be a minimum of two feet. Landfills come under federal, state, and local regulations, and permits must be obtained from health and environmental officials.

Three methods are commonly used for sanitary landfills: the area, ramp, and trench methods. The trench method is generally the most practical for park and recreation areas. With this method, a trench is excavated as deeply as soil and ground water conditions allow. The trench should be twice as wide as the equipment used for compaction and covering. The soil excavated from the trench is used as cover material. The landfill should be convenient to the recreation facilities it serves to reduce the transportation time, but at the same time, it should be located out of sight of public use areas.

In urban areas, a closed municipal or county landfill can provide much needed open space for park and recreational development. Such covered landfills can be used for recreational facilities that do not require heavy structures or level grades. Examples of such recreation developments include golf courses, hiking and bike trails, open play areas and informal play fields, and wildlife preservation areas.

Incineration

Incineration has not been used widely in park and recreation areas. When land is not available for landfill, incineration is an acceptable alternative. Unfortunately, the incinerators that have been used in the past have not met air quality standards. However, a number of relatively small incinerator units are currently available that are completely acceptable for use in park and recreation areas. One such unit is a "starved-air" combustion unit. This unit recirculates hot combustion gases to sustain high temperatures and reduces the total amount of air used in combustion. Units are available that can burn from 200 to 1,200 pounds of solid waste per hour, a capacity sufficient to handle the solid waste from almost any park and recreation development. Operational costs are low because auxiliary fuel is used only to start combustion, and one person can operate these units. It is important to check state laws regarding the use of incinerators.

Recycling

Recycling has finally become a popular method of disposing of solid waste. It is the best of the three methods discussed because the disposed product is reused. Items that can be recycled include aluminum cans, glass bottles and jars, plastic containers, paper, and rubber tires. All of these items, with the possible exception of rubber tires, are commonly found in solid waste generated in park and recreation areas. Recycling is a good land stewardship practice and should be encouraged by park and recreation administrations, even though the method of disposal may be more expensive than the landfill or incineration.

In 1990, the National Park Service developed a pilot program with funding assistance from Dow Chemical Company and Huntsman Chemical Corporation to collect and recycle waste from four national parks: Acadia, Great Smoky, Grand Canyon, and Yosemite. In this program only aluminum, plastic, and glass are recycled.

Finding a local market for recyclable items should not be a problem for park and recreation areas located in urban areas. This may be a more difficult problem for parks in remote locations and the transportation cost may be prohibitive. As recycling becomes more and more economically feasible, park and recreation agencies may find some solid waste items to be a revenue source for park operations and improvements.

Bulk Collection

Another method of trash collection that should be considered in heavily used areas where trash is concentrated in relatively small areas is a bulk collection system. In this system, large in-place units are used for collection at strategically located points, and the entire unit is moved to the disposal point or the unit is emptied into a large disposal vehicle for transportation.

SEWAGE DISPOSAL

The primary purposes of sewage disposal systems are the sanitary disposal of human waste from recreation areas and protection from diseases transmitted through sewage. Problems associated with the selection and design of adequate sewage disposal systems are compounded by recreation areas and facilities that are often in remote locations, have a wide fluctuation in the quantity of sewage being generated because of peak load use on weekends, and the seasonal nature of many of these operations. Urban park and recreation facilities can usually tie into municipal or county sewage systems, while facilities located in rural areas must have self-contained disposal systems.

A basic knowledge of the characteristics of sewage is necessary to understand the methods of treating sewage. Sewage is approximately 99.95 percent water and 0.05 percent solids. Chemically, sewage consists of a wide variety of organic and inorganic materials. Oxygen dissolved in water is required to convert these complex materials into simpler compounds. Fish and other living organisms use this same dissolved oxygen. Therefore, if untreated or improperly treated sewage is discharged into a water course (lake, river, or pond), the dissolved oxygen may be depleted, resulting in the killing of fish and other organisms. The amount of oxygen-using material in sewage is referred to as the Biochemical Oxygen Demand (BOD). The efficiency of a sewage disposal system can be measured by determining the BOD level before and after treatment.

Decomposition of organic matter is biological in character and is dependent upon the action of aerobic and anaerobic bacteria. Aerobic bacteria depend upon the presence of free oxygen for their metabolism. Anaerobic bacteria also depend on oxygen; however, they obtain their oxygen from substances such as sulphates, phosphates, and other organic compounds found in sewage. The action of both types of bacteria is dependent upon warm temperatures above 40 degrees Fahrenheit.

SEWAGE DISPOSAL SYSTEMS

Pit and Chemical Toilets

Pit and chemical toilets are an unattractive and inefficient disposal method. However, they do have a legitimate application in remote areas where water is not available. These methods are unsuitable for heavily used permanent facilities under any conditions. Because of the low developmental cost, the pit toilet has been badly overused by park and recreation agencies, and in many instances, another more suitable disposal system should have been used. When pit and chemical toilets have to be used, they should be made as attractive as possible through the use of high quality building materials and the design of well-lighted and well-ventilated structures.

Composting Toilets

Composting toilets are a relatively new development, resulting from the demand for an ecologically sound sewage disposal method in remote areas. Some of these systems were designed for use in cottages in isolated locations. Their use can easily be adapted for park and recreation applications. In the composting toilet, human waste is mixed with other organic materials such as grass, leaves, bark mulch, or peat moss. The waste is aerobically decomposed either in a container beneath the privy or in a bin separate from the privy. The humus-like material resulting from the aerobic decomposition is relatively pathogen-free and can be spread in a field or on the forest floor. Composting toilets are environmentally sound and can accommodate more users than pit or chemical toilets. They generally require more maintenance than the pit toilet.

Septic Tanks

The septic tank and absorption field is a widely used disposal system for park and recreation facilities. The primary reason for its use is that the system can handle the limited volume of sewage generated by many park and recreation developments. As the developed recreation facilities are designed to handle larger and larger numbers of people, more complex systems must be considered. A limiting factor in the use of septic tanks is the lack of soil percolation, or absorption, in some locations.

The septic tank system consists of an underground waterproof concrete tank of varying size, depending on the volume of sewage anticipated, a distribution box, and a tile drainfield. The drainfield consists of tile placed loosely end-to-end on a bed of gravel. Sludge settles to the bottom of the septic tank where it is digested and liquefied by anaerobic bacterial action. This conversion to a liquid is never complete and the sludge level should be checked annually and pumped out when necessary. The liquid effluent from the tank dissipates into the ground through the absorption field. A percolation test is necessary before an absorption field is installed. This test measures how fast the liquid effluent will filter into various soils, and determines the size of the absorption field.

In locations where soil percolation is very poor, a sand filter normally about three feet thick can be substituted for the normal absorption field. The liquid effluent is distributed over the surface and filters through the sand. When combined with disinfection, this treatment normally produces an effluent that has more than 90 percent removal of BOD. Trickling filters are an effective secondary treatment method in which sewage is sprayed over a rock-filled tank. BOD-producing material is removed by living organisms, such as bacteria, algae, and protozoa, growing on the rock surfaces.

Lagoons

The lagoon (commonly called a stabilization pond or oxidation pond) consists of a pond or basin that, when properly designed and maintained, will provide an environment for the natural reduction of sewage to its stable form through the action of aerobic bacteria. Oxygen dissolved in the pond is replenished with algae growth and from the atmosphere. Effluent from the lagoon must generally be chlorinated. However, no other maintenance is needed. The lagoon should have a water depth of about three to five feet. When operating properly, the lagoon will be odor free. Odor is a sign of overloading, and when it occurs frequently, artificial aeration may be necessary. The lagoon system will handle relatively large amounts of sewage and can be used for a complex of park and recreation facilities. When adequate land area is available, this is the most inexpensive method of treatment of large amounts of sewage.

Aerobic Digestion

Aerobic digestion (also called extended aeration) is technically an activated sludge process. This system is one of the most effective methods for treating sewage, with some systems achieving 95 percent BOD removal. The system consists of two or three components: an aeration tank, a settling tank, and in some instances, local health officials require a sludge-holding tank. The system uses sewage aeration by mechanical means and provides high quality treatment. Raw sewage and activated sludge are mixed together in the aeration tank. Sewage is normally held in the aeration tank with air added for twenty-four hours. Aerobic bacteria break down the organic matter into stable or inorganic material. Solids are then allowed to settle in the settling tank. The liquid effluent from the aerobic digestion system is generally chlorinated before it is discharged into a water course. This system can handle large quantities of sewage and is generally used for a complex of park and recreation facilities. The initial cost of the system is high and requires careful attention by trained personnel. For efficient operation of this system a reasonably steady flow of sewage is needed.

Selecting a Disposal System

Selecting an appropriate sewage disposal system involves careful consideration of the following:

1. Public health requirements. All systems require the approval of the appropriate public health agency.
2. Quantity of sewage to be treated.
3. Initial construction or installation cost.
4. Operating cost.
5. Amount of maintenance required.
6. Land area available consistent with future development plans.
7. Absorption qualities of soil.
8. Water table level.
9. Presence or absence of a water course to handle treated effluent.

Except for pit and chemical toilets, professional engineering help is a legal requisite in planning any sewage disposal system. A park and recreation professional must be able to project the volume of sewage anticipated from the planned recreation facilities. Once this has been determined, sanitary engineers can design an appropriate system to serve the proposed facilities.

Several environmental precautions need to be taken in the development and maintenance of sewage disposal systems. Partially or fully treated sewage that is discharged into a body of water should be additionally treated to lower the bacterial level to the point at which disease-producing organisms are not present. This is often accomplished by adding chlorine to the effluent. When this is done, the treated effluent should be held long enough to allow the chlorine to dissipate before it is discharged into a water course in which high chlorine levels would be toxic to some species of fish.

In campgrounds where recreation vehicle dump stations have been provided, special care is needed. The chemicals used in these tanks are toxic to many organisms and should be thoroughly diluted before entering sewage disposal systems.

WATER SYSTEMS

Potable drinking water (suitable for drinking) is an essential element for any park or recreation facility development. In addition to drinking water, a water supply may be needed for the development of specialized recreation facilities. For example, large quantities of water are needed for a golf course irrigation system, for a swimming pool, or for a ski slope where artificial-snow-making equipment is to be used. The focus here is on the development of potable drinking water for public use.

Sources of potable water include the following:

1. *Natural water supply.* A stream or pond within a protected watershed may provide a natural supply of water that can be used without treatment. Such occurrences are extremely rare and should be undertaken only with the approval of the local health department.
2. *Wells.* The capacity of a water supply system using wells can be increased substantially by adding storage tanks.
3. *Impure water supply.* Water supply generally from a lake or river and an adequate treatment system.

Water treatment is necessary to remove dirt and bacteria and consists of three steps: sedimentation, filtration, and chlorination. In a sedimentation tank or reservoir, suspended dirt particles slowly settle out of the water. Chemicals can be added to speed up this process. In the second step, filtration, the water passes through a sand bed or a mechanical filter. Disinfection, usually using a form of chlorine, is necessary to remove potentially harmful bacteria.

Once an adequate source of water has been found or developed, it is necessary to install a storage and distribution system. Storage tanks can vary from a forty gallon pressure tank for a small building to a large metal storage tank high above the ground. Distribution systems are of two basic types: (1) a gravity system in which the water supply is stored in a holding tank higher than all facilities to be fed, and (2) the use of a pump or pumps. These systems can be designed to use either a submersible well pump and pressure tank or an aboveground pump, also utilizing a pressure tank. Distribution systems for other than potable water for irrigation or other purposes operate on these same principles.

Care must be taken not to cross-connect water lines with other lines that might contaminate the water supply. For example, the main water supply line serving sewage treatment facilities should be equipped with a reduced pressure principle backflow preventer. This is a device that will protect the water supply from a backflow of sewage. This same device can be used in other places where there is a danger of contaminated water backing through an ordinary valve. Hose bibs (the place where a hose connects to the water supply) should be equipped with a hose bib vacuum breaker, which is another device designed to prevent contamination of the water supply.

Properly designed and constructed water systems do not require a great deal of maintenance; however, a good preventive maintenance program should be set up. Routine maintenance must be performed on all pumps and motors and on filtration and chlorination systems as specified by the manufacturer. Storage tanks should be cleaned and disinfected periodically. All metal tanks should be painted to protect against corrosion. Only paints that meet the standards of the American Water Works Association and are acceptable to state and local health departments should be used. Leaks caused by broken or damaged water lines or equipment must be repaired when they occur. The maintenance department must maintain a file indicating when routine maintenance has been performed and also a file of blueprints and drawings accurately locating all water lines, underground storage facilities, and pumps serving park and recreation facilities. Water systems that are chlorinated should be tested daily, and water should undergo a bacteriological analysis periodically.

NIGHT LIGHTING

A large number of outdoor recreation activities require night lighting. Baseball and softball fields, football and soccer fields, tennis courts, swimming pools, par-3 golf courses, and multiple-use game courts are examples of outdoor recreation facilities that are commonly lighted.

There are several advantages to lighting recreation areas and facilities. By extending hours of use, more participants are able to use existing facilities and family members have opportunities to participate together. Activities at night are possible for adults who work during the day. Night lighting may, in some instances, attract people to recreation areas. On the other hand, night lighting recreation facilities in urban areas can be disturbing to residents located close to lighted facilities. The high cost of energy, resulting from lighted facilities greatly increases operational costs. Maintenance also becomes a problem when facilities are used for long periods of time. Not only is it difficult to find a time when a facility is not in use so that maintenance can be performed, but the overuse of a facility may cause additional work especially in the case of the compaction of turf areas.

Technical Lighting Data

The quantitative measure of the output of a light source is a *lumen*. For sports lighting, a reflector is used to concentrate and direct the light energy created by the lamp and project it onto the playing area. The degree of illumination is

Photo supplied by Musco Sports-Lighting, Inc., Muscatine, IA.

FIGURE 6–5 Well-lighted playing fields enhance participation.

measured in footcandles. Thus a *footcandle,* which represents one lumen of light spread over one square foot of surface, indicates the amount of light available in a recreation area where activity takes place. Lighting standards are expressed in terms of footcandles. Light levels are expressed in terms of *initial* and *maintained* footcandles. Initial footcandles refer to the amount of light that is generated during the initial phase of a lighting system's use (the first 25 percent of the rated lamp life). Maintained footcandles refer to the amount of light one can expect to have on the playing surface over the extended life of the lighting system. For example, the standard for lighting recreational tennis courts is to provide 38 initial footcandles and 30 maintained footcandles. Sports lighting should be designed to provide maintained footcandles that ensure the necessary quantity of light throughout the life of the system. Standards have been developed for virtually all forms of recreational activity and are readily available from a variety of sources, including commercial manufacturers of lighting equipment.

Another term commonly used is *luminaire.* A luminaire is a complete lighting unit consisting of a lamp and components designed to distribute light, position and protect the lamp, and to connect the lamp to the necessary power supply. Floodlighting luminaires are designed to produce long, medium, and wide beams of light. This allows flexibility in the design of a lighting system. For example, with a battery of three tennis courts, luminaires with wide beams would be used to light the courts near the light source and medium beams to light the middle courts. In a par-3 golf course or driving range, installation of all three (wide, medium, and long) would be indicated.

Types of Lamps

The incandescent lamp is the oldest lighting system and can still be found in older recreational sports lighting installations. The incandescent lamp produces a very high quality light and the system turns off and on instantly; however, incandescent lamps generate only twenty-five lumens of light per watt of electricity, which means the system is very costly to operate. In addition, the lamp life is relatively short when compared to other systems. The quartz lamp is an improved version of the incandescent system that provides some cost efficiency and longer lamp life; however, this system is outdated by the high intensity discharge systems.

High intensity discharge systems include mercury, metal halide, and high pressure sodium lamps. Metal halide and high pressure sodium lamps are the two lamps used today for sports lighting. With high intensity discharge lamps, light is produced by a continuous electric arc. Inside a discharge lamp there are two electrodes and some form of metal that can be vaporized and broken down into electric particles to conduct current in an electric arc from one electrode to the other. The arc has a negative resistance characteristic in which the resistance drops as current increases. Thus, a ballast must be used to limit the current. Because of the ballast circuit, the high intensity discharge systems are generally more expensive in initial installation cost. This is balanced, however, by a very long lamp life and much lower operating costs. For most sports applications, metal halide lamps are more energy efficient and thus the choice of most lighting engineers. The metal halide lamp generates 100 lumens per watt. The high pressure sodium lamp is even more energy efficient, generating 135 lumens per watt. However, the physical shape of the arc tube and the lack of a focal point make it difficult to project the light efficiently over long distances. In addition, the high pressure sodium lamp produces a noticeable flicker, which can cause a stroboscopic effect on rapidly moving objects.

Installation of Luminaires

The least expensive lighting systems use luminaires affixed to wooden cross arms on wooden poles with overhead wiring. Underground wiring allows the removal of unsightly, and often dangerous guy wires, notwithstanding the obvious aesthetic advantage. Although somewhat more costly, underground wiring should be seriously considered for all recreation night-lighting applications. Use of wooden crossarms was common for incandescent lighting systems. With a high intensity discharge system, fixtures weigh approximately fifty to sixty pounds (compared to fifteen for the incandescent fixture) and installation on a wooden crossarm will cause the crossarm to twist, resulting in misalignment of fixtures. Steel crossarms are more commonly used with high intensity discharge luminaires.

Poles to support the luminaires and crossarms can be made from wood, steel, or concrete. Wood poles are generally the least expensive to purchase and install; however, like the crossarms, they tend to twist and warp as they dry which can create serious fixture alignment problems. Both concrete and steel poles are durable and easy to maintain. A combination of a concrete base with a steel shaft can also be used. Environmental conditions vary in different parts of the country, and a recommendation related to the selection of poles and crossarms should be secured from a local lighting engineer.

Maintenance of Lighting Systems

All electric lamps have a rated lamp life. The rated lamp life is an average figure. Thus, some lamps will burn out before, and some after, the rated lamp life. At the end of rated life, 50 percent of the lamps remain burning; however, only 6 percent of the burning time remains for those lamps still burning. Consequently, it is economical to replace all lamps at the end of the rated lamp life. This is important when organizing a relamping maintenance schedule. Two other considerations should be kept in mind when developing a maintenance schedule. First is the efficiency of the lamp after use over a long period of time. Decrease in lighting efficiency varies with type of lamp used and can be determined from data supplied by the manufacturer.

Second is the dirt that accumulates on the reflective surfaces of the luminaire and the reduction of lighting efficiency. The amount of dirt depreciation can be determined only by experience and can vary depending on environmental conditions. Field tests with a light meter on actual installations are the best guide. Minimizing luminaire dirt depreciation can be done in two ways: (1) installing hermetically sealed and filtered luminaires, and (2) regular cleaning of the luminaire. To be cost efficient, luminaire cleaning and relamping should be scheduled at the same time.

Designing a flexible lighting system at the beginning stages of a new facility will provide for considerable operational cost savings. For example, a driving range system should be designed so that one-half of the lights can be used at any one time to provide for times when the range is lightly used. An 18-hole par-3 golf course should be lighted in sections so that the lights can be turned off as players complete playing portions of the course at closing or so that only nine holes can be used during periods of light use.

Park and recreation administrators must seek professional engineering help when developing night lighting for recreation facilities. Many power companies employ recreation lighting specialists, and manufacturers of lighting equipment provide excellent technical advice. Consulting electrical engineers are also available.

FENCING

The appearance of park and recreation areas should be as natural as possible. Fences of any type tend to destroy the natural quality of the environment and should be avoided whenever possible. Before fencing is used, several alternatives should be considered. One of the most practical alternatives is the use of shrubbery. By careful choice of plant materials, such as barberry, privet, yew, and ornamental and native trees, plantings can be used to control pedestrian traffic or screen unsightly areas. A problem, however, with the use of plant materials is the time required to establish them. This drawback can be overcome by planting mature plant materials, which is extremely expensive, or by erecting an inexpensive type of fencing until the plantings have matured, and then removing the fence. In many instances, fence removal is not necessary because the shrubbery has overgrown the fence.

Other alternatives include the use of water as a barrier. Boulders or rock outcroppings can also be used effectively in combination with other treatments. Grade separations can be used; however, care must be taken not to create untenable maintenance problems.

Despite attempts to keep areas completely natural and to use natural alternatives, the use of fencing is many times the only practical alternative. Factors to be considered in determining the type of fencing to be used include the following:

1. *Function.* Fencing may be used to control access to an area, to direct pedestrian traffic flow, or to control payment of an admission fee, thus determining the height, shape, form, and strength of a particular installation of fencing.
2. *Initial cost of installation.*
3. *Durability.*
4. *Maintenance cost.*
5. *Aesthetic considerations.* How well does the fencing blend into the natural setting?
6. *Safety.* It is important that the fence not create a hazard that might injure persons using park and recreation facilities.

Types of Fencing

Local conditions and availability of materials will often dictate the best fencing for a particular situation. Several of the most commonly used types of fencing and their advantages and disadvantages are discussed here.

Split rail fencing. The advantages of split rail fencing are its natural appearance and long life when locust posts and chestnut, spruce, or sassafras rails are used. It is also easy to mow under the rail fence, and the initial cost is relatively inexpensive. The disadvantages are that it does not provide a very formidable barrier and is climbed easily. It is also relatively weak and easily damaged. This disadvantage is balanced somewhat by its ease of repair.

Chain link fencing. Three types of chain link fencing are commonly used in park and recreation areas: (1) galvanized, (2) aluminum, and (3) vinyl coated. With the galvanized fence, steel wire is coated with zinc using a hotdip process. Aluminum chain link fabric is often used in highly corrosive environments, for example, beach areas where salt will normally damage galvanized fence in a short period of time. With the vinyl coated fence, a plastic or vinyl coating is applied over standard galvanized wire, providing a fabric that is more aesthetically pleasing and that blends with the natural environment, is abrasion resistant, and is even more corrosion resistant than aluminum fencing. It is also considerably more expensive.

Chain link fencing provides a good barrier that is difficult to climb. It is also very strong, durable, and long-lasting when nine- or eleven-gauge fabric is specified. However, the initial costs are high and it has a generally unattractive appearance. Chain link fencing also creates a mowing problem when installed on turf areas. Despite its aesthetic unattractiveness, chain link is widely used in park and recreation areas because of the excellent control and durability features. In addition to the use of the vinyl fabric, chain link fencing can be improved aesthetically by wood slatting or woven plastic strips.

Woven wire fencing. The only advantage of a woven wire fence is its low cost. On

FIGURE 6–6 Split rail fencing is easy to install and maintain.

the debit side, it is not durable, it is easy to climb, it will not last as long as other types of fencing, and it presents the same mowing problem as chain link. Locust or treated posts are a must with a woven wire fence installation.

Post and board fencing. Although painted post and board fencing does not give a natural appearance, its aesthetic qualities are very good in some situations. For example, when used around a riding stable it can be very attractive fencing material. However, it is easy to climb and expensive to maintain.

Solid board fencing. This type of fence is generally used when visual screening is desired. When natural materials such as cedar or redwood are used, very little maintenance is required. It is good fencing to use if a solid barrier is desired to prevent access to an area. But, compared with other alternatives, it will not last as long, and the initial cost is quite high.

Brick, stone, and ornamental iron are other types of fencing that may be used in special situations. Where stone is readily available, it can be used to blend beautifully into a park setting.

Care of vegetative growth under and immediately adjacent to all fencing presents a serious maintenance problem. Ways of easing this problem include chemical sterilization of soil under and six inches on either side of the fence, use of growth retardants, and encasing the fence in an asphalt or concrete strip level with the ground to allow easy mowing. Fencing around tennis courts or multiple-use courts should be inset six inches to eliminate hand mowing.

SIGNS

Signs are used for a variety of purposes in park and recreation areas. They can be used to inform, direct, describe, name, beckon, and prohibit. A good sign system performs all these functions with an air of hospitality, welcome, and dignity. Signs reflect the management philosophy of the agency. If the sign system is done poorly, it can be irritating to the visitor. A primary purpose when developing a sign system should be how *few* signs are needed to achieve the agency's full purpose, not how *many*. A second purpose should be to make the sign system do an adequate job without unwarranted intrusion upon the natural environment of the area. So, the first question that must be asked is, "Is this sign really needed?"

There are also a number of practical considerations that must be taken into account when designing a sign. Signs must be easily and clearly understood. A National Park Service sign, FEE INFORMATION, has caused park visitors to stop and request the "free" information. Messages on signs are important. They should be brief but not abrupt, simple to comprehend but not insulting to the intelligence of the visitor, informative but not wordy, and accurate, particularly when interpreting some feature or story.

Signs must be legible. The style, height, and width of lettering and color contrast are important. The National Recreation and Park Association Management Aids Bulletin, *Signs and Symbols*, is an excellent source and lists legibility standards.

Additional factors that must be considered when selecting sign materials are initial cost, ease of maintenance, and maintenance cost. When wording signs, particularly prohibitive ones, one should word them positively rather than negatively. The "no" and "do not" signs should be avoided whenever possible. Instead of DO NOT PICK THE FLOWERS, a sign saying PLEASE LEAVE FLOWERS FOR OTHERS TO ENJOY conveys a positive message. PICNIC IN DESIGNATED AREAS ONLY is an improvement over the traditional NO PICNICKING. Rather than a sign on a restroom, CLOSED FOR THE SEASON, the message RESTROOMS AVAILABLE AT VISITOR CENTER conveys the management intent. At Coot Bay, a bird sanctuary in Everglades National Park, the sign FISHING IS STRICTLY FOR THE BIRDS has elicited a much more favorable public response than the alternative NO FISHING could have.

The use of symbols on park and recreation area signs can also be effective. The National Park Service arrowhead is easily identified by Park Service visitors nationwide. Many municipal park and recreation departments also make use of symbols, such as pine trees, oak leaves, and shamrocks, to serve as a quick identification for their park and recreation areas and facilities. In addition, symbols are replacing words on signs. Many federal, state, and local recreation and park agencies are using the Federal Recreation Symbols to identify recreation areas along roads and highways.

Types of Signs

Many types of signs are used in park and recreation areas and a variety of materials are used. Signs can be purchased commercially; however, many park and recreation departments manufacture or fabricate a large percentage of their own signs. A number of sign and lettering systems are commercially available, including some with automated systems for lettering and graphics.

Wood is a commonly used material for signs in park and recreation areas. A variety of woods including cedar; redwood; poplar; white, ponderosa, or sugar pine; and cypress can be used. Methods of fabricating wooden signs include the following:

Routing. This method uses a machine with a revolving vertical spindle and cutter for milling out the surface of wood, metal, or plastic. Signs can be hand routed, or commercial sign making machines using templates are available at relatively low cost. The basic sign is routed to a depth of three-eighths of an inch, stained or painted, and the routed letters are painted a contrasting color. The routed sign gives a rustic appearance when appropriate colors are used, and it blends well into most park environments. When using a template, it is possible to purchase many national and international symbols and incorporate them into the routed sign.

Sandblasting. By using sandblasting equipment and special rubber templates, it is possible to fabricate signs with letters and designs that are similar in appearance to routed signs.

Raised letters. Letters and designs are cut out and attached to the painted or stained sign board. The appearance of these signs is also similar to routed signs. Some park administrators believe the raised letter sign is easier to maintain than the routed or sandblasted sign.

Painted or silk screened. A number of commercial kits are available with varying sized and shaped letters and numbers from which attractive signs can be made. Designs, drawings, and photographs can be applied fairly easily by using silk screening.

Metal signs are much more durable than wood, but the initial cost is more expensive. Anodized aluminum and bronze are the two most commonly used materials. The major advantage is permanence, little maintenance, and resistance to vandalism.

For small permanent informational signs, plastic is commonly used. Plastic sign material with two layers of different colored plastic is routed to produce a sign with contrasting colors. These signs can be used effectively for a variety of

FIGURE 6-7 Signs made of anodized aluminum require little maintenance. They are practical for use in remote or unsupervised areas because they are more difficult to vandalize.

applications. They are effective in labeling plant materials in formal gardens, botanical gardens, and arboretums. These signs can also be used to inform and direct park and recreation users in buildings.

The entrance sign is a park and recreation agency's most important sign, giving visitors their first impressions of the facility. Entrance signs should be simple, and they should complement rather than detract from the park environment. Entrance signs with commercial advertising displays are in poor taste and should be avoided regardless of the obvious cost benefit.

Traffic control signs present a minor dilemma. Should these signs be made to blend with other signs in the park and recreation system by using a similar style or should standard highway traffic signs be used? Most park and recreation agencies use standard highway signs because of safety considerations.

Sign Maintenance

A good sign system can be impaired by poor maintenance. Signs must be repainted and replaced when necessary. In most instances, signs that need to be repainted are taken down during the off-season and repainted in the maintenance service center shops, although in some instances repainting in the field is more practical. Duplicates of key signs for areas used on a year-round basis should be considered. A sign maintenance schedule should be developed so that one-third to one-half of all signs are repainted each season.

Signs are a popular target for vandalism. Vandalism can be deterred through the use of high quality materials that are difficult to vandalize. Setting sign posts in concrete or using a "T" or "X" brace underground to prevent removal or turning is a worthwhile precaution to take. This is particularly important in areas with sandy or loose soil. Tamper resistant fasteners should be used when possible. With wooden signs, recess fasteners and plug over them.

Wood Preservation

Wood in its natural form is not a very durable material; however, technology is now available to enable the use of wood in buildings, signs, and fences so that it will require a minimum of care. By injecting preservative chemicals deep into the wood, it is possible to prevent attack by wood-destroying organisms. This process is referred to as pressure treatment. Brushing or spraying preservative chemicals will give short-term protection but should not be confused with pressure treatment. Pressure treatment uses such preservatives as water-borne inorganic arsenicals, creosote, and oil-borne preservatives. Creosote, pentachlorophenol and inorganic arsenicals have been designated as restricted-use pesticides by the Environmental Protection Agency. This means they must be applied under the supervision of a certified pesticide applicator. Creosote- and pentachlorophenol-treated wood should not be used indoors or where it will come in direct contact with drinking water, food stuffs, or bare skin. Pressure treated lumber costs less than naturally durable woods, such as redwood, and is worth the additional expense for fence and sign posts, as well as other outdoor uses that expose wood to the weather.

OUTDOOR RECREATION SURFACES

A recreation surface can have a major impact on the quality of the recreation experience. A smooth, resilient tennis court surface will enhance a game, while a hard, cracked or pitted surface may make the surface extremely unpleasant for the participants. Park and recreation agencies should do everything possible to ensure the best quality outdoor recreation surfaces.

Developing a good outdoor recreation surface starts with planning and development. The subsurface and/or base preparation must be adequate, provisions must be made to handle surface and ground water, and proper materials must be selected for the surface needed. No one surface is satisfactory for all recreation activities. The perfect outdoor recreation surface should have the following qualities:

1. A multiple-use surface, which can be used for a number of different activities.
2. Dustless and stainless.
3. Good durability with good wearing quality despite continued heavy use.
4. Reasonable initial cost.
5. Easy to maintain. Ease of maintenance implies little "down time" when maintenance is performed.
6. Low maintenance cost.
7. A pleasing appearance.
8. Nonabrasive.
9. Resilient.
10. Available for year-round use.
11. Not slippery.

Although a single surface does not exist that meets all of these specifications, this list forms a reasonable set of criteria to consider when evaluating outdoor recreation surfaces.

Types of Outdoor Surface Materials

Earth Surfaces. The earth surface is undoubtedly the oldest and probably one of the most frequently used of all outdoor recreation surfaces. The advantages are its ready availability and low cost (even when a high quality earth surface is developed). Disadvantages include high maintenance cost, easy erosion, problems with weed infestations, and appearance. Perhaps the greatest disadvantage is the dust in dry weather and the mud in wet weather. Long drying time often makes the surface unusable for long periods after a heavy rain.

Turf Surfaces. When appearance and resilience are considered, turf is an attractive recreation surface. For certain activities it is ideal. However, it has high maintenance costs and is not very durable under intensive use. For example, turf would be an ideal material to use under all types of playground apparatus; however, even under relatively light use conditions, it is impossible to maintain adequately.

Aggregates. Surface material called aggregates includes sand, gravel, cinders, and crushed brick or other composition materials. These materials have some good applications for recreation use. For example, a sufficient depth of sand provides adequate impact cushioning in play apparatus areas. From a player's perspective, composition tennis courts are desirable. Gravel pads around a picnic table provide a reasonably durable surface that is porous and allows water to penetrate into the soil. These materials, however, are expensive to maintain and must be replaced frequently.

Concrete and Bituminous Surfaces. Concrete and bituminous (the combination of rock and some type of emulsion) surface materials are widely used as outdoor recreation surfaces because of their excellent durability and low maintenance. If constructed properly with good drainage and good base and sub-base construction, they are long lasting, excellent year-round surfaces and can be used under any weather conditions. Concrete is an excellent surface material when a smooth, level surface is required, for example, for a shuffleboard court. Two qualities that discourage the use of these materials are their lack of resiliency (although bituminous surfaces can be "softened" sufficiently through the use of additives to be attractive surfaces for some types of activity such as tennis) and their abrasiveness.

Synthetic Surfaces. As technology and experience increase, synthetic materials may be the answer to many future outdoor recreation surface problems. The use of materials such as astro-turf, poly-turf, and tartan have been well accepted under certain conditions. Recycled materials such as old tires may have promise for the future. Except for the high initial cost, abrasiveness, and the hardening of the surface as it becomes older (in the case of synthetic turfs), these surfaces meet most of the criteria established for an ideal outdoor recreation surface. When maintenance cost is considered over a period of time, even the high initial cost becomes less important. Applications of various types of synthetic materials are still in the experimental stage, but they hold great promise for the future. Synthetics are being used successfully for surfaces as diverse as under playground apparatus, athletic fields, driving ranges, golf tees and greens, running tracks and for areas around recreation buildings and facilities that are difficult to maintain with any other surface material. While they will play a major role in meeting many present and future outdoor recreation surfacing needs, the artificial appearance of even the high quality synthetics will preclude their widespread use as universal recreation surfaces of the future.

Other types of synthetic surfaces that should be mentioned are artificial ice and snow surfaces. Although not presently in widespread use, artificial surfaces have been developed for skiing and ice skating.

Safety must be a primary concern in the selection and maintenance of any recreation surface. Hardness and abrasiveness of the surface are important safety considerations. When maintaining turf surfaces, the soil composition, frequency of aeration, and type of grass may affect the resiliency of the surface.

What does the future hold? The U.S. Open Golf Tournament is played on a synthetic turf course, the Stanley Cup Hockey Tournament is contested on a plastic rink, and professional champions ski on artificial mountain slopes during the summer. Who would have predicted when the National Professional Baseball League began in 1876 that fewer than 100 years later baseball would be played on a mat of artificial grass?

ROADS AND PARKING LOTS

Park and recreation agencies are responsible for the maintenance of many miles of roads and many acres of parking lots. A road or parking lot system comprises the foundation, the surface, shoulders, and drainage ditches and culverts. Deterioration of these components begins immediately after construction. The job of a maintenance manager is to slow this deterioration to a minimum, extending the useful life of the road or parking lot as long as possible.

The surfaces of roads and parking lots are of two primary types, bituminous and gravel. Proper maintenance should consist primarily of preventive measures. The two surfaces need different maintenance and must be considered separately.

Bituminous Surfaces

Exposure to sunlight, water, heat, and cold causes deterioration of bituminous road and parking lot surfaces. Failure of surfaces, indicated by checking, cracking, and disintegration in the form of potholes, can be traced generally to improper or poor construction. These problems are frequently caused by improper drainage of subgrade and base course material, inadequate thickness or lack of structural strength of the base course material, inadequate thickness of the surface course, or poor subgrade soil conditions.

Even when the road surface or parking lot is adequately constructed, dryness can cause serious problems. Oxidation of the asphalt binder results from the combination of infrared and ultraviolet rays from sunlight. This causes the binder to lose its adhesive and cohesive qualities, and it becomes hard and brittle. The stone aggregates that were held together by the binder become loose from erosion and abrasion. As cracks appear in the pavement, water enters and causes them to increase in size and number during freezing and thawing cycles. Parking lots are subject to additional deteriorating effects from dripping oil, fuel, and grease from parked cars. These substances are solvents and soften the paved surface. For this reason, parking lots should be covered with a good quality sealcoating soon after construction. Roads should also be sealed, but only after they begin to show signs of deterioration.

The durability of a bituminous surface, whether on a road or parking lot, depends largely on the base course. It must be of sufficient thickness, laid on hard subgrade soil, sufficiently compacted, and adequately drained. A good drainage system will prevent water from reaching the paved surface and collecting under it. Good drainage must be provided during the initial construction, but it must also be maintained during the life of the paved surface by keeping all drainage ditches and culverts open. When drainage problems appear, new drainage ditches, culverts, or diversion ditches may be needed to reduce damage to paved areas. Concrete, vitrified clay, and corregated galvanized metal are the materials most frequently used for culverts.

Good preventive maintenance includes early detection of any failure and prompt repair. Failures are best discovered by walking inspections—not many surface failures can be detected from a moving vehicle. Inspection of drainage facilities should be done on a regular basis. It is a good idea to inspect drainage facilities occasionally during heavy rains.

Gravel Surfaces

Gravel can be relatively inexpensive if the material sources are close by. This type of construction may be desirable for park and recreation areas in which the traffic load is light to moderate. However, because of dust problems, poor riding quality, excessive wear to vehicles and tires, high annual maintenance cost, and because it is a source of siltation to adjacent water bodies, park managers should strive to have their gravel roads paved.

Maintenance of gravel surfaced roads differs from maintenance of a bituminous surface in two important respects. The gravel road must be bladed periodically, and some dust control method must be instituted. Blading the road surface is necessary to maintain the road's crown and ensure adequate drainage, and to reduce the wash boarding effect as a result of heavy traffic. Blading may be accomplished with a farm-type tractor and blade or with larger motorized grading equipment. The blading should always be done after a rain when more than average moisture content is present. Under arid conditions, blading must be accomplished when the road is dry. Potholes must be filled as soon as they occur.

Dust on gravel roads can be greatly reduced with the use of calcium chloride, which retains moisture already present in the road surface and absorbs moisture from the air. Calcium chloride should be applied when the surface is damp at a rate of 1½ pounds per square yard. Best results are obtained by mixing the salt with the surface layer of gravel. This can be accomplished by applying the material to the road surface prior to blading. Since calcium chloride is subject to leaching action, it must be replenished periodically.

Another method for controlling dust is the use of a light asphaltic oil, which partially waterproofs the surface, reduces evaporation, and aids in stabilizing the road surface. Used motor oil should not be used for this purpose as it adds toxic chemicals to the soil. Vehicles should be kept off the road until the oil has had a chance to soak into the surface. A freshly oiled road will make a mess of an auto or recreation vehicle.

Another surface material that could be considered for parking lots is porous concrete blocks. These specially designed blocks are laid over the parking lot surface and filled with gravel or earth. This surface has more stability than gravel alone and it also allows water penetration, thus preventing run-off problems associated with paved parking surfaces. In addition to use as a parking lot surface, this material can be used for short driveways that are used infrequently. For aesthetics, turf can be maintained over this surface.

TRAILS

The use of trails in the United States has risen to unprecedented heights in recent years. A great variety of recreation activities use trails, including hiking, horseback riding, cross country skiing, bicycling, nature study, jogging, and off-road vehicles. Government agencies at all levels are seeking to meet this heavy demand. In addition, private nonprofit groups build and maintain many miles of trails in this country. The Appalachian Trail is a good example of how government agencies (primarily the National Park Service, U.S. Forest Service, and a number of state parks) and private nonprofit agencies have worked together to provide an immensely popular trail that receives heavy use. Many of our national parks and forests have extensive trail systems. For example, in 1990, Glacier National Park maintained 730 miles of trails that were used for backpacking and day hikes. Shenandoah National Park provides 500 miles of trails including a ninety-five-mile segment of the Appalachian Trail. A number of states are providing statewide trail systems and many state parks provide trails for a variety of uses.

Greenways

Perhaps the most heavily used trails in the United States are the municipal greenways. The greenway concept originated in England (using the term *greenbelts*). Greenways are a system of interconnected corridors of public or private land that typically follow natural or cultural features, such as watercourses, ridge lines, sewer lines, shorelines, power lines, and abandoned railroads. Greenways are generally left in their natural state to protect the environment and are used primarily for jogging, walking, and biking. The President's Commission on Americans Outdoors in 1987 gave greenways a strong boost with a recommendation that a network of private, local, and state greenways be established to link together the open space of the American landscape. Cities and towns throughout the United States are in the process of developing a system of greenways. Some of the benefits of greenways include the following:

- Helps control soil erosion, stream siltation, water pollution, and flooding by preserving the land in its natural state.
- Provides a habitat for wildlife and areas for nature study by children and adults.
- Provides a safe thoroughfare for pedestrians and bicyclists to walk or ride between homes, schools, parks, offices, and shopping centers.
- Helps to improve air quality by adding oxygen and filtering pollutants.
- Helps reduce noise pollution.
- Provides a buffer for conflicting land use patterns.
- Provides recreation opportunities for all ages.
- Preserves the natural environment of a city or town.

Trail Design and Maintenance

A difficulty in designing an adequate trail system is the accommodation of the variety of trail users. Some of these uses are compatible with each other. Bikes, horseback riders, and hikers can stand some mixing; however, when use by any one group becomes heavy, the recreation experience for the others is greatly diminished. In many instances, separate trails for each group is the only realistic answer to the problem. Whether an agency has one general trail system or multiple-use trails, the following general guidelines apply to any type of trail.

Trail Dimensions

All trails have the following components: (1) trail surface or tread, the surface upon which the person or vehicle makes direct contact; (2) trail corridor, the area on both sides and above the tread that is cleared for the person or vehicle; and (3) buffer zone, lands on each side of the trail corridor that serve to protect and insulate the user from detrimental environmental influences. Table 6–1 indicates the desirable height and width dimensions for a variety of trail types.

TABLE 6–1 Trail dimension chart (preferred distances).

Trail Type	Width	Height
Hiking or Walking	6 ft.	7 ft.
Bicycle	8½ ft.	8½ ft.
Horseback Riding	8–10 ft.	10 ft.
Skateboard	8–10 ft.	8 ft.
Motorcycle	6–10 ft.	8½ ft.
Snowmobile	6–10 ft.	8½ ft.
Cross Country Ski	6–8 ft.	8 ft.

Trail surface (tread). Other than natural cover, the materials used most frequently to stabilize and protect the trail surface are gravel, wood chips, and ground or shredded bark. In some heavily trafficked areas and for bike trails, asphalt paving is often used. In some instances, locally available materials, such as crushed oyster shells, may be used. Regardless of the type of trail surface material, good surface drainage is essential and must be maintained through breaks in grade, water bars, or dips. Water should never be allowed to run unchecked over more than fifty feet of a trail. Check dams, diversion ditches, and culverts must be constructed and maintained where needed to minimize erosion problems.

Grade

The maximum allowable grade for trails depends upon intended trail use. For example, a hiking trail should normally not exceed grades of 5 to 8 percent; however, for short stretches of the trail (approximately 500 feet) maximum grades of 10 to 15 percent are acceptable. By contrast, bicycle trails must be much flatter. A bicycle trail should not exceed a 6 percent slope and should fall into the 4 to 6 percent category only for short stretches of the trail.

Trail Layout

Determining the direction of the trail begins with a careful inventory of the site, which includes soils, water features, topography, geologic features, flora, fauna, archeological sites, and potential safety hazards. By plotting this information into a computerized mapping system, or transparent overlays, the planner can look at alternative routes in order to develop the ideal trail alignment or layout that will take into consideration the landscape and its environmental sensitivities and at the same time provide the best possible experience for the trail user. One-way loop trails are a desirable pattern to follow. Although there are situations when other trail patterns, such as a straight line trail, are indicated, the loop trail has a good application whether it be for a one-quarter-mile nature trail, a five-mile bike trail through an urban park, or a ten-mile wilderness hiking trail. Returning over the same route decreases visitor enjoyment and doubles the traffic load. The loop trail is a relatively simple method for increasing enjoyment of the recreation experience. Multiple loops add the flexibility of providing for the user who is not physically able to walk or ride the entire trail distance, and for the user who is operating under a time constraint.

Trail Markings

A simple, universally recognized, and relatively easy and inexpensive system for marking trails is a blaze formed by scraping the bark of a tree two inches wide and six inches high to form a vertical rectangle and then painting the blaze an appropriate identifying color. Such blazes should be spaced along the trail at distances that are easy to see. Single blaze marks indicate the trail location and double blazes indicate a change in trail direction.

Trail Maintenance

All trails should be inspected periodically for litter, erosion damage, sign damage and deterioration, and fallen trees or limbs. Normally, the trail should be wide enough to accommodate motorized maintenance vehicles (jeep, electric cart). An exception to this might be long hiking trails where rough terrain is encountered. Many hikers enjoy an occasional steep climb or descent, climbing over fallen trees or through tight places in a rock outcropping. To destroy all of these opportunities for the sake of ease of maintenance would be a mistake.

SOIL EROSION

Soil erosion can be classified as two basic types: sheet erosion and gully erosion. Sheet erosion occurs by a gradual wearing away of entire layers of topsoil. Sheet erosion can be caused either by wind or water. In the eastern United States, most erosion is caused by water; however, wind erosion of sandy soils is a problem in many coastal areas. The process of sheet erosion is often scarcely discernible because it occurs over a period of many years. Gully erosion is often the second stage in the erosion process. As small depressions and channels are formed by sheet erosion, they gradually deepen into gullies that cut through the surface structure of the soil.

The secret to solving both types of soil erosion is to slow the movement of water and protect fragile surfaces. Sheet erosion can generally be controlled by establishing a good vegetative cover of grass, shrubs, ground cover, or trees. On long gentle slopes, contour plowing and terracing will slow the flow of water and allow greater absorption. On steep slopes, stabilized mulch and brush strips along the contour of the slope are effective. In either case, control of the watershed above the slope is essential. When large amounts of water are involved, diversion ditches around the slope may be indicated. To control gully

FIGURE 6–8   Soil erosion can be a serious problem.

erosion it is first necessary to control water flow feeding into the gully by stabilizing the watershed above the gully and by diverting the flow of water, perhaps through the use of diversion ditches. The use of concrete, wooden, and brush dams can also be successful. Several references listed in the bibliography at the end of the chapter give good detailed information concerning specific soil erosion control methods.

Soil erosion can be a serious maintenance problem at any outdoor recreation facility. Particular care must be taken during construction. When the natural soil cover is disturbed during the construction of park and recreation facilities, erosion is likely to occur and precautions must be taken. The deteriorative effect is considerably more evident when large land areas are affected, such as during the construction of a golf course or athletic field. The soil loss from these large acreages can cause severe siltation problems to streams, rivers, ponds, and lakes downstream, in addition to the loss of valuable topsoil from the area. Even in small construction sites, efforts to control loss of soil are important considerations. The use of temporary check dams and early soil stabilization will greatly reduce the soil erosion hazard.

Sometimes erosion is caused by heavy recreation use. Heavily used trails, picnic areas, and campgrounds are often affected as the natural ground cover is destroyed, and soil is compacted to the point where absorption of moisture is greatly reduced. Aeration of the soil to reduce compaction and replenishing the ground cover can help alleviate these erosion problems.

Run-off from roads, parking lots, roofs of buildings, paved games surfaces,

FIGURE 6–9   A good ground cover and rip rap have eliminated soil
erosion problems on this lakeshore embankment.

and other artificial surfaces produces, when aggregated, a volume of water that
must be handled by planning for adequate drainage during the construction of
the facility. After adequate drainage from developed facilities has been ensured
through good planning and design, proper maintenance of drainage systems is
essential. Culverts, drainage ditches, and catch basins must be inspected regularly and cleaned out when needed. Many soil erosion problems are caused by
improper maintenance of adequately engineered drainage systems. Water
courses that carry away drain water must also be maintained by clearing sand
and gravel bars and trash accumulations.

The USDA Soil Conservation Service is an excellent source of help with
soil erosion problems.

REVIEW QUESTIONS

1. How serious is the solid waste problem in the United States?
2. What can park administrators do to help solve litter problems in areas
    under their jurisdiction?
3. How do you determine what type of trash receptacle is best for use in park
    and recreation areas?
4. What type of vehicle should be used to pickup trash and litter?

5. What are the acceptable methods of solid waste disposal?
6. How do you determine which is the best sewage disposal system for a park?
7. How can a water system for a rural park be provided?
8. Describe the characteristics of an ideal recreation surface.
9. What surfaces can be used for tennis courts? What are the advantages and disadvantages of each of these surfaces?
10. What types of lighting systems can be used to light a football or base-ball field?
11. What characteristics determine the best type of fencing to be used in park and recreation areas?
12. What is the purpose of signs in park and recreation areas?
13. What factors must be considered when developing a good sign system for park and recreation areas?
14. What factors should be considered when developing a good trail system?
15. Differentiate between sheet and gully erosion.
16. What can be done to control erosion?

CHAPTER BIBLIOGRAPHY

Diaz, Luis F.; Savage, George M.; and Golueke, Clarence G. *Resource Recovery from Municipal Solid Wastes.* Boca Raton, FL: CRC Press, 1982.

Douglas, Robert W. *Forest Recreation.* 3rd ed. Prospect Heights, IL: Waveland Press, 1991.

Helms, Ronald N. *Illumination Engineering for Energy Efficient Luminous Environments.* Englewood Cliffs, NJ: Prentice-Hall, 1980.

Hudson, Mike. *Bicycle Planning.* London: Architectural Press, 1982.

Little, Charles E. *Greenways for America.* Baltimore, MD: The Johns Hopkins University Press, 1990.

Morgan, R. P. C. *Soil Erosion and Conservation.* New York: Wiley, 1986.

Proudman, Robert D., and Rajala, Reuben. *Trail Building and Maintenance.* 2nd ed. Boston: Appalachian Mountain Club, 1989.

Reed, Sherwood C.; Middlebrooks, Joe E.; and Crites, Ronald W. *Natural Systems for Waste Management and Treatment.* New York: McGraw-Hill, 1988.

Untermann, Richard K. *Principles and Practices of Grading, Drainage and Road Alignment: An Ecological Approach.* Reston, VA: Reston Publishing, 1978.

NOTE

1. *Characterization of Municipal Solid Waste in the United States: 1990 Update.* (Washington, DC: Environmental Protection Agency, June 1990).

CHAPTER 7

GROUNDS MAINTENANCE

An important part of park and recreation maintenance is grounds maintenance, a term which generally applies to anything that grows—turf areas, shrubbery, trees. The amount of maintenance required by growing plant materials is compounded considerably by the intensity of recreation use. The mechanics of planting and growing grass, trees, and shrubs in a neighborhood park are not difficult tasks to accomplish. However, when a playground is heavily used or when a softball diamond is used for three or four games a day, maintenance become considerably more complex. Natural environmental conditions can generally be overcome by growing a specialized hybrid grass on a golf course green; however, with 300 golfers a day playing the course, ball marks and turf compaction are problems that must be dealt with successfully if the green is to be maintained in quality condition.

Thus, a grounds maintenance manager deals with a variety of areas, each of which must be treated slightly differently. In areas that are lightly used for nonspecific recreation activities, general principles of grounds maintenance prevail. Heavily used areas and those that need specialized playing surfaces require specialized maintenance. Consequently, a grounds maintenance manager should be professionally trained in horticulture, turf management, or forestry.

This chapter deals with the general turf care, specialized turf care, irrigation systems, the use and care of shrubbery and shade trees, and the park nursery as they relate to grounds maintenance in park and recreation areas.

GENERAL TURF MANAGEMENT

A park, whether it be a 5,000-acre state park or a 15-acre neighborhood park in a city, usually consists of many acres of open land covered with grass. This may include road shoulders and banks, grassed areas around picnic areas, areas around lakes and ponds, and open play areas for a variety of nonspecified recreation activities, such as flying kites, throwing frisbees, neighborhood pick-up touch football games, and so on. Some of these areas are completely open, others are partially wooded for shade and aesthetics.

What is needed to maintain good general turf areas? The five essential elements of good turf care are (1) soil, (2) grass, (3) water, (4) air, and (5) sunlight. To some degree each of these five elements can be manipulated or modified to produce better turf. Soil can be modified by adding nutrients or soil conditioners and by controlling pH. Proper grass can be selected to meet existing environmental conditions. Water is manipulated by providing good drainage and irrigation. Air can be manipulated through aeration of the soil. Control of sunlight is perhaps the most difficult of all, but the elimination of obstacles such as trees so grass can receive adequate sunlight is often possible.

Soil, grass, and water are the elements over which a grounds maintenance supervisor can have the most control. The basic principles of these three elements, then, need to be understood in some depth.

SOIL

Soil Composition

Soil is an important element because it supplies nutrients, water, and oxygen to the roots of grass. Soil consists of two layers, topsoil and subsoil. Topsoil can be broken down into five ingredients: (1) mineral particles (sand, silt, and clay); (2) organic matter (also called humus), formed from dead plants and animals; (3) living plants and animals; (4) air; and (5) water.

Soil texture refers to the proportion of sand, silt, and clay present in the soil. Heavy-textured soils have a high percentage of clay; these soils are more likely to become compacted. When soil is compacted there is very little air space between soil particles, resulting in poor water holding capacity, limited ability to supply nutrient elements to grass roots, and limited aeration. Light-textured soils have a high percentage of sand and also have poor water-holding capacity. The quality of soil can be improved by adding sand to heavy-textured soils and calcined clay or peat to light-textured soils.

Good topsoil has an abundance of organic material or humus. The color of the soil is a good indication of the presence of organic matter—the darker the soil, the more organic matter present. Organic matter provides three major benefits to the soil: (1) it acts as a buffer for materials that are toxic to the grass, including acidic or alkaline conditions; (2) it increases the soil's holding capacity for plant nutrients and water; and (3) it provides a healthy environment for the growth of microorganisms. Microorganisms are essential in the nitrogen cycle, supplying needed nutrients for grass growth.

Soil pH

An important consideration in growing good turf is soil pH, an expression of the concentration of hydrogen ions in soil solutions. A soil's pH factor is measured on a scale of 0 to 14. Zero is the acidic side and 14 the alkaline. A pH of 7.0 is neutral. Most turfgrasses do well with a pH condition between 6.0 and 8.0. A pH factor below 5.5 has an adverse effect on grass. Both nitrogen and phosphorus in fertilizer are affected by low pH; fertilizer loses its effectiveness in a low pH condition. In addition, acidic soil is relatively impermeable to moisture, and dead grass roots decay very slowly. The pH factor of soil can be raised with the addition of lime. Lime tends to move downward in the soil with little lateral movement; thus, when spreading lime, thorough coverage is important. Soil pH can be lowered by adding sulphur, although under certain soil conditions (high organic content) the addition of sulphur is not as effective.

Soil Preparation

One of the best ways to ensure good turf stands is through adequate initial soil preparation. Problems arising from inadequate soil preparation can be difficult to correct after a recreation facility has been developed. Steps to follow in preparing soil for seeding turfgrass are as follows:

1. Test the soil. A soil test measures the pH and nutrient content of the soil in the area to be planted. Soil testing is done in most states by the department of agriculture. Soil testing is extremely important, and it is a step that should not be overlooked. Guessing at the correct application of lime or fertilizer is foolish. At best it may be a waste of money; at worst, it may create a soil condition that is not conducive to the growth of turfgrass. The soil test should be repeated for general turf areas every two years. For specialized turf areas, such as a golf course green, the soil should be tested annually.

2. Grade area to desired slope to ensure adequate drainage and remove any large materials such as rocks and stumps. The development of sophisticated earth moving equipment allows major modifications of the land if the developer desires. The best example of this is landscape modification that has taken place in the development of many golf courses constructed during the past five to ten years. If significant grade changes are made, to facilitate mowing, slopes greater than one to four should be avoided.

3. Remove undesirable plant materials by sterilization if necessary. If the final grade of an area to be established in turf is severely altered by grading, the topsoil from the area should be stripped and stockpiled until the proper grade of the subsoil has been established. While it is stockpiled, sterilization can take place. Methyl bromide is generally used for sterilization. The soil to be treated is covered with plastic and should be treated for 24 hours. After treatment, it is best to wait three to four weeks before planting grass. Methyl bromide will do an effective job of killing most weed seeds in the soil. It will also kill nematodes and control some diseases. The weather should be warm (above 50°) for the methyl bromide application.

4. Add one-half of the lime as indicated by soil test. Do not apply a total of

more than fifty pounds of limestone per 1,000 square feet of turf area. If more lime is needed to raise the soil pH to the acceptable level, additional limestone should be added in six months or one year.

5. Plow the entire area to be seeded. Plowing will normally turn up soil to a depth of four to six inches. Where heavy topsoil or subsoil conditions exist, subsoiling to a depth of twelve to eighteen inches will ultimately produce a healthier turf. Grass roots normally grow to a depth of eight to twelve inches.

6. Add the second half of the lime, soil conditioners, and nutrients as indicated by soil test.

7. Rototill or plow lightly in two directions to thoroughly mix added materials.

8. Smooth surface with cultipacker or rake.

9. Plant grass by broadcasting seed on the prepared area.

10. Roll with light roller or rake.

11. Mulch with a seed-free material.

12. Water to a depth of four inches.

13. When grass has grown about two inches, lightly topdress with a high nitrogen fertilizer.

14. Mow by setting mower higher than normal (2½ to 3 inches) for first few mowings.

Nutrient Elements

There are three major nutrients needed for healthy turfgrass:

1. *Nitrogen*—promotes leaf or blade growth. With a nitrogen deficiency, the blade of grass turns a light green or greenish-yellow color. When nitrogen is not properly balanced with phosphorous, potassium, and lime, a succulent, tender growth is produced. Principle sources of nitrate used in fertilizer are from urea, ammonium nitrate, calcium nitrate, and sodium nitrate.

2. *Phosphorus*—produces healthy root growth. An inadequate supply of phosphorus will retard or even halt growth of grass roots.

3. *Potassium* (also commonly called potash)—important ingredient in the manufacture of sugars, starches, and proteins. Potassium gives the grass general vigor, strengthens the plant stems, and provides resistance to disease. Potassium deficiency is indicated by browning of grass tips and blade margins.

In addition to the three major nutrients, other elements, often referred to as trace elements, are necessary for high quality turf. These elements include calcium, magnesium, sulphur, iron, zinc, manganese, copper, molybdenum, and boron.

Nutrients are provided naturally in the soil and by the use of fertilizers.

There are two general classes of fertilizer, organic and inorganic. Organic fertilizer can be subdivided further into two groups: natural and synthetic. Natural organic fertilizers include animal manures, sewage sludges, fish meal, composts, cotton seed meal, and tobacco stems. Compared with inorganic fertilizers, the natural organic fertilizers are relatively low in nutrient value. The natural organic fertilizers have an advantage of slow release of nutrient elements. Inorganic fertilizer, by contrast, is used up much more quickly. Because of the obvious problem of people coming in contact with animal manures and sludges, these two forms of natural organic fertilizer are seldom appropriate for intensively used park and recreation areas.

Synthetic organic fertilizers are manufactured by treating urea with formaldehyde. Untreated urea is highly soluble in water, and the nitrogen is used up by the grass blade or passes through the soil too quickly. By adding formaldehyde, the release of nutrients is slowed considerably. This type of fertilizer is often called ureaform. A good formulation of ureaform fertilizer will provide for quick and slow release of nitrogen. When buying, it is important to know the percentage of quick and slow release fertilizer contained. Ideally, a bag of ureaform fertilizer should contain 35 percent W.I.N. (Water Insoluble Nitrogen).

Inorganic fertilizers are manufactured from chemical salts. Commercially packaged fertilizers must show, by law, the guaranteed percentage of each nutrient. These are shown in percentage by weight of nitrogen, phosphorus, and potassium, in that order. Thus, a bag of fertilizer labeled 5-10-10 will contain five pounds of nitrogen, ten pounds of phosphorus, and ten pounds of potassium per 100 pounds.

How and When to Fertilize

Cool season grasses are normally fertilized in fall and/or spring. Some turf experts are now recommending one heavy fall fertilization and none in the spring. Warm season grasses are also generally fertilized in the fall and spring with supplemental fertilization during the late spring and summer with a high nitrogen fertilizer. Fertilizer must be spread uniformly only when grass is dry. There is a danger of fertilizer burn if too much fertilizer is applied at one time or if fertilizer is applied to wet grass. If fertilizer is applied to wet grass, burning can be avoided by watering after application.

TURFGRASSES

Grass Selection

Selection of the proper grass variety is the first step toward developing a high quality turf. A grounds superintendent must choose from an ever widening variety of grasses depending upon environmental conditions and the anticipated use or activity. The first consideration in selecting the best turfgrass must be the general environmental conditions—temperature, soil condition, humidity, disease resistance, and drought tolerance when the turf area is not irrigated. Some grasses are more shade tolerant than others and some bear traffic better than others. Resistance to wear is an important consideration in virtually all recreation areas. The days of "Keep off the grass" signs no longer exist in parks; even areas planted as general lawns can expect a moderate amount of traffic from people using the park facilities. Wearability is an especially important consideration when selecting grasses for playgrounds and athletic fields where intensive use can be anticipated. Another important consideration in grass selection is the amount of maintenance required. Frequency of mowing, fertilization requirements, and other special care needed to maintain some grasses in top condition is costly. Planting a high budget grass without the fiscal resources to maintain it is poor management.

All grasses can be classified into two types—warm- and cool-season grasses. Warm-season grasses have their period of greatest growth during the summer months of June, July, and August. These grasses are dormant during the winter and turn brown from October to early May. Warm-season grasses have their best application in the southern states. Cool-season grasses have their period of most active growth in the spring and fall and are relatively dormant during the summer months of July and August.

Grasses are in the family Poaceae. The scientific name refers to the genus and species of the grass. For example, the scientific name of Creeping bentgrass is *Agrostis palustris.* Agrostis is the genus of all the bentgrasses and palustris is the species name for Creeping bentgrass. Bentgrass can be further subdivided into varieties or cultivars. For example, Seaside is a variety of bentgrass. Some of the more common warm- and cool-season grasses will be described, indicating their advantages, disadvantages, and applications. New varieties are constantly being developed and tested. As these new varieties prove to be superior to the old, they will come into common usage. A grounds maintenance manager should keep in touch with new turfgrass developments through workshops and periodical literature.

Cool-Season Grasses

Fescue. The fescues can be divided into two groups—tall and fine. Both are drought tolerant, grow well in moderate shade, do well in poor soil, handle traffic well, and are disease resistant. Because of low maintenance requirements, the fescues are commonly planted in general lawn areas. All fescues can be grown from seed. The fine fescues have a good application for shaded lawn areas with sandy soil and limited maintenance. The tall fescues are coarser than fine fescue or bluegrass but when seeded heavily can make a presentable lawn grass or athletic field. Winterkill may be a problem with some tall fescues in northern locations. Common varieties are:

- Kentucky 31, Alta, Rebel, and Olympic (tall fescue)
- Pennlawn, Creeping Red, and Chewings (fine fescue)

Kentucky Bluegrass. This grass gets its name from its bluish color. It does well in fertile, limed, well-drained soils, in full sunlight or moderate shade. It spreads rapidly with creeping underground stems (rhizomes). It does not wear particularly well. Common varieties are:

- Common
- Merion (low growing and disease resistant)
- Newport and Windsor

Bentgrass. The fine texture of the bentgrass family produces high quality turf; however, it is a high maintenance grass, requiring low mowing, fertilization, pest control, watering, and thinning. The common types of bentgrass are Creeping bent, Colonial bent, and Redtop. Bentgrass spreads by aboveground stems (stolons) and, if not properly maintained, produces a mat and/or thatch condition. When high quality playing surfaces are desired, such as golf course greens and tees, tennis courts, and bowling greens, bentgrass is commonly used. Creeping bentgrass must be frequently watered and requires almost full sunlight. Common varieties are:

- Highland Colonial (good for overseeding)
- Penncross
- Penneagle
- Redtop

Penncross has become widely used on golf courses because of its consistent texture and disease resistance. Colonial bentgrass is used for general lawn areas and is often mixed with bluegrass and fescue. Redtop is also commonly used in grass mixtures because of its quick growth characteristic. It seldom lives more than three years, making it undesirable as a permanent grass.

Ryegrass. Ryegrass is a fine textured grass during its first year of growth. It is not drought or shade tolerant and does not do well in wet or acidic soils. It germinates more quickly than other grass and for this reason is commonly used as a cover grass, while slower growing grasses become established. It is also used to overseed warm-season grasses to give color during their dormant season. Common varieties are:

- Annual or Common
- Perennial

Warm-Season Grasses

Bermuda. Common bermudagrass is a very hardy grass. It bears traffic well, and for this reason is often used on playgrounds and athletic fields. It is fast growing and spreads by rhizomes and stolons. Common bermuda can be planted from seed. The hybrid bermudagrasses are finer textured than common bermuda and are produced principally at the Coastal Plain Experimental Station in Tifton, Georgia. In recent years, a number of excellent varieties of hybrid bermudagrass have been developed for golf course tees, greens, and fairways and are widely used throughout the South. Hybrid bermudagrass is also commonly used for high quality athletic fields, such as football stadiums, in the South. In addition to the problem of all warm season grasses of turning brown in the fall, bermudagrass is not shade tolerant and requires heavy fertilization. Common varieties are:

- Ormond
- Tifgreen
- Tifway
- Tifdwarf
- Common
- Santa Ana

Zoysia. Zoysia is also a hardy warm-season grass. Some varieties do well in northern climates because it is more cold tolerant than other warm-season grasses. This grass has good wear resistance and does well in moderate shade. It also has moderate fertility and moisture requirements. Like bermuda, it spreads by rhizomes and stolons but is considerably slower growing and takes longer to establish.
Common varieties are:

- Meyer
- Matrella
- Emerald
- Midwest

Carpetgrass. Carpetgrass is a relatively coarse-textured grass that does well in moist places and adapts well to sandy soils. It has moderate shade tolerance and has low fertility requirements. Carpetgrass is much less cold tolerant than bermuda.

St. Augustine. St. Augustine is a coarse-textured grass found widely in coastal areas of the South. This grass has good shade tolerance but is especially vulnerable to insects and leaf diseases. It is a low growing grass that spreads by rhizomes and stolons.

Centipedegrass. The major advantage of centipedegrass is that it grows well on soils of low fertility and requires little maintenance. It does well in moderate shade. It is less drought and cold tolerant than bermuda. It has very poor wear resistance.

Bahiagrass. Bahia is not a particularly desirable lawn grass because of its coarse texture; however, it is widely used on road shoulders because it requires little maintenance and grows under poor soil conditions. It is relatively shade tolerant. The major problem with bahiagrass is that it produces a seedhead that makes the grass unattractive.

Planting Turfgrass

Four methods can be used to establish turfgrass: (1) seeding, (2) vegetative propagation, (3) plugging, and (4) sodding.

Seeding. Seeding is the most commonly used method to establish turfgrass and generally the least expensive. All of the cool-season grasses, in addition to common bermuda and carpetgrass, are commonly established by seeding. Soil preparation for seeding was discussed earlier in this chapter (see pages 177–178). Different varieties of grass have different germination times. Fescue and rye seed germinate rather quickly, generally in about eight days. The blue-grasses are considerably slower and require fourteen to twenty-one days to germinate. When buying grass seed, it is important to recognize that seed is bought by weight rather than by seed count. The number of seeds per pound varies greatly depending upon the variety. Rye and tall fescue seed is large with about 227,000 seeds per pound. Kentucky Bluegrass seed is much smaller with slightly over two million seeds per pound. Bentgrass seed is even smaller with five to nine million seeds per pound depending on the variety. The seed rate per 1,000 square feet depends on the number of seeds per pound. Cool-season grasses are generally planted in the fall, although spring planting is possible. Warm-season grasses are planted when the temperature is high enough to germinate seed promptly (generally about 55°F).

Hydroseeding is a relatively recent development and is widely used. Specialized equipment is used that includes a large (500 to 1,500 gallon) tank, agitator, pump, hose, and nozzle. A mixture of seed, water, mulch, and fertilizer are sprayed onto the area to be seeded. An alternative procedure applies seed and fertilizer in one operation and follows with equipment that blows chopped mulch (generally straw or wood-fiber) along with an adhesive such as bitumen. Hydroseeding is a particularly good technique for seeding road shoulders, steep slopes, stream banks, and other hard-to-reach areas.

Vegetative Propagation. Vegetative propagation is commonly called sprigging. Some varieties of grass typically grow through creeping stems. These grasses spread by underground stems called rhizomes and aboveground stems called stolons. These creeping stems are used in vegetative propagation, which is accomplished by taking sod from the grass to be planted, running it through a soil shredder, and broadcasting or spreading it over the area to be established. The chopped up grass is then lightly topdressed, rolled, and watered. It is extremely important for the grass to be kept moist until it has taken root and the new turf is well established.

Plugging. A third method of establishing new turf is by plugging. Plugs of turf generally $1\frac{1}{2}$ to 3 inches in diameter are placed in the ground 12 to 18 inches apart. The lateral growth pattern of the turfgrass then covers the entire area. This method is slower than vegetative propagation, but requires less material and can be used effectively when coverage time is not critical. This method is used to establish athletic fields and to repair spots of golf greens where grass has died.

Sodding. Sodding is by far the most expensive method of establishing turf. Any type of turfgrass can be established by sodding. This method is used when mature turf is needed in a hurry or where traffic will not allow the use of one of the other methods. Sod is cut at about $1\frac{1}{2}$-inch thick in lengths and widths that can be easily handled. The entire area is covered with sod, rolled with a light (150 to 200 lb.) roller, and watered.

Aeration

The purpose of aeration is to provide air to the roots of the grass. In normal turf, aeration should be performed once a year (in the spring), when the soil is soft but not muddy. Where compaction is a problem, aeration should be performed more frequently. The aerifier should remove a soil core to a depth of six to ten inches. These soil cores should be broken up and spread over the surface. This can be accomplished by dragging the area with a flexible steel mat. Aeration should be done before fertilizing and liming.

Mowing

Grass is healthier if it is allowed to grow to its normal height. Cutting turf areas too closely reduces the depth of the root system. Grass should be cut so that not more than one-third of the blade of the grass is cut during the mowing. Height of cut depends on the type of grass. General turf areas should be cut at $1\frac{1}{4}$ to $1\frac{1}{2}$ inches. Some varieties can be cut from $\frac{3}{4}$ to 1 inch, or even shorter. It is important to vary the pattern of cut of a lawn area, and turf should be mowed with a sharp mower. A dull mower tears the grass blade and exposes it to disease.

Thatch Management

Thatch is the tightly interwoven layer of living and dead grass tissue found between the green blades of grass and the soil surface. A thin layer of thatch can be beneficial because it helps reduce soil compaction, increases the resiliency of turf, is more tolerant of recreation use, and insulates the soil surface beneath the thatch layers, thus protecting the grass from heat and cold. Problems with increased thatch thickness include (1) a more hospitable medium for insects and disease to multiply; (2) grass intolerance of temperature changes; (3) inefficient water use; (4) reduced effectiveness of pesticides, herbicides, and fertilizer. The thatch problem is generally more severe in warm-season grasses. The best way to control excessive thatching is through periodic vertical mowing. The use of a power rake, aeration, and topdressing are also helpful in controlling thatch build-up.

Turf Pests

Turfgrass is susceptible to attack from insects, disease, and weeds. Maintaining good healthy turf will reduce, but not eliminate, the danger from each of these three pests. Healthy turf can be maintained by proper aeration, fertilization, and watering; by maintaining sharp mowing equipment; and by thatch removal when needed. If pests become a problem, they can be controlled in one of four ways: (1) biological control utilizing beneficial predators, (2) cultural controls utilizing genetic manipulation, (3) mechanical controls utilizing trapping or physical removal by hand, and (4) chemical controls utilizing pesticides. The choice of control method should be predicated on safety, both to the operator and to the general environment; effectiveness; and economy.

The best approach to turf pests is integrated pest management, which emphasizes the balanced use of all available methods to keep pests from reaching damaging levels. The goal is to produce a good turf and minimize the influence of pesticides on people, the environment, and the turf. Integrated pest management methods include (1) careful attention to the selection of the best adapted grasses; (2) proper use of cultural practices, such as watering, mowing, and fertilization; and (3) proper selection and use of pesticides when necessary. Early detection and prevention will minimize pest damage. Should a problem occur, determine the cause or causes, then choose the safest, most effective control or controls available.

When chemical control is necessary, select the proper pesticide, follow label directions, and apply when the pest is most susceptible. Treat only those areas in need. Regard pesticides as only one of many tools available for turf care.

When insecticides are used, they should be applied in late summer or early fall when insects are young and easily killed. Some examples of common insect problems on lawn areas include grubworms, cutworms, sod webworms, mole crickets, and clinchbugs.

Diseases are the most difficult of the pests to control. Some diseases can destroy turf in a matter of several hours. Fungicides should be used to control diseases and should be applied after mowing. Some examples of common disease problems include leaf spot, root rot, brownpatch, dollar spot, powdery mildew, and snow mold.

Herbicides are used to chemically control weeds. Two types are used: (1) pre-emergence, applied a couple of weeks before weeds appear, and (2) post-emergence, applied when weeds are beginning to grow. Weeds can also be controlled by using high quality weed-free grass seed. Some examples of common weeds include crabgrass, chickweed, dandelion, cinquefoil, nutgrass, white clover, and wild onion. Contact the state agricultural university or the county Agricultural Extension Office for the most current information related to controls and integrated pest management.

Irrigation Systems

Water is an essential ingredient in maintaining high quality turfgrass. The only way to ensure an adequate amount of moisture in the soil is through the installation and use of a permanent, underground irrigation system. Permanent irrigation systems can be classified into three types: (1) spray, (2) rotary, and (3) snap valve. All three of these systems can be controlled manually or automatically. The manual system requires the operator to physically operate the system. The automatic systems are electronically controlled and can be operated by a clock.

The spray system utilizes pop-up sprinkler heads that discharge a fine uniform spray. Sprinkler heads are spaced fifteen to twenty-five feet apart. This system has a good application for highly manicured lawn areas but is not appropriate for sports fields and other recreation areas because the large number of sprinkler heads provide a hazard for activity. The major advantage of this system is excellent control of the pattern or area being watered, providing optimum use of water.

The rotary system also utilizes pop-up sprinkler heads. Water is distributed by two orifices within the nozzle, which slowly rotates so that a high velocity stream sweeps over a large circular area. This system will throw a stream of water thirty to sixty feet. Part circle heads are also available. This system is used extensively on golf courses and park facilities.

The snap valve system utilizes a long-arm rotating sprinkler head. It has the greatest range and will throw water 80 to 200 feet. This system is also widely used on golf courses and large park areas. The initial cost of this system is the lowest of the three discussed; however, the operator must physically put the sprinkler arms in place, and labor cost to maintain the system is extremely high when compared with the other two systems. When the high cost of labor is considered over time, the rotary system has proved to be more economical.

A portable irrigation system operates the same way as the snap valve system except the pipe is located above ground rather than underground. This system is expensive to operate because of the high labor cost to move the system from one location to another. The system, however, has a good application for park and recreation facilities. The system can be used effectively when establishing new turf areas, in times of extreme drought, and to prepare turf areas for special events. The flexibility of the system allows its use in many areas throughout the park and recreation system rather than in one specific area as with the permanent underground systems.

Regardless of the type of irrigation system used, a hydrometer should be used to measure the moisture content of the soil. In many instances, soil that appears to be dry will be dry on the surface only; two to three inches underground sufficient water may be present so that irrigation is not needed.

SPECIALIZED TURF AREAS

Although the principles for general lawn care already discussed apply to specialized turf areas as well, specialized areas, such as golf courses, tennis courts, bowling greens, and athletic fields, do present some unique problems that make maintenance more complex. Golf course maintenance will be used to illustrate the complexity of specialized turf care.

First of all, a variety of grasses are used on different parts of the golf course. Golf greens are generally planted with either a hybrid bermuda or Creeping bentgrass; grass on tees may be hybrid bermuda, Creeping bentgrass, or Kentucky bluegrass. Fairways may be planted with Kentucky bluegrass, common or hybrid bermuda, or zoysia. On courses using warm-season grass greens, they are commonly overseeded in the fall with a combination of bentgrass, fescue, and rye. Rye is also used to overseed fairways.

The cut height of the grass will vary with different parts of the course. Greens are generally cut to $1/4$ to $3/8$ inch, tees $1/2$ inch, fairways $3/4$ inch, and rough areas 2 to 3 inches. Rough areas can be maintained at a somewhat shorter height (1 to 2 inches) to speed up play.

Compaction, caused by foot traffic on greens and by golf carts beside tees and greens, can be a serious problem on a golf course. This problem can be solved by moving cup positions on greens every two to three days, by aerating and fertilizing more frequently, and by constructing cart paths in areas that are heavily used.

Thatching, too, causes difficulties. A heavily thatched golf green will produce a surface on which a putted golf ball will bounce unless perfectly struck. Golfers dislike the inconsistency of such a putting surface. Thatching can be dealt with by vertical mowing two or three times per year or by using mowing equipment that straightens the grass as it is cut.

FIGURE 7–1 Maintaining good turf on a golf course is a complex
and time-consuming job.

Turf on a golf tee is subject to considerable use and abuse by the golfer. This is particularly true on a par-3 hole where irons are used for tee shots. Good design of tees will provide large tee areas so that tee markers can be moved daily if necessary to allow the turf to recover.

Because of ball marks and scuff marks from clubs and shoes, indentations gradually develop on golf greens. In order to ensure golfers a smooth putting surface, the green must be topdressed periodically. Topdressing is done by spreading about ¼ inch of soil of the same texture as the soil used in the construction of the green. This material is worked into the surface by dragging with a flexible steel mat. Topdressing is done two to five times per year.

On a well-maintained course, greens must be cut daily. On a heavily used course it is important that the mowing be done before the course is open for play.

Golf course grass is not as healthy as normal turf because of the closely mowed greens, tees, and fairways. Golf courses, then, should be fertilized more often with high nitrogen fertilizer, and special attention needs to be given to insect, disease, and weed control.

A well-maintained golf course requires a large amount of water under normal environmental conditions. Most greenskeepers agree that early morning is the best time to regularly water the course because there is less wind, less water demand when a municipal system is being used and thus better water pressure, and less danger of turf disease from a green or tee staying wet all night from a late evening watering. Bentgrass greens must be syringed (lightly watered) early each morning to remove dew accumulations. This procedure should be repeated during the day when the weather is hot.

At times, a golf course should be closed to play to safeguard the condition of the course. In very wet weather, golfers and golf carts may do irreparable damage to the course. In cold weather, turf may be seriously damaged by golfers walking on lightly frozen greens. The decision of when to close the course should be left up to the course greens superintendent because he or she is ultimately responsible for the condition of the course.

BALL FIELDS

The maintenance of softball and baseball diamonds is another area of specialized maintenance that involves many municipal and county park and recreation departments. It is important to construct and develop quality facilities from the start. Three key elements should be carefully considered as the field is being developed. The first is drainage. Both surface and subsurface drainage must be considered. A 1 to 2 percent slope, generally a crown, should be established. If the existing soil drains poorly, its composition may be altered by adding or replacing material and/or installing a subsurface drainage system. The second critical element is soil composition. Soil composition is important because it is a factor in establishing good drainage, and it affects soil stability and resilience. The third concern is the choice of turfgrass. When a cool-season grass is used, one of the tall fescues or Kentucky bluegrass is generally the choice. When a warm-season grass is used, a bermudagrass variety such as Tifway, Tifway II, or Vamont are good choices. Adequate research should be conducted on the best varieties of turfgrass before a decision is made for use.

Ball fields, when used for competitive league play, require a great deal of care and attention. Maintenance on these facilities is conducted on a daily, weekly, and seasonal basis.

Daily maintenance includes routine jobs such as litter pickup, trash collection, and rest-room and locker room cleaning. The skinned (non-turf) portion of the infield should be dragged every day. Many park and recreation departments use homemade drags constructed from flexible steel mats, landscaping rakes, and boards covered with carpet. In addition, several commercially made drags are on the market. It is best to remove the bases, water the infield to control dust, and drag from the outside in. Holes in the pitcher's mound, batter's boxes, and areas around the bases should be filled, compacted, and raked smooth. Base lines and batter's boxes must also be lined each day with a material that will not harm either the players or the turf. Frequently, park and recreation departments with a large number of ball fields to maintain will employ one or more specialized crews that maintain all ball fields in the system by traveling from one location to another. Game bases are generally put out by a field supervisor or umpire rather than the maintenance crew to ensure that the field will not be used until the scheduled teams are ready to play. In addition, it serves as a deterrent to vandalism.

Weekly maintenance includes mowing grass in the infield, outfield, and borders of the field and checks for safety and needed repairs to dugouts or players' benches, stands, fences, backstops, rest-rooms, and locker rooms should be made. Dust from a dry field can make playing on such a surface unpleasant. Wetting the infield daily can help solve the problem; however, broadcasting calcium chloride on the dirt portion of the infield every week or two is a more practical solution. Calcium chloride increases the water holding capacity of the soil and does a good job reducing dust.

Ball fields that do not dry quickly after a rain present a maintenance headache. The best solution to this problem is good initial construction of a ball field, with enough slope on the infield and outfield to allow adequate drainage from the playing surfaces. Proper soil composition is also important. Many departments construct their infields from a sand-clay mixture. A mixture of 60 percent clay and 40 percent sand has proved to be satisfactory, although this will vary somewhat in different sections of the country.

Seasonal maintenance includes good turf maintenance as discussed earlier in this chapter. In the spring, about ten cubic yards of soil should be added to the infield to replenish soil lost during the previous season. With heavily used ball fields, some soil replacement during the playing season may also be necessary. Major repair work, such as replacing bleacher seats, repainting, and replacing fencing, should take place during the off season so that all facilities are in excellent condition by the beginning of the baseball season.

TURF MANAGEMENT AND MODERN TECHNOLOGY

Maintenance managers should take advantage of advancing technology as they seek to maintain high quality turf areas for recreation use. Modern managers should consider the following:

- Computer applications to turfgrass management. Computers can be used for such tasks as recording and scheduling fertilization, seeding, aeration, and topdressing. Computerized irrigation systems can apply water based on soil moisture levels and climatic conditions. As new software is developed, computers should become even more valuable management tools.
- New turfgrass varieties. Developments in genetic engineering and tissue culture promise the development of turfgrass for recreational uses that will better withstand heavy use, will have better recuperative potential, will be able to withstand low mowing, and will be easier to establish.
- New ground cover materials (geotextiles or landscape fabrics). These materials help protect turf during periods of severe wear (for example, a stadium that is used for a concert). They can also be used effectively for weed

control and erosion control.

- Changes and improvements in equipment used to maintain turfgrass.
- Techniques that protect the environment.
- New developments in slow release fertilizers and chemicals. These developments should be monitored because this technology is changing rapidly.
- Professional organizations to maintain and improve knowledge of turfgrass management. Organizations such as the Golf Course Superintendents Association of America and the Sport Turf Managers Association should be considered. Managers should take advantage of the services of the University Agricultural Extension Service in their state. Short courses and workshops should be budgeted for turfgrass managers as part of their in-service training programs.

TREES AND SHRUBBERY

Trees and shrubs have become an important part of urban and rural environments, planted around residences, along streets and highways, in and around shopping centers, and in city parks and greenways. Aesthetically, attractive landscaping provides a pleasant environment in which to live and work. The appearance of park and recreation areas should be as natural as possible, and developed facilities should blend into this natural environment. Also, landscaping can be used to create areas of beauty where none existed before. Restoration of blighted landscapes calls for creation of beauty rather than preservation of natural beauty.

In addition to aesthetics, trees and shrubs provide some practical functions. Trees and shrubbery can act in some ways as climatic controls. Trees provide shade and thus relief from solar radiation. Plants can be used as a windbreak, or they can guide wind flow to provide maximum cooling in the summer months. Throughout the Midwest, trees protect farm buildings from winter winds. Air temperature can be moderated by woodlands. During the summer months, central city temperatures are almost always higher than the surrounding suburban areas because trees produce a cooling effect from the shade they provide and as a result of evapo-transpiration.

Trees and shrubs replace oxygen in the air, recycle water, and reduce air pollution by absorbing dust and chemical pollutants, such as nitrogen oxide, sulfur dioxide, carbon monoxide, halogens, ammonia, and ozone. Plants help control soil erosion. Trees and shrubbery help reduce noise in parks coming from outside sources, such as traffic or commercial establishments, and may help reduce noise generated within the parks, for example, from a playground that may be objectionable in residential neighborhoods. Leaves, twigs, and branches absorb sound energy. Plants absorb high frequencies at a greater rate than low frequencies. Human hearing is more sensitive to high frequencies,

Metropolitan Board of Parks and Recreation, Nashville, TN.

FIGURE 7–2 Formal gardens are attractive but expensive to maintain.

thus plants filter out bothersome noise. Trees and shrubbery can be used to control pedestrian traffic flow and to screen unattractive areas from public view. Finally, properly selected plants also may provide food for animals and birds.

Trees and shrubbery also have disadvantages. Trees produce leaves that fall and must be raked and hauled away. Landscaping is generally costly, including the initial cost of plant materials, as well as cost to maintain these materials once they have been planted. Also, landscaping generally increases mowing time of turf areas by creating islands and uneven borders that require careful trimming and mowing with smaller equipment.

Landscaping in park and recreation areas has gradually changed over the years. Traditionally, many municipal park departments maintained beds of annual plants that were changed with the season. A bed might contain pansies in the spring, dahlias in the summer, and chrysanthemums in the fall. Although this seasonal rotation is still used for formal gardens and selected park areas, a gradual shift has been toward permanent plantings that are just as attractive and much less costly to maintain.

The planning of landscaped areas should be done by a landscape architect. Many large park and recreation agencies employ landscape architects as part of their permanent planning staff. Other departments use consultants on a job-to-job basis.

The selection of plant materials for park and recreation areas is a critical decision. Environmental conditions such as temperature, soil type, moisture, sunlight requirements, and wind resistance must be primary considerations.

Raleigh Parks and Recreation Department, Raleigh, NC.

FIGURE 7–3   Interior landscaping enhances the work environment
of this park headquarters.

Disease- and insect-resistant plants must be selected. Size, shape, and growth characteristics are important, depending upon the function of a plant or tree. Some plants are more compaction tolerant and better able to cope with such urban problems as exhaust emissions, smoke, and road salt. Some species of trees and shrubs are more smog and pollution tolerant than others. An ideal shrub or ornamental tree is one that has an attractive flower, attractive foliage, attractive fruit (unattractive, messy fruit may eliminate the plant), and good fall color. Few plants meet all of these criteria. An example of an ornamental tree that does is flowering dogwood (*Cornus florida*).

URBAN FORESTRY

Urban forestry includes street trees, trees on residential property, and park and greenway trees. It involves three primary functions: (1) planting, (2) maintenance, and (3) removal. Many municipal park and recreation departments are responsible for trees and shrubbery on city rights-of-way, as well as greenways and park and recreation property. The responsibility for planting includes identification of sites suitable for planting and selecting and planting appropriate species. Well-designed plants create an attractive environment in any community. However, improper use and design can create some of the problems listed below:

- Planting trees and shrubs can create blind intersections that block a driver's sight line from oncoming traffic, creating a safety hazard. Avoid this problem by proper selection and placement of trees and shrubs.
- Tall growing trees can block street lights and stop lights. Proper placement of trees and street lights avoids the situation in which trees must be constantly pruned.
- Roots can damage sidewalks and power lines, resulting in costly repairs. The trend in recent years has been to avoid planting in the strip between the street and sidewalk. Also, careful attention should be paid to the pattern of root growth of trees planted in areas where these problems are likely to occur.
- Trees can grow into utility lines, creating a maintenance nightmare. Underground utilities in many communities have eliminated this problem. Where overhead utility lines exist, planting low growing varieties of trees is a much better solution than constant pruning that results in misshapen trees.
- Leaves can stop up drainage systems.
- Limbs can fall on parked vehicles and other property. Careful tree selection and the pruning of dead limbs will help alleviate this problem.
- Removal of dead trees can be costly. In some instances, having individuals or private contractors remove the trees for use as firewood or timber can provide a cost savings.

In recent years, landscape architects have been used to fit plantings to street locations. A downtown area, an area of light commercial use, and a residential area, call for different landscape treatments. The use of a larger variety of trees for street planting is becoming more widespread. The traditional shade tree of the 1920s and 1930s was the American elm. Unfortunately, Dutch elm disease denuded many U.S. cities of almost all of their shade trees. In Columbus, Ohio, 70,000 trees were destroyed by the disease. Planting a variety of trees will prevent this kind of catastrophe in the future. Ornamental trees have also become popular. The use of dogwood, redbud, flowering crabs, and flowering cherries is becoming common. An alternative to municipal maintenance responsibility is to encourage private property owners to plant trees on their property rather than on the city right-of-way. Property owners receive advice on what trees to plant and how to plant, and in some instances, small trees are provided free of charge or at a low cost.

In order for a municipality to manage an urban forestry program, a tree ordinance is essential. Such an ordinance is the legal basis for the program, providing guidelines for managing trees on public and private property and delineating the authority and responsibility of the municipal department charged with its operation. The managing department can be the parks and recreation department, public works departments, urban forestry department, or some other municipal department. A tree ordinance will generally include the following: (1) planting requirements such as spacing and location; (2) maintenance (particularly pruning) requirements including responsibility of adjacent property owners; (3) tree removal requirements, including condemnation of trees on private property; (4) requirements related to public utilities; and (5) licensing and insurance requirements for private tree care firms. The International Society of Arboriculture (P. O. Box 71, Urbana, Illinois, 61801) has developed a model municipal tree ordinance that has been modified for local use by many communities.

In addition to tree ordinances, some communities have enacted vegetation protection ordinances that are broader in scope and are designed to protect trees and ecosystems during land development, construction, and utility installation. Also, it is not unusual for governments to have zoning laws and subdivision ordinances designed to protect wetlands, agricultural land, and other environmentally sensitive areas from development.

Planting and Maintaining Trees and Shrubs

Proper care when planting trees and shrubs is essential if a high survival rate is to be expected. Trees and shrubs may be planted bare-root or balled and burlapped. Large-sized plants are usually sold as balled and burlapped nursery stock. Some varieties of plants do well when planted from bare-root stock, and shipping charges from nurseries are greatly reduced. Bare-root plants should be planted while dormant and watered during dry periods through the first growing season.

An old park maxim says, "Plant a ten cent plant in a one dollar hole but never, never plant a one dollar plant in a ten cent hole." The economics may be outdated, but the message is still a valid one. When planting, a rule of thumb is that the hole should be six to twelve inches wider on each side and six inches deeper than the ball of the plant. Width is critical because root growth is primarily lateral. Holes dug much deeper than root balls often result in settling and affect the plant as if it were planted too deeply, suffocating the root system. Some settling of the plant must be anticipated. After settling, the root collar of the plant should be level with the surrounding terrain. Holes for trees and shrubs are generally dug with an auger, either hand held or operated from the power-takeoff of a tractor. Augers up to thirty-six inches in diameter are available. If augers are used to prepare planting holes, it is a good idea to use a shovel to "rough up" the sides of the hole to allow opportunity for roots to penetrate the planting pit wall. For large trees, a specially engineered tree spade may be needed. Adequate drainage around the hole and through the bottom and sides of the hole is essential. The plant should be watered thoroughly at the time of planting. However, nitrogen fertilization is not generally recommended until the plant has become established. Nitrogen fertilization at planting tends to burn exposed roots. Damaged or broken branches should be pruned; however, extensive pruning at planting should be avoided.

Small trees and shrubs generally do not need to be supported after planting. Larger trees (seven to ten feet or more) should be supported by staking or using guy wires. In areas where heavy use can be anticipated, such as a playground, smaller trees may also need protection. Under these circumstances, guy wires present a safety hazard and staking is recommended. In areas exposed to direct sunlight, young trees should be protected from the climate. This is accomplished by using tree-wrap paper or burlap.

When a large number of small shrubs are planted in the same bed, it is often more practical to rototill the entire plant bed rather than dig individual holes for each plant. When drainage is poor, and with plants, such as azaleas, that require excellent drainage, raising the entire bed may be indicated.

After planting, mulching is essential. The mulches can be organic or inorganic. Commonly used organic mulches include pine straw, wood chips, bark, composted leaves, and coarse peat. Inorganic mulch generally consists of gravel or small rocks. Mulch is important in shrubbery beds because it holds moisture and slows runoff of water. A heavy mulch will reduce weed growth. However, care must be taken not to apply too much mulch because excessive use of mulch around shallow rooted plants can suffocate them. Organic mulches add some organic matter to the soil, and they have considerable aesthetic value.

After planting, the essentials of caring for trees and shrubs include mulching, weeding, watering, pruning, fertilizing, and controlling insects and disease. Mulching simply involves replacing mulch as it is needed. Organic mulches, depending upon the type used, will generally last two to three years. If a good mulch is maintained, very little weeding of shrubbery beds should be necessary. Weeding shrubbery beds is considerably more costly than the cost of maintaining an adequate mulch. Even with a good mulch, some weeding will be necessary in most beds. Watering is especially important during the first two years after trees and shrubs have been planted. Slow, deep watering is much more effective than frequent shallow watering.

Pruning trees and shrubs is more time consuming than any other maintenance task. Pruning may have three purposes: (1) shaping the tree or shrub, (2) rejuvenation, and (3) removal of dead wood. Pruning for shaping may be necessary in some instances. However, trees and shrubs in parks should be allowed to grow into their natural shape. Topiary, the art of pruning trees and shrubs in various shapes and designs, may have a place in specialized areas, such as formal gardens, but should not be used in parks. Severe pruning of any shrub or tree gives it an artificial or synthetic appearance and detracts from the park environment. Pruning for rejuvenation varies with different plants. Some shrubs require periodic light pruning; others do best with a severe cutback each year. Pruning dead limbs from trees in intensively used areas of parks is critical from a safety standpoint. This work should be done by an experienced in-house crew or by contract.

Fertilization of trees and shrubs should be based on a soil test. Most trees and shrubs do best in slightly acidic soils. However, the preference range varies with different plant varieties. Trees and shrubs should be fertilized in the late fall or early spring. Fertilizer is generally applied to trees by one of the following methods: (1) punch-bar, (2) drilled holes, or (3) surface application. When using either the punch-bar or drilled holes method, holes should be about two feet apart and twelve to eighteen inches deep. Shrubbery beds can be fertilized by broadcasting, but in small plantings, plants may be treated individually; this method provides less environmental impact from nutrient loss. Shrubbery historically has been fertilized annually, but plant appearance may indicate that only every other year is necessary.

It is difficult to justify fertilization of street trees much beyond the establishment period. Fertilization of a few specimen trees may be indicated; however, widespread fertilization is not cost effective.

Control of disease and insect problems begins with the selection of disease-resistant trees. Do everything possible to ensure a healthy tree to avoid unnecessary problems. Once a problem has been discovered, it is important to obtain a correct diagnosis. Few park and recreation departments have a staff person who is knowledgeable about all insect and disease problems, but help can be secured through the local USDA Cooperative Extension Service office. Furthermore, applications of pesticides requires specialized equipment and licensed operators. While large departments will have enough use to justify these resources, smaller park and recreation agencies can handle their spray programs by contract.

Tree Removal

Another aspect of an urban forestry program is tree removal. When trees die, tree and stump removal is a costly process. Trees should be removed before they become a hazard to persons or property. Trees must often be removed limb by limb when there is a danger to surrounding property. Stump removal is accomplished by grinding to below grade and backfilling with soil and sawdust to slightly above-grade level to allow for settling. Chemicals can be used to speed the decay process for stumps in noncritical areas.

Tree Inventory

Departments responsible for large numbers of mature trees should keep a tree inventory. The inventory should include the following information:

- Site description of tree location—includes restrictive environmental conditions such as wetlands or overhead wiring.
- Tree species.
- Tree size—diameter is the most frequently used measure of tree size; however, height, crown, and spread might also be recorded.

- Condition of trees—general description of tree vigor, health, or damage.
- Planting dates.
- Dates of performed maintenance.
- Needed maintenance—for example, a tree should be sprayed for insect or disease problem.

Tree inventories can be kept on index cards or in a notebook; however, the best format in most instances is a computerized system. Specific tree inventory software is available.

THE PARK NURSERY

Many park and recreation departments operate their own plant nurseries. In many instances, the nursery may be economically feasible if the department saves money by propagating and growing its own nursery stock. One reason for maintaining a nursery is if the desired variety of plants is not available from commercial nurseries. Another reason for establishing a nursery is to test and evaluate new plants before committing to extensive use in park plantings. When deciding whether or not a park and recreation department should establish its own plant nursery, the following should be considered:

1. *Volume of plants needed.* An agency must use enough plants to justify the investment in equipment, facilities, and personnel needed to operate its own nursery. A park and recreation agency with extensive tree and shrubbery plantings, a large formal garden or gardens, and responsibility for landscaping streets and highways may save substantial amounts of money each year by operating its own nursery. A small department with a relatively low demand for trees and shrubs will have difficulty justifying the nursery on the basis of economic feasibility.

2. *Commercial plant sources.* There are many excellent commercial nurseries in the United States, and they may be able to supply higher quality plants at lower cost. If a park and recreation agency communicates anticipated needs to local nursery operators, their commercial growers usually are willing to grow the variety of plants needed by the agency. The possibility of plants supplied by commercial nurseries should not be overlooked. The commercial nursery can supply a highly professional service that need not be duplicated by the park and recreation agency.

3. *Land availability.* Ideally, land for a nursery operation should be located near the maintenance service center so that the cost of transporting equipment to maintain the nursery can be eliminated.

4. *Capital financing.* Financing should be available for developing needed buildings, facilities, and purchasing the necessary equipment.

5. *Availability of qualified personnel.* A professional staff person trained in ornamental horticulture is needed.

The facilities necessary to maintain a high quality park nursery are expensive. If an agency is going to do its own propagation, a greenhouse is necessary. Cold frames can be substituted but these are not entirely satisfactory. Considering the high cost of energy, the operating cost of a greenhouse is extremely expensive. After plants have been propagated in the greenhouse or cold frames, they are generally moved to a shade house where small plants are grown until they are of sufficient size to be moved to the nursery beds. The park and recreation agency can eliminate the need for a greenhouse by purchasing rooted cuttings (lining-out stock) from commercial sources. This eliminates a costly facility from the operation. However, securing the desired variety of rooted cuttings is difficult without the close cooperation of commercial nurseries. An irrigation system is essential to a successful nursery operation. With adequate facilities and staff, a park nursery can be a valuable addition to a park and recreation system.

REVIEW QUESTIONS

1. Describe the best soil conditions for growing turfgrass.
2. How do you prepare soil for planting turf areas?
3. Why, how, and when should you aerate soil?
4. Describe the importance of nutrient elements in the care of turfgrass.
5. What kinds of irrigation systems can be used for turf areas?
6. Describe the methods of establishing turfgrass.
7. How do you determine what variety of turfgrass is best for a particular park and recreation area?
8. What are some of the problems that make care of a golf course more complex than general lawn care?
9. What is the value of landscaping park and recreation areas?
10. How do you determine what plants are best for park plantings?
11. What must be done to properly care for shrubbery?
12. Should a park and recreation department develop its own plant nursery?
13. What facilities are needed for a nursery operation?
14. What responsibility does a park and recreation department have for street and highway plantings?
15. What are the current park practices with regard to urban forestry?

CHAPTER BIBLIOGRAPHY

Arnold, Henry F. *Trees in Urban Design.* New York: Van Nostrand Reinhold, 1980.

Beard, James B. *Turf Management for Golf Courses.* Minneapolis, MN: Burgess Publishing, 1982.

Carpenter, Philip L., and Walker, Theodore D. *Plants in the Landscape.* 2nd ed. New York: W. H. Freeman, 1990.

Emmons, Robert D. *Turfgrass Science and Management.* Albany, NY: Delmar Publishers, 1984.

Gerhold, H. D.; Wandell, W. N.; Lacasse, N. L.; and Schein, R. D., eds. *Street Tree Factsheets.* University Park, PA: The Pennsylvania State University, 1989.

Harris, Richard W. *Arboriculture.* Englewood Cliffs, NJ: Prentice-Hall, 1983.

Hudak, Joseph. *Trees for Every Purpose.* New York: McGraw-Hill, 1980.

James, N. D. G. *The Arboriculturalist's Companion.* Cambridge, MA: Basil Blackwell, 1990.

Madison, John H. *Principles of Turfgrass Culture.* Malabar, FL: Robert E. Krieger Publishing, 1982.

Manion, Paul. *Tree Disease Concepts.* Englewood Cliffs, NJ: Prentice-Hall, 1981.

Miller, Robert W. *Urban Forestry.* Englewood Cliffs, NJ: Prentice-Hall, 1988.

Newton, Michael, and Knight, Fred B. *Handbook of Weed and Insect Control Chemicals for Forest Resource Managers.* Beaverton, OR: Timber Press, 1981.

Pirone, P. P. *Tree Maintenance.* 5th ed. New York: Oxford University Press, 1978.

Shigo, Alex L. *A New Tree Biology.* Durham, NH: Shigo and Trees, Associates, 1989.

Whitcomb, Carl E. *Landscape Plant Production.* Stillwater, OK: Lacebark Productions, 1986.

CHAPTER 8

MAINTENANCE EQUIPMENT

U ntil a few years ago, the majority of park maintenance work was done manually. Ditches were dug by hand. Grass along road shoulders was cut with scythes. Trucks were loaded with shovels. Litter was picked up by hand. Sand in golf course traps was raked by hand. Watering was done with hand-held hoses or with sprinklers that had to be manually put in place and moved to ensure even coverage. Edging was done with a hoe, and holes for planting trees and shrubs were dug by hand. Because of recent technological advances, park and recreation agencies today employ a variety of mechanized equipment to perform maintenance functions. Departments are constantly looking for new and more refined equipment to reduce maintenance labor costs.

This chapter surveys some of the most commonly used maintenance equipment, discusses the selection and care of equipment and the importance of maintenance records, reviews the function of the maintenance service center, and discusses energy conservation.

SURVEY OF EQUIPMENT

Maintenance Vehicles

Maintenance vehicles, including trucks, jeeps, or other four-wheel drive vehicles and tractors, are used to transport personnel, supplies, equipment, and materials to locations within a park and recreation system. As with all maintenance equipment, vehicle selection must be based on the function to be performed by a particular maintenance unit.

One vehicle that has a good application in some park and recreation operations is similar to a golf cart. This vehicle can transport one or two people and a small amount of equipment more economically than any other. It may be electrically or gasoline powered. This type vehicle is great for litter pickup on trails, transporting one- or two-person repair crews, and transporting personnel for facility inspections.

A variety of trucks, from the pickup to large dump trucks, are useful, as well. When facilities are widely spaced and transportation time is important, these vehicles are extremely practical. There is no substitute for trucks when heavy and bulky supplies, equipment, and materials must be moved from place to place.

The tractor is still one of the most versatile pieces of maintenance equipment; with attachments, it can perform a great variety of maintenance jobs. Both gasoline- and diesel-powered tractors are commonly used. When many hours of continuous operation are indicated, such as when a tractor is used almost exclusively for mowing operations, the diesel tractor may be the most economical vehicle because of lower operating costs. With appropriate attachments, maintenance jobs that can be performed with a tractor include mowing; digging trenches and holes for trees, shrubbery, and posts; dragging baseball and softball infields; hauling; light grading; scraping; snow removal; loading soil, sand, and other materials; sweeping roads and parking lots; spreading fertilizer; sawing wood; plowing; and subsoiling and total seedbed preparation. No other piece of equipment can come close to matching such versatility.

Mowing Equipment

Mowing turf areas is the most expensive item in a typical park and recreation maintenance budget. So, it is important that a grounds maintenance supervisor select equipment that can handle this time-consuming job most efficiently. For example, an eighteen-inch hand-operated power mower will require about five hours to cut one acre, under normal conditions. A thirty-inch mower will reduce mowing time to about three hours. A tractor-drawn eighty-inch rotary mower can cut this one acre of grass in about forty-five minutes.

There are four basic types of mowing equipment: rotary, reel, flail, and sickle bar. All four types of mowers may be pulled by, or mounted on, a tractor or other vehicle, or they may be self-contained with their own power sources. All four types of mowers also can be purchased in a variety of sizes, from small eighteen- to twenty-one-inch units up to units that cut a fifteen- to seventeen-foot swath.

Rotary mowers are used for general purpose cutting, and do a good job cutting coarse grass and weeds. A rotary mower can be used when a cutting height of one inch or more is desired. The reel mower gives the best quality cut and is used when low, smooth turf is desired. However, the terrain must be relatively smooth for the reel mower to be effective. Reel mowers have a cutting height range from about $\frac{1}{2}$ to $2\frac{1}{2}$ inches. Specialized units can be purchased for lower or higher cutting. The flail mower has come into more widespread use for general mowing because of its safety features. Unlike the rotary mower, the flail mower, because of its design, will not throw foreign objects that may injure persons or damage property. The sickle bar (also called cutterbar) mower is used primarily for very tall grass such as on road shoulders and banks. Smaller sickle bar units are also valuable when trimming under post and board or split rail fences; the slender cutting unit will fit under the low boards of these fences.

The size of the area to be mowed, and obstacles, terrain, and type of turf to be maintained determine the size and type of mowing unit best suited for a particular area. Naturally, a grounds maintenance manager wants to use the largest equipment that is practical to cut a particular turf area. Large expanses of turf can be maintained most economically with large tractor-drawn equipment; confined areas must be cut with small hand-operated equipment. For intermediate areas too confined for large tractor-drawn equipment, the self-propelled riding mower with twenty-five- to seventy-two-inch width has proved to be excellent.

Turf Maintenance Equipment

In addition to mowing equipment, a variety of equipment is needed for proper care of general and specialized turf areas, including aerifiers and spikers used on compacted soil. An aerifier is a metal drum with spring-loaded hollow core tines attached. The diameter of a tine can vary according to how large a plug of earth the operator wants to remove. The spiker is similar but has a solid steel spike that simply makes a hole in the ground pushing soil particles together.

The Toro Co., Minneapolis, MN.

FIGURE 8–1   This mowing unit is capable of handling large turf areas.

Photo by C.W. McIver, Charlotte, NC.

FIGURE 8–2   A hydroseeder allows quick coverage of large
and inaccessible areas.

Under the majority of soil conditions, the aerifier is preferred in reducing compaction. A verticut machine is a unit with vertical knives that cut stolons and alleviate matting and thatch problems. A renovator is used to prepare existing turf areas for reseeding. The topdresser and fertilizer spreader are similar pieces of equipment used to spread soil mixtures and nutrient elements. Other useful types of turf conditioning equipment include rollers, sod cutters, shredders, seeders, hydroseeders used on road shoulders and banks, mulchers, and edgers. Most of the equipment listed can be purchased to operate behind a tractor or other vehicle, or the equipment can be self-propelled independent units.

Spray Equipment

When selecting spray equipment for chemical sprays, it is extremely important to select equipment that will permit effective use of smaller dosages and will reduce drift of harmful residues. Despite present technology, the use of chemical sprays for the control of some insect, disease, and weed problems is still indicated. As knowledge and application of other control methods become more sophisticated, we may be able to reduce the use of chemical sprays even further. However, in many instances, the use of chemical sprays is the only effective control measure known.

The spray equipment operator is also important. This person should be well trained in the use of spray equipment. In a number of states, certification for operators is required. This practice will become more widespread in the future.

Generally, a sprayer consists of a storage tank in which the solution to be used is agitated by a mechanical or hydraulic system, a pump, a power source, a pressure regulator, and a distribution system usually consisting of one or more spray nozzles. A spray unit must be able to handle a variety of chemical sprays, including those with water and oil bases, oil-water emulsions, and wettable powders that are insoluble. Many of the chemicals used are quite corrosive; thus, the equipment must be constructed with corrosive-resistant materials and cleaned thoroughly after each use.

Four types of sprayers are commonly used in park and recreation areas:

1. *Fogging units*—generate an atomized aerosol spray by thermal or mechanical means. Commonly used for insect control in picnic areas, campgrounds, and other outdoor recreation areas where a large population of insect pests persists.

2. *Boom-type sprayers*—operate under relatively low pressure (40–100 psi) and are trailed behind a tractor or other vehicle. Used primarily on turf areas to dispense insect-, weed-, and disease-control chemicals.

3. *High-pressure general purpose sprayers*—hydraulic units that operate under high pressure (generally 400–800 psi) and are used for general-

FIGURE 8–3 A rotary mower on a hydraulic arm is well suited for areas that are difficult to reach.

purpose spraying in smaller turf areas and shrubbery.

4. *Mist sprayers*—used primarily for spraying trees. Utilize an air stream to carry spray droplets and are effective for spraying greater distances with less wind deflection.

Another type of sprayer not included above is the power duster. Dusts have a greater drift hazard and, generally, are not recommended for use in park and recreation areas. Application of one of the four spray types mentioned previously should handle the needs of park and recreation agency spray programs.

Hand-Held Power Equipment

Hand-held power equipment is largely designed for use in remote areas when the use of large mechanized equipment is not practical and for small jobs in areas that are delicate. This type of equipment includes post hole diggers, chain saws, backpack vacuums and blowers, pruning shears, chemical spray equipment, and paint spray equipment. Improvements are constantly being made to increase the efficiency and ease of operation of such equipment.

A valuable addition to hand-held maintenance equipment is the string trimmer. This unit is powered by a small gasoline or electric motor, and it uses a nylon filament or blade that rotates at high speed to trim grass and weeds in hard-to-reach places, such as around tree trunks and along fences, backstops,

Photo courtesy of The John Deere Co.

FIGURE 8–4 The string trimmer can save many hours of hand labor.

walks, and buildings. This piece of equipment replaces the labor consumptive sling blade and hand clippers. The unit is safe to use and does an excellent job on small areas that need to be manicured.

Miscellaneous Maintenance Equipment

Several pieces of equipment do not fit any of the categories discussed. One valuable piece of equipment used by many park and recreation maintenance departments is the hydraulic bucket. Departments that have responsibility for shade trees usually have one or more such units. They are especially valuable for pruning high tree limbs and for tree removal. In addition, they are useful for working on electric lines and for replacing light bulbs and cleaning outdoor lighting fixtures. Another piece of equipment used by departments with shade tree responsibility is the chipper. This is a fast and economical way to dispose of brush and tree limbs. The wood chips produced are good for replacing ground covers in picnic areas, campgrounds, and playgrounds. Blowers and power vacuum units are valuable for leaf and litter removal. In many instances, these two types of units have greatly reduced the need for raking. Blowers are commonly used to pile leaves, litter, and debris into rows, so they can be picked up easily by vacuum units. A final group of miscellaneous equipment is used in connection with winter sports and includes snow removal equipment, ice resurfacing equipment, and equipment needed to maintain ski and toboggan slopes.

FIGURE 8–5 Specialized equipment is needed for winter sports areas.

SELECTING MAINTENANCE EQUIPMENT

The first step in purchasing a fleet of maintenance equipment is the selection of proper equipment. The following subjective criteria should be used as a guide when selecting equipment:

1. *Purchase functional equipment.* Equipment must be capable of doing the job. The following questions should be asked: What is the task that needs to be performed? Under what conditions is the equipment going to be used? How often and for what duration of time will the equipment be used? For example, a prime consideration for selecting equipment to mow an area with many trees and shrubbery is maneuverability: A mower with a short turning radius is needed. When purchasing a hydraulic bucket for pruning and maintaining electrical fixtures, the equipment selected should reach the heights needed. Equipment should be field tested when its capabilities are in question.

Versatility is another quality to consider. When possible, select equipment that can be used for more than one purpose. Single-purpose equipment has a place when the job demands it; however, purchasing expensive equipment that will be used infrequently is not good economics. If a piece of equipment will be used once a month or several times a year, it may be more economical to lease or rent or to have the job done on a contractual basis.

2. *Purchase quality equipment.* Generally, industrial- or commercial-grade equipment that has a long life span when properly cared for is the best buy. Attention should be given to the dependability of the manufacturer, and one should be selected with a proven track record. When making this decision, experience with the equipment can be helpful—maintenance records are an invaluable aid in this respect. When a maintenance department has experience with equipment to be purchased, and records to back it up, a better value judgment can be made. Other agencies who use the equipment can also be helpful; the department should benefit from their experience by soliciting their advice.

3. *Consider availability of parts and service.* The most functional and durable piece of maintenance equipment is useless if parts and service are not available. It is important to ascertain if the local distributor carries a full line of parts for the equipment to be purchased. Time spent waiting for parts to be shipped by the manufacturer is costly.

4. *Consider fuel economy and energy conservation.* With the rising cost of all forms of energy, fuel efficiency becomes an important economic concern. When purchasing automotive equipment, miles (or hours) per gallon should be investigated. The energy standard of comparison for electrically operated equipment would be kilowatt hours. The use of less expensive alternative fuels should also be considered.

5. *Check for safety.* There are at least two important aspects to safety: the operator using the equipment, and the park and recreation user. In many instances, equipment must be operated in park and recreation areas that are

heavily used. When this is true, the safety of the park and recreation patron must be given a high priority.

6. *Consider standardization of equipment.* The advantages of equipment standardization generally outweigh the disadvantages. One advantage is the ability to interchange operators without additional training. Also, the mechanic's job is greatly simplified when repairing identical or similar equipment made by the same manufacturer and the department can stock parts that are frequently used without having to maintain an enormous inventory. In addition, when one piece of equipment is worn out or damaged beyond repair, usable parts can be salvaged for other machines.

However, if a department standardizes with one manufacturer, it becomes "locked into" their equipment. When another manufacturer develops a better line of equipment, the maintenance department may not be aware of the equipment because of the lack of experience with it. Also, it is difficult to find a manufacturer that produces the "best" equipment in all types. One manufacturer may produce excellent reel mowing equipment, yet their rotary mowers may be inferior to other brands. If a department decides to standardize most of its equipment, it is desirable to take bids on a large quantity of equipment at one time.

7. *Investigate cost and ease of maintenance.* Consultation with the mechanics who must maintain the equipment and with the operators who must use it is important.

8. *Consider cost of the equipment.* It is important to think in terms of long-term cost rather than immediate cost. When the other criteria already discussed are considered, saving $100 on a $1,500 piece of equipment may be false economy.

CARE AND MAINTENANCE OF EQUIPMENT

Once selection of quality equipment has been accomplished, care and maintenance must be addressed. Two important aspects of care and maintenance of equipment are *preventive maintenance and repair.* If a park and recreation agency wants to get maximum life from its equipment, both aspects must be incorporated into a maintenance program.

Preventive Maintenance

Preventive maintenance is the ongoing maintenance necessary to keep equipment in optimum working condition. The goals of preventive maintenance are listed below:

1. *Prevent safety hazards.* Keeping equipment safe for the operator and for the people around whom it is operated is important. Regular preventive

maintenance, including safety checks, will ensure top condition.

2. *Prevent or reduce number of breakdowns.* Downtime because of equipment failures is costly. Good daily maintenance will spot problems that can be corrected before they become serious.

3. *Reduce operating costs.* Good preventive maintenance will prolong equipment life. In addition, well-maintained equipment operates more efficiently and thus costs less to operate.

Tasks in a preventive maintenance program include lubricating, changing oil, washing, checking water level of the battery and radiator, checking tire pressure for proper inflation, checking safety features of the equipment, keeping proper adjustments and tuning, replacing expendable items such as air and fuel filters, checking emission control system, checking metal parts subject to corrosion and repainting when appropriate, and inspecting brake linings.

The responsibility to see that preventive maintenance is performed is at least twofold. Equipment operators and a department's mechanical staff should share the responsibility of preventive maintenance. The equipment operator is perhaps the most important element in achieving good equipment care and maintenance. Responsibility for a single piece of equipment should be assigned to one employee. Merit salary increases should be partially based on how well the employee cares for equipment. Some time must be spent in staff training convincing employees of the importance of good preventive maintenance and in developing pride in the way the employees care for equipment assigned to them.

The responsibility for specific preventive maintenance tasks must be clearly delineated between the operator and maintenance staff. Normally, the routine daily tasks, such as greasing, washing, and checking water, oil, and tire pressure, are the responsibilities of the equipment operator. Tasks such as oil changes, tune-ups, and checking brake linings are handled by a qualified mechanic. Having an untrained operator do mechanical work will probably create problems that can be avoided by an understanding of who is responsible for what types of preventive maintenance jobs. Key elements in all equipment care are the operational and maintenance manuals that accompany equipment. Both the operator and mechanic should read the manuals and should be thoroughly familiar with the instructions prepared by the manufacturer.

Repairing Equipment

Despite preventive care, parts wear out and must be replaced and equipment failures happen. Many small departments have repair work performed by commercial garages. Larger agencies maintain their own garage facilities as part of a maintenance service center (see page 215). The capital investment to adequately equip and operate a garage is substantial; however, when an agency owns a large fleet of maintenance equipment, it is practical, in terms of economy and convenience, to operate a garage. The garage must be well equipped and well staffed if the needed services are to be provided. Finding mechanics who are capable of working on the variety of equipment operated by a typical park and recreation agency is difficult. A mechanic must be able to handle repair work on small motors, tractors, automotive vehicles, buses, and generators. Many equipment manufacturers operate excellent training programs for mechanics. Local technical institutes also provide valuable training in specific mechanical technology that may be needed to supplement a good mechanic's basic training. Time and money spent by a park and recreation agency for this type of continuing education is well spent.

If a garage is to operate efficiently, a policy must be established to deal with priority of repair requests. When five pieces of equipment are simultaneously brought to the garage for repair, each operator is convinced that his or her repair request is the most important. To establish a priority policy, consider the following: time required to accomplish needed repair, effect on park users if repair is delayed, economic consequences of putting off the repair, and available alternatives such as using another piece of equipment or having the repair done commercially. Such value judgments are not easily made. However, if guidelines for determining priorities are established and understood by equipment operators and supervisory personnel before the controversy stage is reached, chances of disruption of an agency's operation is lessened.

REPLACING EQUIPMENT

Good fiscal management dictates the establishment of a system for equipment replacement. In many park and recreation agencies, funds for equipment replacement are the most difficult to secure. As a result, maintenance equipment is used long after its optimum life has been reached. This situation exemplifies poor management for several reasons: (1) the safety of the operator and/or park and recreation user may be endangered; (2) the routine operating cost may be higher because the equipment no longer operates at near optimum efficiency; (3) the cost to repair and keep the equipment in operating condition is in most instances expensive; and (4) the quality of maintenance performed by worn out equipment may be substandard.

Budgeting for equipment replacement is typically handled in one of three ways: (1) replacement of specific equipment items is included in the regular park and recreation operating budget; (2) replacement of specific equipment items is included in a separate budget with a separate budget designation, for example, it might be called a "supplementary" or "B" budget; or (3) a separate maintenance fund (also referred to as a sinking fund) is established and a percentage of the operating budget is allocated for nonspecific equipment replacement and is used "as needed" during the year. The problem with the first two methods is the time frame in which equipment replacement decisions must be made. Budget preparation generally takes place at least one year and quite often two or three years before the actual replacement is to be made. It is difficult to anticipate equipment replacement needs this far in advance if securing optimum use from a given piece of equipment is the management goal.

In recent years, the maintenance fund concept has become more widely accepted and used. When this system is used, each item of maintenance equipment is depreciated and an equivalent amount of money is set aside each year for the replacement of that piece of equipment. The money for the fund comes from the agency's operating budget but is set aside in a special maintenance fund to be used for equipment replacement only. At the end of a given fiscal year, unspent money in the maintenance fund is carried over to the next year. Thus, the spend-it-or-lose-it dilemma is eliminated. The fund can be used for nonspecific equipment, so that any piece of equipment that is judged to need replacement can be replaced. This method is a valuable management tool because it allows a park and recreation department to get optimum life from its equipment.

Using the maintenance fund, equipment is not replaced just because it is budgeted for replacement nor is it used beyond its useful lifespan because funds are not available for replacement. One of the secrets of any equipment replacement system is establishing realistic depreciation schedules that indicate when a piece of equipment should be replaced. Experience with a particular type of equipment makes this task easier. With new types of equipment and unusual one-of-a-kind equipment (when the experience factor is not available), the judgment becomes considerably more subjective. Consulting the manufacturer and investigating the experience of other departments is a valid means of establishing these schedules.

EQUIPMENT RECORDS

The primary requisite for a records system is that the information obtained be usable. In addition, the record-keeping system should be as simple as possible to produce readily available useful information. For some departments, a fairly elaborate computerized system may be needed to produce this result; in small departments, a much simpler system designed by a knowledgeable supervisor or administrator may be just as effective.

Equipment records can generally be classified into two groups: (1) inventory records and (2) operational records. Inventory records should begin with a general list of all equipment owned and operated by a park and recreation agency. Inventory records for each piece of equipment owned should include details such as date of purchase, price, serial number, model number, warranty, bid advertisement, and specifications. Operational records should include records of performed preventive maintenance (dates of oil changes, tune up, lubrication); fuel consumption; and repair records, including cost of parts and labor.

Equipment records are valuable when budgeting operating costs for the coming year. They are also helpful when purchasing new equipment. They are useful when assessing the care by the equipment operator and valuable when planning and executing preventive maintenance. They are necessary, in case of theft, to determine license number and/or equipment serial number, and they are helpful in determining economy of operation and effectiveness of the maintenance function. To be entirely useful, equipment records must be intelligently analyzed. Analysis can be done manually, using a calculator or other mechanical device, or by computer. Many large departments have developed computerized systems for equipment records. When adequately programmed to produce usable information and when the operational staff is trained to use the computerized results, this technique can be a valuable management tool.

MAINTENANCE SERVICE CENTERS

Park and recreation agencies have used a variety of names to describe the facilities that serve as the hub of their maintenance departments. The terms *maintenance center, service center, central garage,* and *park shop* are all commonly used. We have chosen to use the term *maintenance service center* because it seems to be the most descriptive.

Park and recreation agencies use a number of different arrangements when establishing a maintenance service center, based on their particular mode of operation. When the area being serviced is relatively small, one center will serve all maintenance functions for the agency. In a large municipality or a state park system where facilities are scattered over a wide area, it is quite common to find district or regional maintenance service centers. In many instances, the district centers are complete facilities handling all of the maintenance service needs, while in other instances, the district center provides basic services and another central facility provides specialized kinds of maintenance service. Another arrangement used in some state park systems is to have the district or regional maintenance service center provide the specialized function while the basic maintenance services are provided in smaller centers located in individual parks.

In a majority of cases, the maintenance service center is a self-contained facility that provides services for one intensively developed park, a regionalized group of facilities, or the entire park and recreation system. Normally two or three functions are carried out by the maintenance service center.

Routine maintenance. The maintenance service center serves as a central location for specialized maintenance crews whose jobs may be garbage and trash collection, janitorial services, general park cleanup, lawn care, or care of trees and shrubs. The specialized crews may provide for some combination of these services. The maintenance service center provides a place for storage of equipment and supplies for these crews. It provides a place where the employees report for work each day to receive work assignments and where supervisory staff is housed.

Major and minor repair work. A variety of shops are located in the maintenance service center and many items are brought to the center for repair. The same repair personnel will often have to go to specific park and recreation facilities to make repairs. For example, a tractor or mower will generally be brought to the center for repair work while repairs to a broken water line or replacing a broken window in a community center building will be done on site.

Construction crew function. When a separate construction crew operation is maintained, it will often be responsible for major repair work such as reshingling a roof on a picnic shelter.

In some park and recreation agencies, the maintenance service center may also house nonmaintenance but related functions, such as security or park police.

Site Selection

To determine the site for a maintenance service center, the following should be considered:

1. *Geographic location.* A site should be central to the park and recreation facilities to be served. Selecting a remote location requiring extensive travel time would not be wise. Driving time is a more important consideration than lineal distance.
2. *Accessibility to utilities.* The site must have good access to water, sewage, electricity, and telephone.
3. *Good topography.* The site must present no severe grading problems and must be free of rock outcroppings or other environmental conditions that will incur high developmental costs.
4. *Size.* The site must be large enough to provide for present facilities and anticipated expansion.
5. *Aesthetics.* Maintenance buildings and facilities need not be architectural gems, but at the same time, they should not be eyesores. Function is more important than architectural beauty for a maintenance service center. With care in site selection and/or effective screening, this objective can usually be accomplished without great difficulty.

Development of Buildings and Facilities

The buildings and facilities needed for a maintenance service center will depend on function and how the service center is to be used. A normal, well-developed maintenance service center will generally include the following types of buildings and facilities.

Workshops. Again, depending on the function and scope of the department's operation, a maintenance service center may include a variety of workshops, including carpentry, paint, electrical, plumbing, and metal shops. In a small department, one workshop may be sufficient to house all of these functions, while in a large maintenance service center, workshops for each of the functions may be highly developed with sophisticated equipment for each.

Garage. A garage for servicing maintenance equipment is a basic feature of the maintenance service center. Equipment in the garage will depend upon the scope of the operation but will generally include diagnostic equipment, grease rack, welding equipment, and sharpening equipment. Equipment for wheel alignment and body work is generally too specialized for the garage. When needed, this work should be handled by commercial garages.

Storage buildings. A variety of storage space is necessary in the maintenance service center. Locked storage space must be provided for items such as janitorial supplies, spare parts, small hand equipment and tools, chemicals, and fertilizer. Storage for flammable substances such as paint should be separated from other equipment and supplies. Underground storage is a good alternative for dangerous substances. Adequate shed storage is needed for vehicles and larger equipment. Depending on location and the danger of theft and vandalism, this type of storage area may be open or closed. The entire maintenance service center can be isolated by fencing or blocking the entrance road. In these instances, open shed storage for equipment is satisfactory.

Outside storage space. Many maintenance items, such as drain tile; bricks; sand and gravel; lumber; galvanized, concrete-asbestos, and plastic pipe, when adequately protected from vandalism and theft, do not need to be stored in a building. An area in the maintenance service center that is easily accessible for maintenance vehicles must be provided.

Fuel storage. The center should have gasoline pumps for maintenance equipment. Underground storage is essential for pumps located away from buildings to reduce fire hazard.

Wash pits. If equipment is to be kept clean, a well-drained area for washing vehicles and equipment is essential.

Facilities for employee comfort. A well-developed center should include toilets, showers, locker and lounge facilities for employee comfort and convenience.

When developing a high quality maintenance service center, there are a number of desirable features that should be considered during the planning process. Construction materials used in building should require minimal maintenance. Concrete block is such a material used for many maintenance buildings. Traditionally, because of aesthetic considerations, wood has been widely used. Because of the danger of fire associated with many maintenance functions, fire-resistant or retardant walls and roofs should be considered.

The maintenance service center has many potentially dangerous areas, and an effective employee safety program is essential. OSHA standards must be incorporated into the planning of maintenance facilities. (See Chapter 4 for more on this topic.)

All indoor work areas must be well lighted. Lighting engineers recommend twenty footcandles for general workshop lighting and fifty footcandles for areas where delicate or detailed work is performed, such as in a sign shop or where bench repair work is done.

Workshops and garages in maintenance service centers must be planned according to function. Functional planning involves such things as installing twelve-foot wide garage doors so that bulky items can be handled easily; sequencing equipment in a carpentry shop so the operator can use a saw, planner, and sander in a logical sequence rather than moving from one part of the shop to another; locating doors directly opposite each other so long pieces of lumber can be handled in the carpentry shop; and providing the garage and wash pit areas with drive-through capability so that equipment with trailers does not have to be driven in reverse. Agricultural engineers and shop equipment manufacturers have studied the problems of functional planning of workshops extensively, and literature from these sources can be helpful for planning workshops and other maintenance facilities.

Buildings should be designed so that expansion is easily possible. This is particularly important for buildings used to store equipment. As the park and recreation agency constructs new facilities, the impact on the maintenance service center must be considered.

Adequate heating, air conditioning, and ventilation is essential throughout maintenance center buildings. The type of fuel used for heating and air conditioning should be the most economical for that section of the country. When practical, solar applications should be considered. Ventilation is particularly important in areas used for welding and spray painting. Heating and air conditioning engineers recommend that a system be installed capable of handling one cubic foot of air per minute for each square foot of floor space.

Adequate electrical service must be provided. Electrical service should provide a 240-volt service so that three-phase power, which is more economical, can be utilized. Savings in initial equipment cost and operational cost is well worth the initial cost of developing this power source. When aggregated, the power requirements for the maintenance service center are quite high, and every economy in operational cost savings should be carefully considered. In addition, consideration of details such as providing an adequate quantity of electrical outlets for small machinery and equipment will make the maintenance employee's job much easier.

In recent years, the psychological value of color in work areas has been proven through laboratory testing, which indicates that color affects the work performance, health, and safety of employees. Major paint companies can be helpful in selecting a color scheme that will improve the quality of the workshop environment. This should be accomplished as the maintenance buildings are initially constructed; however, it can also be done when repainting becomes necessary in existing buildings.

COMMUNICATIONS SYSTEMS

The need for good communication between park and recreation units is not limited to the maintenance function, although the application to the maintenance function is an important one. The administrative, program, security or police, and maintenance functions must be linked through a network that provides an effective communication channel. Between fixed locations, such as a community center, swimming pool, golf course, maintenance service center, or administrative and supervisory offices, a good telephone system must be developed. Between vehicles and mobile personnel that move frequently from one location to another, a mobile communications system must be developed.

Mobile communications are particularly valuable and can increase the effectiveness and efficiency of the maintenance operation. Mobile communication is needed between a maintenance supervisor and departmental administration, a maintenance supervisor and a program supervisor, and a maintenance supervisor and staff. The system should not be used as a crutch for poor organization and work assignment; however, many instances arise when atypical and emergency situations dictate changes in maintenance work assignments. In these instances, a good mobile communications system can prevent many wasted hours of labor.

Mobile communication is best used when it is available to maintenance supervisory personnel, roving work crews, and individuals carrying out repair functions. Normally, it is not necessary to provide mobile communication to all maintenance personnel. An individual operating a mower or a building janitor should require little deviation from the work schedule established at the beginning of the day, and communication with these types of personnel is seldom needed.

Mobile communications can be divided into three principal categories:

1. *Mobile telephone service.* Cellular telephones placed in administrative or maintenance vehicles can provide an excellent and flexible communication network.

2. *Two-way radios.* These are mobile units that can be used with or without a base station or stations at a fixed location. This system is often referred to as a dispatch service. Generally, the mobile units are affixed to maintenance vehicles; however, portable hand-held units are also available. Communication is possible between the base station and mobile units or between mobile units. Mobile units attached to vehicles are appropriate for maintenance supervisors and roving crews using a vehicle for transportation because much of their work

will be done within hearing distance of their vehicle.

The Federal Communication Commission (FCC) regulates all radio communications in the United States. A license is required to operate transmitting units except low powered walkie-talkies. Some park and recreation agencies use the Citizen's Band wave length; however, range is limited, and in most sections of the country, traffic is very heavy and its use is not practical. A much better system is an assigned frequency on the Public Service band either in the VHF or UHF bands. Preference is generally given to the VHF band because it gives a strong signal that does not skip readily, and the equipment is less expensive.

3. *Paging system.* This is a compact radio receiver that buzzes when the unit is activated. Limited voice communication is possible with some equipment. When the unit is activated, the employee goes to the nearest telephone or two-way radio and contacts a predesignated unit. The paging system is appropriate for individuals who frequently move from place to place in their work.

When selecting mobile communications equipment, seek the advice of an expert. Salespeople and manufacturers' representatives can also be helpful in designing a system to meet agency needs. Consultants are also available; if a large system is involved, they should be considered. Even a small radio system is relatively complex, and items such as number of units needed, wattage, range, and antenna type and height for the base station should be considered carefully.

Normally, mobile communications equipment is purchased by competitive bidding. If an agency has financial constraints, purchasing used equipment and modifying it is a possible alternative. Equipment is also available on a lease or a lease-purchase basis. Whatever alternative is chosen by a park and recreation agency, it must be sure that the equipment selected will be adequate for the job.

Once a park and recreation agency acquires a mobile communications system, personnel need to be trained in its use. Employees should understand the basic operation of the equipment; they should learn some of the basic code signals commonly used in the ten-code message system; and they should learn basic radio courtesy and appropriate FCC regulations governing radio transmission.

ENERGY CONSERVATION

Prior to the 1970s, most people in the United States considered the energy supply to be inexhaustible. Energy prices were relatively inexpensive, and few people were concerned with any form of energy conservation. Since that time, prices of all forms of energy have skyrocketed, and we are in grave danger of exhausting the supply of petroleum and natural gas within the foreseeable future.

Because energy costs have become such a major item in park and recreation budgets (only the cost of personnel has risen more rapidly), an administrator must look for ways to economize. There are numerous ways to conserve energy, and a concerted effort by a park and recreation agency may save a considerable amount of energy and money. All park and recreation agencies should develop an energy management plan. Such a plan generally involves two major steps. The first step is an inventory phase in which the agency carefully inventories all uses of energy. This is followed by a management plan that seeks to reduce and find alternatives to energy use. One program developed cooperatively by the National Park Service and the U.S. Department of Energy entitled "Energy Management and Planning Program" provides excellent guidelines for any park and recreation agency. The program was designed specifically for park and recreation personnel to assist with the development of a plan to reduce energy usage.

In most park and recreation operations, vehicles are one of the greatest energy consumers. Vehicles are used in a variety of operations from routine ranger patrolling, transportation to maintenance work, and cutting grass. The amount of energy consumed can be reduced in one of two basic ways: (1) reduction of miles traveled (or hours in use in the case of some equipment), or (2) increasing vehicle operating efficiency. Careful study of each activity requiring energy use will determine if one or both of these savings can be applied. In all instances, gasoline and electric motors should be properly maintained for optimum efficiency. Good maintenance can extend the life of equipment by one-third. Maintaining proper tire pressure can have an economic payoff. Low tire pressure reduces fuel economy and tire life. Reduction of roadside mowing is one means of saving energy. Substituting ground covers or wildflower plantings are good alternatives.

Proper construction and maintenance of buildings can yield energy savings. All buildings should be properly weather stripped around doors and windows; windows should be caulked; cracks in walls and floors should be sealed; leaks in all faucets and toilet fixtures should be repaired. Spring loaded faucets should be used. Buildings that are heated in winter should have storm windows or thermopane glass. Walls, ceilings, and floors should be properly insulated. Steps should be taken to keep sunlight from penetrating windows in the summer and allowing sunlight to enter during the seasons when the building is heated. This can be accomplished by installing venetian blinds and curtains or by planting deciduous trees to provide summer shade, while allowing sunlight to enter buildings during winter and early spring. Devices to control electric consumption by water heaters and/or pumps should be considered. Lowering the thermostat settings during the winter and raising them during the summer can provide substantial savings.

One place to look for significant energy savings is interior and exterior lighting. All lights and electrical equipment should be turned off when not in use. This includes fluorescent lights when they will be unused for twenty minutes or longer. The level of lighting should be measured and reduced when appropriate. Many offices, hallways, and activity rooms have considerably more light than is needed. Elimination of excess lighting can provide dual savings. Energy is saved through direct reduction of kilowatts used; energy is also saved by reducing the load of air conditioning units during the hot months of the year. Conversion of lighting systems from incandescent to more energy efficient systems such as fluorescent indoors and metal halide or sodium vapor outdoors should be given serious consideration. Major savings in operational costs are possible through these conversions.

As shown, a multitude of specific energy saving techniques can be considered when planning an energy conservation program for a park and recreation agency. Each of these techniques should be examined with practicality and cost effectiveness in mind.

As new park areas and facilities are planned, energy should be a primary consideration. Location is an important consideration. Recreation facilities should be located near population centers or in close proximity to good public transportation. Internal road systems should be as compact as possible to reduce transportation costs. Recreation facility development can be designed to encourage low energy forms of recreation, such as canoeing, walking and hiking, sailing, and bicycling. Planning and development of new facilities should take advantage of modern technology and consider applications for using renewable energy resources such as wood, solar, and wind. Demonstration and interpretation of these energy saving systems provide an excellent educational opportunity for park and recreation agencies.

REVIEW QUESTIONS

1. Describe the four different types of equipment that can be used for mowing turf areas.
2. What is turf conditioning equipment?
3. What factors must be considered when selecting maintenance equipment?
4. What is involved in caring for the equipment that is owned by a park and recreation department?
5. What records should be kept for maintenance equipment?
6. Why are maintenance equipment records important?
7. Should a park and recreation department maintain its own garage?
8. What is the function of a maintenance service center?
9. What considerations should be given to site selection for a maintenance service center?
10. What buildings and equipment would you expect to find in a well-equipped maintenance service center?
11. Under what conditions would a radio communications system be valuable for a park and recreation agency?
12. What energy conservation measures can your local park and recreation agency put into effect to lower energy costs?

13. In what ways can facility and site planning considerations help reduce energy consumption?

CHAPTER BIBLIOGRAPHY

Energy Planning and Management for Parks and Recreation. Washington, DC: U.S. Department of Interior, Park and Recreation Technical Services, n.d.

Luetzelschwab, John. *Household Energy Use and Conservation.* Chicago: Nelson Hall, 1980.

Mashburn, William H. *Managing Energy Resources in Times of Dynamic Change.* Liburn, GA: The Fairmont Press, 1989.

1982 Public Works Manual. Ridgewood, NJ: Public Works Journal Corporation, 1982.

Turner, Wayne C., ed. *Energy Management Handbook.* New York: Wiley, 1982.

CHAPTER 9

MAINTENANCE AND THE PUBLIC

P ark and recreation maintenance exists for the purpose of serving the public. If we are to serve well it is imperative that we have the enthusiastic understanding and support of the public. Such understanding and support can best be established and maintained by serving in such an unobtrusive manner that the public is hardly aware of our presence and certainly not irritated by it. This chapter addresses areas affecting maintenance and the general public, specifically, public liability, public safety, vandalism, and public relations management.

PUBLIC LIABILITY

During the past fifty years, from World War II to the present, recreation as an industry has experienced unparalleled growth. However, this growth trend in the recreation industry has slowed from time to time due to inflation, financial recession, and a nationwide tax-cutting fever. These factors have resulted in reduced government revenues, necessitating reductions in the numbers of public recreation workers and decreases in leisure expenditures by the government. Such circumstances emphasize the need to eliminate, or at least minimize, unnecessary expenditures within the recreation industry.

The relationship between budget cuts, noneconomical operation, and poor recreation maintenance practice is best illustrated by the fact that almost all lawsuits involving park organizations, their officers, or employees are concerned with maintenance practice. It is also factual that the payment of just one moderately large legal award to an injured party might bankrupt a recreation enterprise.

Operations within the recreation industry are administered by any one of a variety of sponsors, including public, nonprofit, charitable, and profit-making commercial organizations or a combination of these. The legal responsibilities and legal duties associated with the operation of a business within any industry also apply to recreation. Consequently, persons responsible for the operation of a recreation enterprise should be aware of those aspects of their operation that subject themselves and their personnel to liability, responsibility, and duty considerations.

Constant vigilance through careful systematic inspection and preventive maintenance will go far toward the discovery of hazardous equipment, structures, areas, and facilities that might injure users. However, oversights occur and accidents do happen. When injury does result from the use of a recreation facility, the parties involved are subject to the same legal rules that determine fault and responsibility for injury in nonrecreational cases. Legal liability infers a responsibility, which the courts recognize and enforce, between parties.

Because we are specifically concerned with legal responsibility attached to park and recreation maintenance practices, the following discussion will be concerned with tort liability only. A *tort* is a legal wrong and includes a large variety of acts that are deemed to have unreasonably interfered with the interest of others. In cases where a tort is proven, compensation is made to the individual who is injured in person, property, or reputation. Most legal action, in connection with tort law, is brought on the basis of *negligent* conduct. Fewer actions are brought on the basis of *nuisance*—a condition that leads to injury. The general legal principles or doctrines that relate to liability are derived from common law. If we are to understand the basis for liability, it is necessary to develop familiarity with some of these legal principles.

Negligence

A generally accepted definition of negligence is *failure to act as a reasonable and prudent person would have acted under the circumstances.* A more precise and legal definition that appears in Corpus Juris[1] states that "negligence is an unintentional breach of legal duty, causing damage reasonably foreseeable without which breach damage would have not occurred." The standard used to determine negligence in the case of a park or recreation professional would exceed the standard of behavior that would be regarded as reasonable for a nonprofessional person. A jury, of course, makes this determination and decides whether or not the defendant's behavior conforms to the standard.

Elements Essential to Prove Negligence

In order to successfully bring a liability suit based upon negligent conduct, the following four elements must be proven to recover from the wrongdoer:

1. A duty or obligation (recognized by law) to conform to a standard of behavior to protect others from unreasonable risks.
2. A breach of duty caused by failure to meet the standard required under the circumstances.

3. A close causal connection between the conduct and the resulting injury.

4. An actual injury or loss suffered by the plaintiff.

Care Owed to Visitors

The duty of a recreation operator to protect a visitor from injury changes markedly according to the legal status of the visitor at the time of injury. There are three legal status classifications of persons who enter the premises of another. These are *trespasser, licensee,* or *invitee.*

The Trespasser

A trespasser is one who enters the property of another without permission and not for the benefit of the property owner. In general, the only duty owed a trespasser is to use due care to avoid injury to the trespasser if this person's presence is known. If the recreation operator does this, he or she is in little danger of a legal action if an accident befalls the trespasser. The only obligation of the operator is to protect the trespasser from intentional injury, such as a shooting or setting traps that might be injurious. Should the trespasser be discovered, care should be taken to make the person aware of dangers such as a mining operation, blasting, or other dangerous activity. If forceful eviction is required to remove the trespasser from the premises, this should be done by a law enforcement agent.

The Licensee

A licensee is one who enters a property with the operator's permission but not for any economic benefit to the operator. The visitor who asks permission to hunt, ride, or ski an area and is given permission to do so becomes a licensee. Should the hunter fall into an open pit, or should the skier become injured by running into a stump hidden by snow, or should the rider's horse break a leg by stepping into an unseen hole, the licensee cannot claim damages for himself or herself, the equipment, or the horse.

The landowner is under no obligation to inspect the premises for unknown dangers, nor is he or she obliged to make the premises safe for the licensee. However, a hidden hazard known to the operator, such as a concealed mine shaft, a dynamiting operation, or an ill-tempered animal, requires that the operator exercise reasonable care to see that the licensee is aware of the danger. If the danger has been made known to the licensee or is by its nature obvious, then the risk is assumed by the licensee, and the owner has no further duty to the licensee.

The Invitee

This classification of visitor includes all of those who frequent public parks, public playgrounds, and other public recreation areas to use them for the purposes for which these facilities were developed and to participate in programs provided thereon. In addition, an invitee is a business visitor invited or permitted to enter the private property of another for purposes that benefit the landowner or for the mutual advantage of the landowner and the invitee. Guests who pay fees for the use of recreation facilities are, therefore, classified as invitees. Legally, invitees are owed the highest level of care to prevent injury to them. The private landowner or the public recreation operator is obliged to be aware of any dangers; the landowner must search out dangers and warn the invitee of them. The implication of common law toward the invitee by recreation operators is evident. The safety of patrons depends upon the condition of the premises and the facilities provided for public use. The prudent operator must not only warn or instruct the patron about existing dangers, but must also make periodic and thorough inspections of the premises and facilities, promptly making necessary repairs or safety provisions. The operator who fails to exercise such ordinary care and further fails to keep a written and dated record of inspection and repair will not have a good defense against any legal action arising from injury sustained while using a recreation area.

The obligation of the owner or recreation operator to render the area's facilities safe, however, pertains only to that part of the premises to which the invitation is extended. Once invitees go beyond the area to which they are invited, they lose their status as invitees and become licensees or trespassers. Therefore, the recreation operator or the private landowner need not protect the visitor from absolute danger except as indicated for a licensee or trespasser. Two classic examples of failed legal action against recreation operators in these types of situations are a 1940 Connecticut case[2] and a 1944 Iowa case.[3] The Connecticut case centered around two inexperienced skiers who went beyond the area open for skiing and were injured when they skiied over a hidden ledge and fell. The Iowa case considered a situation wherein a young man and a female companion were injured when they left a dance held at the municipal golf course clubhouse and proceeded to the back of the building to find a dark location, whereupon they fell into an open basement and were injured. In both cases, the courts held that the injured plaintiffs had lost their status as invitees and became licensees when they went beyond the location to which they were invited and, therefore, took the premises as they found them.

Doctrine of Attractive Place or Nuisance

An old legal concept holds that a landowner or operator owes no duty or care to trespassers. Obviously, under these circumstances any and all kinds of hazards could be allowed to exist on any premises regardless of the area's proximity to schools or other locations frequented by children. The old rule of no duty to trespassers was later modified to exempt trespassers who were children. Therefore, landowners and operators are required to keep their premises free from hazardous conditions that might be harmful to child trespassers.

In order to qualify for legal recovery under this doctrine, it is essential to establish three conditions: (1) that the child was, in fact, a trespasser; (2) that the owner or the operator of the land should have known that children would be attracted to the property because of something on the property; and (3) that the dangerous condition that attracted the child onto the premises was a man-made condition rather than a natural one.

Numerous attempts at recovery on behalf of injured children have failed when the injury occurred on a public park or playground because the child is almost always an invitee and rarely a trespasser when on public park lands or in a public playground.

Doctrine of Governmental Immunity

Our law is a product of English Common Law. The premise of governmental immunity first emerged from the eighteenth-century case of law, *Russell* v. *the Men of Devon*. In this classic case, Russell brought suit against all the men of Devon County, England, for damages to his wagon occurring from the collapse of a bridge, which was the county's duty to maintain. Despite this, the court ruled against Russell, instituting the following rationale: To rule for the plaintiff would lead to an infinity of actions; there was no precedent for such a suit; liability of this kind should be imposed only by the legislature; there are no county funds out of which to satisfy the claim. The court concluded that it is better that an individual sustain an injury than that the public should suffer an inconvenience. This reasoning still provides the nucleus for progovernmental immunity arguments.

At present, marked differences in governmental liability exist from state to state. Betty Van der Smissen,[4] in her 1967 study of the fifty states and governmental immunity to tort liability and her 1975 update of that study,[5] found that since 1960, there has been considerable judicial and legislative activity toward abrogating the doctrine of governmental immunity. Many states have enacted legislation authorizing liability insurance. The trend is to provide a remedy for the injured, yet protect the tax funds of the municipality through insurance authorization and prohibit the dragging along of suits filed many years after the cause of action by procedural statutes of notice and statutes of limitations. In most instances, it has not been a matter of changing the doctrine of governmental immunity per se, but providing that governmental immunity may not be used as a defense by the insurance company to the extent of the insurance carried.

Another emerging trend relates to the basis of liability. Rather than applying the governmental-proprietary test to the function, recent statutory enactments and court decisions seem to be turning to the nature of the act performed; that is, whether or not the act is a discretionary one of policy formulation and planning being performed (no liability) or a ministerial duty of policy execution or operational decision making (potential liability). The governmental-proprietary function distinction is not in direct contrast to the new discretionary-ministerial distinction because both types of duties are performed for proprietary functions and for governmental functions. It is also important to note that the doctrine of governmental immunity protected the corporate entity alone, while an individual now may be protected when he or she performs a discretionary (immune) duty within the "discretionary-ministerial" distinction. There also appears to be greater support for the liability for dangerous and defective conditions; several of the recent laws have specific provisions relating to inspections.

James J. Bonifas, deputy corporation counsel for the Milwaukee County Park Commission, has indicated that in his home state of Wisconsin there has been total abolition of governmental, charitable, and religious immunity to tort liability.[6] Bonifas further stated that the fault system, which to varying degrees involves assessment of negligence, is under sharp attack and that the humanitarian social conscience today is much more concerned with the victims of society's progress and the shifting of financial losses than with the legal distinctions of immunity to suit those that were formulated in the Victorian era. The attempt to socialize all loss is evident and simply involves transferring the financial burden from individuals to society. In short, for a recreation or park organization to depend upon the doctrine of governmental immunity as a guarantee against responsibility and liability is to invite a sad and abrupt awakening.

Assumption of Risk

One who participates in an activity is expected to understand the hazards and potential injury risks and to assume such risks. Risks or hazards due to defective equipment or dangerous areas are not assumed by an individual unless such hazards are completely obvious and the individual uses the defective equipment or dangerous area in spite of it, knowing fully what he or she is doing. The courts denied the allegation of assumption of risk as a defense when a party was injured by stepping on a broken bottle in a dressing room,[7] when a ring holding a swing broke resulting in injury to a nine-year-old girl,[8] and when a pedestrian walking through a park fell into a hole covered by snow and was injured.[9]

On the other hand, the defense of assumption of risk was upheld by the court when it was shown that the injured knew of the hazard. This occurred in connection with cases involving the playing of softball on an area formerly used for tennis with an old post bracket still remaining on the field,[10] a basketball player colliding with a brick wall two feet behind a basketball goal,[11] and a ball player when he tripped on a curb around a ball diamond which was used to retain water for ice skating in the winter.[12]

Assumption of risk is based on the legal theory that no harm is done to one who consents. Of course, the injured's own knowledge and the ability of an injured individual to understand the risks involved are important. In this connection, a child is not expected to have the same capability of accepting a given risk as is an adult. This is reflected in the fact that most cases where assumption of risk is used as a defense against negligence involve individuals in their teens or older. Van der Smissen believes that the courts are placing a stronger emphasis upon communication of the risk involved and the appreciation of the risk by the participant than in the past.

Contributory Negligence

Contributory negligence is different from negligence only insofar as there is no duty owed to another. However, the other tests of negligence apply. Plaintiffs must conduct themselves as reasonable and prudent persons in behalf of their own protection from injury. The standard, of course, is different for children and for adults. A child must exercise a degree of care for his or her own safety commensurate with capacity, age, experience, and intelligence. Some courts have held that a very young child, such as the five-year-old boy who was killed playing in a park on some corrugated metal pipes which rolled down and crushed his head, was not capable of contributory negligence because he did not realize or understand the hazard and danger involved.[13] Generally speaking, children below the age of eight are regarded by the courts as incapable of exercising understanding and reason, while children between the ages of eight and twelve are regarded as being capable of some understanding though not full understanding of the care required for their safety. Situations in which contributory negligence has been used as a defense include a softball player who carelessly and dangerously slid into a permanent post being used as a base,[14] a small boy who had his feet crossed under a teeter totter, resulting in injury when the board came down,[15] and a girl who was bitten when attempting to feed a bear which was chained to a tree.[16] Contributory negligence was also alleged in court cases involving an individual using stairs or hallways in darkness,[17] exceeding a proper speed,[18] doing something after being warned or forbidden to do so,[19] walking on steps known to be insecure,[20] failure to be cautious when a reasonable person might anticipate a dangerous condition, such as entering a shower room[21] or diving into water.[22]

The Statute of Limitations

Many states have a statute of limitations for tort actions stating that any suits must be filed before a given period of time following the accident or situation that gave rise to the suit. The usual length is two years. The state of Vermont has enacted a short statute of limitation of one year for skiing accidents. In North Carolina, there is a three-year statute of limitations; however, it is important to note that in connection with all such limitations the one-, two-, or three-year period does not begin for children until after they have reached legal majority at age eighteen.

Insurance

In the operation of commercial or private recreation enterprise, insurance can transfer the risk of the financial settlement from an individual to a professional risk bearer who is able to shoulder an economic loss. In essence, insurance substitutes a known loss for an unknown loss. Budgeting a recreation enterprise is important; this can be done with insurance because the insurance premium is a fixed cost that can be included in planning a budget.

To avoid the risk of staggering losses, liability insurance is indispensable to the private and commercial recreation operator. The shock of the large financial judgment may completely destroy the financial foundation of a recreation agency. Even small damage claims can seriously affect the financial stability of an enterprise. The most prudent and careful recreation operator should not assume that he or she will not be sued; a court decides whether the case is justified. Even though a defendant may not be proven negligent and liable, he or she may be faced with high defense and legal fees. Liability insurance can provide protection against such legal costs. The insurance company can also represent the defendant in a lawsuit so that the defendant does not have to appear in court. Private operators may wish to consider incorporation of their enterprise. Their liability may be limited to the value of the property and all other assets that are part of the corporation. Liability insurance costs may also be less, but a lawyer should be consulted about other considerations and limitations before deciding to incorporate.

Presently, more than one-half of the states have authorized, through legislative enactment, park and recreation agencies to carry some kind of liability insurance. Such statutes usually fall into one of three categories: (1) authorization of insurance with governmental immunity maintained, but immunity may be waived as a defense; (2) general insurance authorization; and (3) authorization to carry insurance in behalf of employees, administrators, board members, personal companies, or professional service organizations related to parks and recreation.

North Carolina state law, like a number of other states, authorizes municipalities to carry liability insurance. However, the courts hold that through the act of securing liability insurance, governmental immunity is waived to the extent of the insurance for torts of agents or employees when acting within the scope of their authority. It should be noted that this situation is viewed with considerable apprehension on the part of many park and recreation administrators because they believe that the purchase of liability insurance to cover employees only invites liability suits. Therefore, park and recreation officials tend to recommend the private purchase of individual liability insurance by employees rather than blanket liability insurance coverage for employees from a policy paid for by the public jurisdiction.

Availability of Liability Insurance

Since public and private providers of leisure services are considered to be high risk, all leisure service providers are affected by liability insurance availability and affordability. Insurance companies are charging higher rates for risk coverage and selecting those risks they will offer to insure. In the recent past, insurers have canceled policies midterm or increased rates by 200 to 400 percent or more. Such high rates have forced recreation providers either to curtail or eliminate park and recreation program offerings. Participation fees are often increased significantly to cover higher insurance costs.

Nuisance

A nuisance is defined as whatever is injurious to health, indecent or offensive to the senses, or an obstruction to the free use of property so as to interfere with the comfortable enjoyment of life and property. Distinguished from negligence, nuisance is considered a continuing danger or permanent condition that might inflict injury, while negligence rests on an act or failure to act as an individual. A civil action by ordinary court proceedings may be brought to stop or abate a nuisance and to recover damages sustained because of the nuisance.

Only 15 percent of cases relating to parks and recreation allege nuisance as the basis for liability, and the recovery experience for injured plaintiffs in nuisance cases is only one out of four.[23] Until 1967, at least eighteen states had direct indications that nuisance is a basis for liability suits; however, only ten of these states have cases where the judgment actually held for the injured plaintiff. In the following five years, six states (Georgia, Kentucky, Kansas, New Hampshire, Tennessee, Wyoming) held, either through court decisions alone or in relation to statutes, that nuisance was actionable regardless of governmental immunity.[24]

Regardless of the liability or immunity of a governmental agency for negligence, generally, it has been held by the courts that a governing body has no right to maintain a nuisance, and where such is created and maintained, liability will ensue. For this reason, many attempts have been made to allege nuisance rather than negligence in order to recover for injury. However, such allegations have not been highly successful because most courts decided that nuisance is a condition and not an act or the failure to act. In other words, most accidents and injuries to persons occur as a result of negligent conduct—failing to inspect and repair. Most courts, viewing faulty playground equipment, reason that although the faulty equipment is a condition, it is, nevertheless, the failure to inspect and repair (which is in fact negligence) that has caused the injury. Nuisance cases seem to distribute themselves into several categories relating to maintenance practice and operation. These are (1) water areas, (2) playground apparatus, and (3) other nuisance cases in various situations.

Water Areas

There are, on record, a number of court cases wherein the depth of water was regarded as too shallow for diving, thereby constituting a nuisance.[25] Faulty construction and layout was the basis of alleged nuisance in other cases involving water areas. However, as stated by the court in *Stein* v. *West Chicago Park Commissioners* (1928), ponds and lagoons in parks have become too well recognized as means of decoration and recreation to be considered a public nuisance.

Playground Apparatus

With only two exceptions, involving a slide[26] and a swing,[27] defective playground apparatus has not been regarded by the courts as constituting a nuisance. Unblocked metal pipes[28] and a hole at the end of a park slide[29] were held to be nuisances.

A merry-go-round pivot post that caused an injury to a sixteen-year-old boy who ran into it while playing football was declared not to be a nuisance.[30] The court contended that injury was the result of contributory negligence on the part of the boy who did not care for his personal safety.

Other Nuisance Cases

A great variety of situations and conditions are found in court cases in which nuisance is alleged as the cause of injury. For example, dry unslaked lime used to line a football field burned the face of a player but was held not to constitute a nuisance.[31] Neither a truck left unattended and running on a park trail,[32] nor the negligent operation of a power lawn mower in a park[33] were held to constitute nuisances. On the other hand, the court held that a small grass sprinkler pipe rising out of the ground, which caused injury to a person who tripped and fell, constituted an actionable nuisance.[34]

Legal Actions Directly Related to Maintenance Practices

It is important to note that the courts will look for precedents or previous legal decisions, in related or similar situations, and use these as guides before making a legal judgment with respect to a particular case. Many legal actions involving park and recreation activities have been a direct result of situations created by maintenance practices in connection with equipment, areas and facilities, and recreation structures.

Inadequate maintenance of playground equipment such as swings, teeter totters, and slides makes up the great bulk of legal actions brought for the purpose of recovery for injury. Suits have been brought for injury resulting from defective chains,[35] defective supports, deteriorated footings and worn out fittings.[36] Protruding and unguarded sharp objects extending from playground equipment,[37] and dangerous defects in the surfacing beneath playground apparatus[38] have served as important bases for legal action to recover for injury. With respect to recreation areas and facilities, nearly all such legal cases have alleged poor maintenance practice. The improper construction[39] and inspection[40] of bleachers and grandstands resulting in their collapse and injury to spectators is an area in which many lawsuits have been brought.

Most of the foregoing conditions and situations seem to suggest that simple, regular maintenance practice is all that is necessary to avoid the legal backlash that results from injury to a patron. This analysis is undoubtedly correct in the majority of situations; however, we need only to look at the great number of legal actions that have been brought regarding improper maintenance practice to realize that common sense preventive maintenance programs are simply not followed in too many situations. Preventive maintenance should include regular, systematic, thorough inspections with the replacement of worn parts and material that through decay and corrosion have lost their strength and constitute a potential hazard.

The surface condition and guard rails for walkways, paths, and trails have provided the basis for a number of suits that have been filed on behalf of injured parties.[41] For the most part, the courts hold that a defective pathway or walk surface should be maintained in a safe condition and should not present a hazard.

Slippery surfaces,[42] improperly maintained baseball backstops,[43] gates,[44] railings,[45] and fences[46] have been the subjects of attention by the courts. In addition, cases have been filed in connection with improper handling and storage of explosive substances[47] and hot coals and ashes.[48] The courts have held that there is a definite responsibility to care for trees[49] to the extent that if a defective condition is obvious, it should be taken care of to avoid injury to persons who might be struck by falling limbs. The courts have also indicated that there is a duty to remove a fallen tree that might obstruct a walkway or road,[50] and that tree stumps constitute a hazard if not cared for properly.[51]

One of the greatest legal issues debated involves the use of barriers in natural areas for the protection of park and recreation area visitors.[52] The argument of whether or not a barrier should be erected as a protective device, or whether or not the object is itself sufficient to give warning, or is in a location where it should be considered a part of the hazards of the natural environment, still rages. Accidents that have resulted in the death of a number of visitors to our national parks in the past several years have rekindled the interest in this issue, and it is a topic of considerable interest and concern for congressional investigative committees that have reviewed the situation and recommended a conservative (more barrier protection) approach. Good housekeeping practices should be followed that will result in the prompt elimination of hazardous rubbish and rubble, and facilities and equipment needing repair should be serviced without delay. Some would argue that regular systematic preventive maintenance programs are prohibitive from the standpoint of cost. However, just one judgment against the recreation operator for injury to a patron could pay for the actual cost of many years of systematic preventive maintenance very easily. Again, it should be emphasized that almost all liability suits involving park and recreation areas are related to maintenance practice.

Preventive Maintenance and Lawsuits

Recreation officials can do much to protect the recreation agency, agency personnel, and themselves from lawsuits, including the following:

1. Acquaint maintenance personnel with the legal liability aspects of recreation.
2. Supply each employee with a pamphlet or other literature containing essential liability material covered during an orientation period. Such orientation literature should include explanation of each individual's legal responsibilities. In addition, this literature should cite court cases involving the various phases of the recreation maintenance program.

The implications of liability for personnel and their responsibilities under these conditions should be discussed with all new employees and volunteers. Hopefully, this approach might save the recreation agency or individual employees from a financially disastrous and professionally embarrassing loss.

PUBLIC SAFETY

Unfortunately, overall accident data for park visitors and recreation participants in general is not readily available. However, accident data provided by the National Park Service for the calendar year period 1980 through 1990 were analyzed and revealed the following information.

Of more than 3.5 billion visitors to the national parks during the ten-year period 1980–1990, 1,704 were killed in accidents. This represents less than one fatality (0.49) per million visitors. According to John Fleming, manager of Government Services for the National Safety Council, more persons were killed on U.S. roads over a ten-day period than were killed in all of the national parks in a ten-year period.

Drownings, motor vehicle accidents, and falls accounted for 85 percent of all visitor fatalities. Between 1980 and 1990, drownings, motor vehicle accidents, and falls accounted for 654, 530, and 264 fatalities, respectively, or 1,448 of the total 1,704 fatalities that occurred in national parks. Clearly, drownings, motor vehicle accidents, and falls must be the primary targets in any program intended to reduce visitor fatalities in U.S. national parks.

The Accident Prevention Program

Safety coordinator. The first step in an organized safety program is the appointment of a safety coordinator by the maintenance manager. Safety officers need reasonable authoritative clout since they must review safety procedures in all departments and assign responsibility for specific problems. Their range of influence includes activities as diverse as employee safety training, purchasing new equipment, revising work practices, and ensuring public safety. To accomplish this, they need unwavering administrative support.

Safety committee. A safety committee can also help. It should meet periodically, perhaps monthly, to read accident summaries and reports. It can also review the work of the safety coordinator.

Safety records. Records are most important to help safety officers answer certain questions such as: What are the most frequent kinds of accidents? Where do they occur? Without such information, safety officers are operating in a vacuum. Usually, operating and program personnel in the recreation organization provide the needed information. As coordinators, they must arrange a reporting procedure that will channel relevant information to them.

Patron and nonemployee injury records. A primary responsibility of the safety officer should be the establishment and maintenance of an accident record system that will identify trouble spots and accident frequencies. Such data will give the safety coordinator an indication of the effectiveness of the existing accident prevention program. If, for example, the accident frequency rate is rising out of proportion to patron use, the safety officer knows that the program needs redirection. In brief, records of accidents are essential to efficient operations because they are the foundation of any effective accident prevention program.

The American National Standards Institute has published a "Method of Measuring and Recording Patron and Non-Employee Injury Statistics," (ANSI Standard Z 108.1).[53] This system was developed to provide an orderly and uniform method of handling patron injury data for comparative purposes.

Dealing with injuries. Each recreation organization should have a set of standard procedures to follow in case of an injury. These should be reviewed often in inservice training programs to keep all staff members (especially seasonal employees) familiar with procedures. Although such procedures might vary according to local conditions and services available, the following suggestions are offered as a guide.

General procedures:

1. First aid kits should be on hand and readily accessible at each activity area: centers, playgrounds, athletic contests.
2. Maintain a schedule for checking the contents of the first aid kit.
3. Obtain a list of several physicians who agree to be on call to the department or agency. Having more than one or two will protect you when one is unable to come. Ask them to let you know if they are out of town or otherwise unavailable.
4. Register participants whenever this is feasible, including the name, address, telephone (business and home) numbers of parents or guardians, and the name and telephone number of the family physician.

In case of serious injury or illness:

1. Render first aid immediately *providing you know what to do.* (It is desirable to have maintenance personnel trained in first aid.)
2. Call an ambulance or rescue squad if one is needed. Directions to the person receiving the call should include a brief description of the injury, first aid administered, and clear, specific directions as to how to get to the injured person. Have someone ready to direct the arriving ambulance to the injured person. In some cities, a central emergency setup exists to which all calls for emergency help are made, so that the appropriate emergency vehicle is sent. This is a great help in most cases. One of the greatest advantages is that one telephone call will bring an emergency vehicle. With this system, the central control knows the whereabouts and availability of all emergency vehicles.
3. If the injured is transported to a hospital, call ahead indicating that the injured is en route, and give name of family physician if available. (Refer to registration card.)
4. Call the parent or guardian indicating action taken.
5. Try to avoid causing anxiety. Care should be exercised when calling a parent about an injury. It is better to understate the seriousness of the injury. If the victim has been sent to a physician or hospital, tell the parent where.
6. If an ambulance is not needed, have parent transport victim.
7. Fill out an accident report. (Be sure to record the names of all witnesses.) See Figure 9–1.
8. Eliminate the cause of the accident. If an area, facility, or piece of equipment is hazardous, its use should be prohibited until the dangerous condition is removed.
9. If the accident is serious, a verbal report should be made to the system manager immediately.
10. The staff should be advised that no admission of fault should be expressed. In some cases, it might be wise to call the agency attorney if there is the

least likelihood that negligence will be charged. In any event, the attorney should be informed in writing of all injuries. (A copy of the accident report will suffice.)

11. Show a personal interest in the injured person, even after you have been relieved of all responsibility regarding the accident and injury.

Other Aspects of the Accident Prevention Program

In addition to patron injury records and an established policy for dealing with visitors' injuries, other important elements need to be included in the safety

```
Department of Parks and Recreation, Safetyville, Anywhere
Area or Division Reporting . . . . . . . . . . . . . . Injury Report No. . . . . . . . . . . .
    1.  Name of Injured. . . . . . . . . . . . . . . . . . . . . Sex. . . . . Age. . . . . . . . . . . . . .
                            Last,    First,    Initial
    2.  Address of Injured . . . . . . . . . . . . . . . . . . . . . . . . . . . . . . . . . . . . . . . . . . . . . .
    3.  Extent of Injury? Burn . . . . . .; Cut . . . . . .; Fracture . . . . .; Sprain . . . . ,
        Other, specify . . . . . . . . . . . . . . . . . . . . . . . . . . . . . . . . . . . . . . . . . . . . . . . . . .
    4.  Part Injured? Arm. .; Face. .; Foot. .; Hand. .; Head. .; Leg. .; Other. . . . . ,
        specify. . . . . . . . . . . . . . . . . . . . . . . . . . . . . . . . . . . . . . . . . . . . . . . . . . . . . . . . .
    5.  What Immediate Action was taken?
        a.  First Aid Given: . . . . . . . . . . . . . . . . . . . . . . . . . . . . . . . . . . . . . . . . . . . . .
        b.  Injured, seen by physician? Yes. . . . No. . . . If yes, where?. . . . . . . . . .
                . . . . . . . . . . . . . . and by whose authority? . . . . . . . . . . . . . . . . . . . . . . .
        c.  Injured sent to hospital? Yes. . . . No. . . . If yes, how transported. . . . .
                . . . . . . . . . . . . . . and by whose authority? . . . . . . . . . . . . . . . . . . . . . .
        d.  Parents Notified? Yes. . . . No. . . .
        e.  Division Head Notified? Yes. . . . No. . . .
    6.  What Activity was injured engaged in?. . . . . . . . . . . . . . . . . . . . . . . . . . . . .
    7.  What physical cause was involved?, for example, equipment, design, playing
        surface, etc. . . . . . . . . . . . . . . . . . . . . . . . . . . . . . . . . . . . . . . . . . . . . . . . . . . .
    8.  Has physical cause been corrected? Yes. . . No. . . If not, why . . . . . . . . . .
        . . . . . . . . . . . . . . . . . . . . . . . . . . . . . . . . . . . . . . . . . . . . . . . . . . . . . . . . . . . . . .
    9.  What personal deficiency did injured have that should have kept him from.
        from participating in activity . . . . . . . . . . . . . . . . . . . . . . . . . . . . . . . . . . . . .
   10.  What unsafe act, on the part of the injured, contributed to the injury? . . . .
   11.  Was leader present? Yes. . . . No. . . . If no, Why?. . . . . . . . . . . . . . . . . . . .
        . . . . . . . . . . . . . . . . . . . . . . . . . . . . . . . . . . . . . . . . . . . . . . . . . . . . . . . . . . . . . .
   12.  Describe events leading to injury? . . . . . . . . . . . . . . . . . . . . . . . . . . . . . . . .
   13.  How could accident have been prevented?. . . . . . . . . . . . . . . . . . . . . . . . . .
        . . . . . . . . . . . . . . . . . . . . . . . . . . . . . . . . . . . . . . . . . . . . . . . . . . . . . . . . . . . . . .
   14.  What follow up preventive action has been taken?. . . . . . . . . . . . . . . . . . . .
        . . . . . . . . . . . . . . . . . . . . . . . . . . . . . . . . . . . . . . . . . . . . . . . . . . . . . . . . . . . . . .
   15.  Names and addresses of witnesses:. . . . . . . . . . . . . . . . . . . . . . . . . . . . . . . .
        . . . . . . . . . . . . . . . . . . . . . . . . . . . . . . . . . . . . . . . . . . . . . . . . . . . . . . . . . . . . . .
        . . . . . . . . . . . . . . . . . . . . . . . . . . . . . . . . . . . . . . . . . . . . . . . . . . . . . . . . . . . . . .
        . . . . . . . . . . . . . . . . . . . . . . . . . . . . . . . . . . . . . . . . . . . . . . . . . . . . . . . . . . . . . .

Signature. . . . . . . . . . . . . . . . . . . .           . . . . . . . . . . . . . . . . . . . . . . . . . . . . . . .
                Person Reporting                                    Division Head

                . . . . . . . . . . . . . . . . . . . . . . . .
                Safety Director
```

FIGURE 9–1   Visitor-participant injury report.

Source: Walter L. Cook, "Manual for Public Safety for Park and Recreation Departments." American Institute of Park Executives Management Aid Bulletin No. 20, 1962–1963, p. 41.

program to protect the visiting public. These elements, discussed below, include building plan review, safety hazard inspection, fire protection, building plan review for fire protection, fire hazard survey inspection, and fire protection equipment.

Building Plan Review

Before facilities are constructed, it is worthwhile to hire a safety expert to review the plans. A safety expert can save lives and money by pointing out safety hazards in construction drawings and traffic patterns. Because safety is this person's specialty, the expert can find the danger spots that produce fires in buildings and cause injuries to visitors and to employees. By ensuring in advance that a planned project complies with building safety and fire protection codes, the safety expert can save the park and recreation organization money that might otherwise go into expensive post-completion changes.

To conduct an effective plan review, the safety coordinator must build and maintain a current library of reference materials from the National Safety Council, National Fire Protection Association, and the local OSHA office. In addition, he or she must keep current with legislation requiring new and remodeled public buildings to be architecturally barrier free by incorporating ramps rather than stairs and curbs, railings, grab bars, and other design features that facilitate access and circulation for handicapped people.[54]

Safety Hazard Inspections

A regular inspection schedule is the heart of any effective safety program. In many cases, the safety coordinator must bring in specialists such as fire marshals and safety engineers to inspect the premises. Periodically, insurance companies also send representatives to determine whether or not the organization is complying with insurance protection requirements. Such experts provide the safety coordinator with information to prepare action lists that detail all important corrections, such as remedial remodeling, extra fire doors, and installation of fire dampers in ventilating ducts. On the basis of this information, the safety coordinator can compile a safety checklist to guide his or her own inspection tours. Particular attention should be paid to potential hazards related to high risk activities such as skiing, horseback riding, white water canoeing and rafting, sport parachute jumping, motocross, archery, riflery, and snow and water ski jumping.

The Americans with Disabilities Act of 1990 has created a new area of concern for safety on the playground. Play equipment and surfacing must now be chosen to provide play opportunities for all children, sometimes causing problems for our varied population of users. Do ramps, which make it possible for wheelchair users to enter onto play equipment now provide an invitation for skateboard and bicycle users? The hard surface that accommodates wheelchairs and assistance devices may be too hard to cushion falls from platforms and slides. While still in the working stage, it is hoped that compliance regulations will provide the means for some adaptations that will allow accessibility and safety for all children.

Fire Protection

Most municipal park and recreation organizations rely on local fire departments; however, rural, isolated park systems to a considerable extent depend on their own personnel and equipment to fight fires on their premises. Yet, the most important initial consideration in fire protection is not a good fire department, but an effective prevention program. This work requires more time than any other safety job. Only very large park and recreation organizations can afford a full-time, well-trained fire protection expert. But, every organization must assign at least one part-time, partially trained person to the job. It is this individual's task to coordinate all fire protection activities and to call in specialists to help with complex problems.

Review the Building Plan for Fire Protection

The fire protection expert's job logically begins when a building begins. All basic construction drawings should cross this person's desk for approval before ground is broken. This expert checks all plans against codes required by the federal and state agencies as well as the codes recommended by such organizations as the National Fire Protection Association, The American Society for Testing Materials, and the American National Standards Institute. In light of their provisions, the planned building can be evaluated by checking for features such as corridors that provide alternate escape routes, fire doors that retard the spread of flames and smoke, sprinkler systems that adequately cover all areas, and fire extinguishers that are appropriate to building materials and equipment.

Fire Hazard Survey Inspection

Usually, the fire protection expert begins with existing buildings, many of which were designed prior to the existence of current fire codes, fire protection features, and fire-fighting methods. The first step, therefore, should be an extensive survey of the recreation system structures. On such a tour, potential fire hazards are identified in structures and housekeeping procedures for handling rubbish, chemicals, and flammable materials. The expert also examines and evaluates alarms, extinguishers, sprinklers, fire doors, and escape routes. This survey will inevitably produce a list of remedial work for immediate and long-term action.

Additional inspections should follow at regular intervals. For some inspections, the safety director should call in the local fire chief. On such tours, the fire chief can learn the layout of recreation system buildings, and the safety supervisor can develop closer working relationships with the department and learn more about the fire chief's specialty—protecting people. From insurance inspectors, who also tour the system periodically, the supervisor can learn more about this inspector's specialty—protecting property.

Fire Protection Equipment

Fire alarms. The alarms should be designed into the wiring of a building during its planning stage. Ideally, all systems should connect with the park and recreation security office, and local fire and police departments. With cutoff switches, alarms can be tested periodically without disturbing public agencies. More sophisticated systems have both local alarms, within the buildings, and an annunciator in each main entrance hall to show where in the building the fire originated.

Fire sprinkler systems. These systems can involve complicated design decisions. Architects and engineers work out basic calculations to determine the number of sprinkler heads, the area each head should cover, and the size of the water piping required. The safety officer works with these professionals and reviews their efforts for final approval. To adequately protect the recreation system's interests during this critical planning process, the safety supervisor must be as knowledgeable about the technology of sprinklers as possible, asking every question as it occurs and insisting that designers clearly explain all options. A key choice is between a wet or a dry system. A wet system holds water all the time for instant discharge but risks occasional freezing. A dry system eliminates this risk but does not respond as quickly.

Another major decision centers on how the system should be activated. Most sprinklers are heat-activated but cause considerable water damage when responding to small or localized fires. The supervisor, therefore, must decide how to shut off the system and who should have this authority. Testing sprinklers, of course, is another question that he or she must research before making any recommendations.

Fire extinguishers. Extinguishers are needed even though a building may be well equipped with alarms, sprinklers, and other sophisticated fire protection devices. With a good portable extinguisher, even an untrained person often can put out a small blaze before it activates the sprinklers. An extinguisher may even slow the spread of a large fire until professionals arrive. The right extinguisher in the right place at the right time can save lives, lost work time, valuable equipment, and money needed for other purposes. The technology of fire fighting is complicated, however, requiring that the safety supervisor develop considerable expertise about extinguishers before buying, placing, and maintaining them.

Extinguishers come in a wide variety of types, each of which is designed for certain kinds of fires. Because no extinguisher is suitable for every fire, it is essential that each piece be clearly identified and properly labeled to avoid misplacement and misuse.

- *Class A extinguishers* are used on common fires: wood, paper, rubber, and many plastics. They contain water, loaded stream, foam, or a combination of dry chemicals. Maximum travel distance to this extinguisher should not exceed 75 feet, and maximum coverage should average 3,000 square feet.
- *Class B extinguishers* are suitable for fires of flammable liquids, gases, and greases. They hold loaded stream, foam, compressed gas (bromotrifluoromethane and carbon dioxide), dry chemicals, multipurpose dry chemicals, and vaporizing liquids. The maximum travel distance to this extinguisher should be 50 feet.
- *Class C extinguishers* are designed primarily for fires originating from or surrounding electrical equipment. Spraying water on this kind of blaze could electrocute the firefighter. An extinguisher with nonconducting flame suppressants is required for such fires.
- *Class D extinguishers* work effectively on fires of combustible metals such as magnesium, titanium, zirconium, sodium, and potassium. The nameplate for each piece should explain its relative effectiveness for each kind of metal fire.

For additional information regarding fire extinguishers, safety supervisors should consult local authorities and write to such agencies as listed below:

The National Association of Fire Equipment Distributors, Inc.
111 East Wacker Drive
Chicago, Illinois 60610
National Safety Council
1121 Spring Lake Dr.
Itasca, IL 60143-3201

Maintaining fire extinguishers. The safety office cannot simply install an extinguisher and forget it. As time passes, both parts and materials may decay enough to render it inoperable. Someone, therefore, must periodically examine the device, and repair, recharge, or replace it if necessary. That person could be the safety officer, a subordinate, or possibly a private contractor. Because this maintenance can be frequent and repetitious, many recreation systems find it simplest to hire a commercial firm to handle it.

The major maintenance chore is an annual examination of each piece of equipment. At that time, a maintenance worker thoroughly checks the mechanical parts for breakage and corrosion, examining the contents for deterioration and leakage. The worker repairs what is broken, replaces what is missing, and records the work on a dated tag affixed to the extinguisher. Whoever performs this work will need all the technical data pertinent to each type extinguisher.

A monthly inspection is also necessary to see that each extinguisher is in its designated place, that it is visible, accessible, undamaged, and free from defects. On this tour, an inspector also verifies that the maintenance tag is up to date.

VANDALISM

Vandalism—the willful and often pointless destruction, defacement, or defilement of property—is a serious problem in the United States. The total cost of vandalism in the United States is estimated at more than a billion dollars a year.[55] Governmental authorities are spending increasing amounts each year in an effort to reduce vandalism, but they are not succeeding. Park and recreation organizations are particularly hard hit with repair and replacement costs due to vandalism.

The rapid escalation of vandalism is apparent on our federal lands. The National Park Service, U.S. Forest Service, and Bureau of Land Management reported that out of a total of 135,815 known sites, more than 43,000 or 32 percent already had been affected by vandalism, and another 33 percent were in unknown condition. National Park Service statistics showed a 51 percent increase in the number of vandalism violations between 1985 and 1987.[56]

A vandalism survey of the ten National Recreation and Park Association (NRPA) Southern Regional States found that almost 2 percent of the total operations and maintenance budget of the responding 171 park and recreation departments was spent for vandalism repair. The per capita cost to the population served was 10.3 cents.[57]

A vandalism study in eight rural parks managed by the Vicksburg District U.S. Army Corps of Engineers reported a $63,000 expenditure in vandalism repair due to more than 460 individual vandalistic acts during 1980.[58] Charles Nutter, New Orleans recreation director, stated that 30 percent of all park maintenance is cleaning up or repairing vandalism.[59]

Analysis of only the economic impact of vandalism on recreation underestimates the total loss. Consider the impact of vandalism on the recreation environment which in turn diminishes the recreation experience. It is not possible to attach a dollar value loss on permanent defacement of natural features such as trees and rocks or irreplaceable historical or cultural artifacts.[60]

Causes of Vandalism

Most of what has been written about vandalism can be classified as rhetorical opinion rather than factual research information based on data objectively gathered and analyzed.

Most of the existing research describes vandalism behavior, general motivations, peer influences, and who commits the acts where and when. While such information is of interest to recreation providers, such things as parental and peer influence are beyond the control of park professionals.

What is needed by park and recreation practitioners is evaluative research that involves explicit evaluation of the effectiveness of specific programs, strategies, or managerial techniques for controlling vandalism at specific areas and facilities. Unfortunately evaluative research information based on specific antivandalism programs or management strategies is, at best, extremely limited.

Solutions and Strategies

Managers should attempt to solve vandalism problems in their own situations by conducting evaluative research. This research would involve evaluation of the effectiveness of specific programs or strategies for controlling vandalism, including methodology and cost effectiveness. The demonstration of cause and effect allows a manager/researcher to see which program or strategy works under specific conditions and circumstances. As such, evaluative research provides important information from the manager's perspective because it is the manager who is trying to control the problem and, therefore, reduce unnecessary vandalism repair and replacement costs.

Vandalism control programs and strategies to be considered for application to local situations include:

- Public education
- Staff education
- Participant and visitor involvement
- Facility design and construction
- Detection enforcement and security
- Prompt repair or replacement
- User fees
- Removal of vandalism opportunity
- Covering vandalism costs by surcharge

Available research information and "expert opinion" regarding these suggested programs and strategies follows.

Public Education

A continuous public education program is required if the public (remember that the public changes with each new generation) is to be enlisted in an active antivandalism program. Finger waving or chastising is not the answer. The public must be reminded constantly that they paid for and own park and recreation facilities, and that use will be curtailed if vandalism continues. Traditionally, we have attempted to instill in the public proper values and attitudes toward vandalism. However, a vast discrepancy exists between attitudes and vandalistic behavior. New innovative public education approaches are needed.

Staff Education

The first line of defense against vandalism may be well-trained enthusiastic staff members who are sensitive to the needs and desires of recreation participant/ users. Much effort is needed to enlighten the staff, particularly middle-age and older members. Positive attitudes toward the visiting public and understanding causes of vandalism are important. When staff members believe that vandalism can be curbed and that the public can appreciate good facilities and treat them properly, a manager has come a long way toward improving the situation.

Participant/Visitor Involvement

Research on depreciative behavior, including vandalism in recreation settings, indicates that public involvement has considerable potential for reducing the problem. The objective is to find ways to change users' behavior to reduce their own vandalistic acts as well as those of other people. An excellent approach would be to include patrons in the choice and planning of recreation facilities. This can be accomplished through public hearings, consultation with concerned citizens, and discussions with organized citizen groups. Rules for the use of recreation facilities developed with the assistance of participants/users more quickly gain public support and commitment. There are a variety of ways to involve the public in, for example, reducing vandalism in forest campgrounds:[61]

Involve the victim informally. Encourage users to handle a vandalism problem themselves and/or show them how to contact proper authorities.

Involve the culprit. Provide a constructive alternative to destructive behavior. This can be done by organizing the suspected culprit(s) and requesting help in stopping vandalism.

Involve people in formal programs. The U.S. Forest Service "Campground Host" program is a good example of this approach. Volunteer hosts, usually retired married couples, live on campgrounds and offer information and assistance to visitors/users. The presence of campground hosts is reported to have decreased vandalism problems in a variety of campground situations.

Facility Design and Construction

Considerable effort has been directed toward the design and construction of "vandal proof" facilities and equipment with many isolated successes. The problem seems to be that most antivandalism design and construction features that seem to work well in one situation fail in other situations. What is needed is evaluation of new antivandalism design/construction ideas in different locations to prove their universal worth. A study of eighty-six municipal parks by Monty Christiansen[62] identified the frequency and severity of park facilities vandalized. (See Table 9–1.)

TABLE 9–1   Facilities vandalized, according to degree of damage, listed in descending rank order of frequency of parks observed as having each vandalized item. (Items shown in boldface were found in all categories of vandalism.)

Facilities Receiving Minor Cosmetic or Repairable Vandalism	Facilities Receiving Nonrepairable Vandalism, but Still Functional	Facilities Completely Dysfunctional Because of Vandalism
Restrooms (doors, screens, interior walls & partitions)	**Restrooms** (roofs & doors)	**Drinking Fountains**
		Lights
	Benches	**Waste Containers**
Shelters	Electric Meters	Swings
Picnic Tables	**Waste Containers**	Plantings
Waste Containers	**Lights**	**Benches**
Benches	Walls	**Restrooms** (plumbing)
Basketball Backstops	**Electric Outlets**	Signs
Walls	**Drinking Fountains**	Flagpoles
Drinking Fountains	**Bleachers**	**Fencing**
Lights	Wooden Climbers	Whirls
Electric Outlets	Flagpoles	**Electric Outlets**
Fencing	Guard Railings	Electric Meters
Signs	Play Apparatus	Guard Railings
Wooden Climbers	Bike Racks	**Bleachers**
Bleachers	**Fencing**	Teeters

Source: Reprinted from Park Maintenance, 32, no. 9 (September 1979): 11. Box 1936, Appleton, Wisconsin 54913.

The identification of the most commonly vandalized park facilities can be used by a manager to alert planners and designers. In addition, these items should be given special attention in plans and specification reviews to avoid use of vandalism-prone products and materials.

Detection, Enforcement, and Security

Increased detection and strict enforcement of laws, policies, and rules are often cited as an arena to deter vandalism. Jeffery[63] found that detection and enforcement to be effective as a deterrent must result in punishment. The potential vandal must realize that he or she will probably be seen, caught, and punished. Unfortunately, this chain of events is often not the case in most recreation areas according to the research evidence that we do have.

Security systems available for indoor and outdoor recreation areas and facilities include personnel who serve as park rangers, guards, exchange station and registration attendants, guard animals and electronic/mechanical surveillance equipment. Before a decision is made to institute any security system, Burton[64] recommends that the following questions be reviewed and answered:

1. What is the dollar value of the property to be protected?

2. What is the probability of vandalism to the facility?
3. What are the probable losses to vandals?
4. How much protection can we afford?
5. Is insurance protection available?
6. Are insurance premium discounts available if a security system is used?
7. What protection does a system actually afford?
8. How much does a system cost?

If answers to these questions suggest work force utilization, it is important that their patrolling and surveillance be randomized so as to avoid prediction. It is also important that local law enforcement officers be aware of their presence and be familiar with their activities in a given area.

Guard dogs provided on a rental basis have been used increasingly in facilities subject to frequent breaking and entering. The advertised presence of a dog is a strong deterrent to vandals, but should be properly handled by trained personnel to eliminate the possibility of a bad public image or legal liability due to a dog's interference with persons approaching on legitimate business. In considering a mechanical security system, it is important to utilize the services of a qualified, capable consultant to study the particular circumstances and make appropriate recommendations. Many school systems have expert school security directors capable of providing needed assistance. It may be possible to have recreation facilities serviced and monitored by local school security equipment.

User Fees

The use of fees as a deterrent to vandalism is believed by some managers to be quite effective. Their rationale is based on the idea that fee payment on the part of the patron makes for greater protective ownership feelings and, consequently, will result in fewer vandalistic acts. Other managers believe the opposite and rationalize that fee payment is often interpreted by the patron as a license or permit to vandalize. Which of these viewpoints is supported by objective research evidence? Neither. We simply don't know.

Prompt Repair or Replacement

The repair and replacement strategy is based on the theory that immediate repair or replacement following discovery of vandalism to facilities will result in no future vandalistic attempts at that location. There is widespread belief that this antivandalism procedure is effective. However, there is little verification to indicate the extent to which this strategy results in reducing vandalism.

Removal of Vandalism Opportunity

Predictably, removing facilities, closing areas, or hiding what can be vandalized does work as an absolute deterrent to vandalism. However, removal or closing simply circumvents the problem of vandalism rather than attempting to solve it. By removal of equipment and closing facilities we are not properly serving the public. We are actually penalizing the users who are not responsible for the problem. Despite the negative aspects of facility closing, a good case can be made for closing a recreation area or facility during periods when the facility is not usable for its intended purpose, particularly when experience demonstrates that vandalistic acts and misuse of the facility occur more frequently during those time periods.

Covering Vandalism Costs by Surcharge

Clark[65] suggests that we "treat vandalism as a cost of doing business, i.e., treat it like shop lifting." After we have done everything possible to stop vandalism, we must assume that some will still occur, and we should charge facility users the resulting cost.

A maintenance manager can reasonably argue that a vandalism surcharge will avoid further reductions in the already scarce maintenance dollars. Certainly, a vandalism surcharge would make users clearly aware of the financial impact of vandalism.

Seeking Help and Communicating Results

If it is difficult to set up an analytical framework and research design for the evaluation of a program or strategy, help is available, usually from the closest educational institution. A vandalism problem may even be suggested as a graduate student research project.

Once the evaluative research effort is completed, share findings by submitting them for publication in a state or national professional journal. This final step of communicating is critical if we are to succeed in significantly reducing vandalism by sharing information.

In summary, it is important to recognize that vandalism is a complex problem with little available proven information as to the "best approach" for control. There is a critical need for evaluative research on various antivandalism programs, managerial strategies, and techniques in a variety of park situations under varying circumstances.

If a park and recreation manager waits for "someone else" to provide the solutions to local vandalism problems, in all likelihood it will not happen soon. Park and recreation managers are in the best position to identify vandalism problems in local parks.

Managers should apply one or more antivandalism programs or strategies on an experimental/control basis. They should then closely monitor the effects based on the incidence and cost effectiveness of the effort.

Finally, when dealing with a problem as complex and frustrating as vandalism, a manager must maintain a positive attitude. The problem began sixteen hundred years ago with vandals ransacking Europe and is not likely to disappear soon. Managers must believe that tomorrow's evaluative research will solve some of today's vandalism problems. "Keep the faith" and do the necessary *homework.*

PUBLIC RELATIONS MANAGEMENT

Lawrence A. Appley writes, "Whatever an organization does that affects the opinions of its various publics toward it is public relations."[66] This definition is useful for several reasons. First, it points out that whether or not it has a public relations program, every organization has public relations because it is involved with individuals and groups of people who have opinions about the organization. Appley makes the distinction between public relations and public relations administration as the intelligent, conscious effort to influence publics in a positive way.

Second, Appley's definition of public relations makes reference to multiple publics, not a single public. Certainly, the concept of publics applies to recreation maintenance organizations because they constantly deal with many different groups. This makes public relations management difficult because, in connection with maintenance operations, it is not always possible to comply with all requests for service from each public, because of repair work priorities, scheduling limitations, and other restricting circumstances.

Maintenance is not glamorous. Recreation activities, program events, cultural presentations, even innovative administration procedures are capable of capturing the attention of the press and the public much more readily than routine maintenance operations. This simply means that maintenance departments must try harder.

The essence of good public relations management for maintenance is projecting the image (an honest image) of a unit or agency dedicated to serving the public better. Despite infinite possibilities and varied approaches, this is still the prime goal. The rather conservative mentality of most maintenance agencies has been a problem over the years. "Who needs that nonsense!" is often the comment of a maintenance chief when asked to make a special public relations effort. Unfortunately, this attitude may cost money, personnel, and operational authorization when governing authorities have the overall operating budgets and proposals under consideration.

Sound public relations management is not a gimmick; it is not dishonest. It does not lie or color facts. It consists of communicating ideas, concepts, philosophies in a manner that will enlighten citizens, groups, elected officials, public bodies as to the purposes, goals, and operating techniques of a maintenance organization. It tells a true story, but it tells it effectively, in a way that will encourage favorable action by employees, citizens, and authorizing committees.

The Employee and the Multiplier Principle

Alert maintenance managers have long recognized that individual workers are key to good public relations because they create the public image of the recreation system. The suggestion that each employee accentuate the positive follows the powerful voice-and-ear method of influencing others. It capitalizes on the multiplier principle, taking advantage of every contact made by recreation department employees—inside and outside the organization. Surveys indicate that each staff member associates with an average of 50 persons, including members of his or her immediate family, church associates, and members of service clubs or social groups and similar organizations. It is interesting to speculate on what could happen if every member of the staff would make it a point to say just one favorable thing about the recreation system, its staff, its policies, and its services to each of these 50 persons. Everyone who hears the recreation story tends to repeat it to others, and according to the laws of mathematical progression, a miracle could result for the system. The only thing an individual would have to do is to start this chain of communication. Then, it is a simple suggestion that the maintenance manager encourage employees to accentuate the positive by telling folks what is good about their public recreation program. Therefore, urge employees to make it their business to make friends for themselves and the recreation system. Never underestimate the importance of a single employee's personal influence. However, employees must be convinced through repeated experience that their organization is truly concerned with their personal and professional welfare before their manager can reasonably expect them to speak favorably about the organization. Negative experiences are just as likely to be repeated if this is not the case.

Minimizing User Conflicts

Generally, the typical user of recreation areas and facilities is not concerned about maintenance problems. Having little knowledge or interest in what is involved, the public's main concern is that the facility is available and in good condition. Haven't we all expressed a similar attitude when we have wanted a suit altered, driven our cars into a garage for quick repairs, or found the paper towel container empty in a restroom? However, we sometimes resent this attitude, when we are on the receiving end of a user complaint or demand. We must constantly bear in mind that these users are the same people who pay for the facilities and make maintenance jobs possible and necessary. The following eight considerations are taken from the concluding portion of a public relations manual developed by the late Oka Hester, then director of Recreation and Parks, Greensboro, North Carolina:

1. A citizen [or user] is not a person with whom to argue or match wits.

Arguing wastes time and convinces no one of anything but your own lack of intelligence.

2. A citizen is the most important person to enter this office, in person, by mail, or by telephone.

3. A citizen is not dependent on us. On the contrary, we are dependent on him.

4. A citizen is not an interruption to our work; he is the purpose of it.

5. A citizen is not an outsider in our work; he is part of it.

6. A citizen is not (and this is most important to remember) a cold statistic. He is a flesh and blood human being with feelings and emotions like our own.

7. The citizen is the most important person with whom we deal.

8. A citizen is a person who brings us his problems. It is our job to handle them in such a way as to be beneficial to him and to ourselves.[67]

For these reasons, every effort must be made by the park and recreation maintenance management team to minimize user conflict in their combined operations.

The overall problem facing us is how to perform the necessary maintenance and repair tasks with a minimum of conflict? There is no easy answer to this question because each operation has conditions peculiar to that particular situation. Factors such as weather, daily and seasonal operation of programs, preparation of specialized facilities, hours of operation anticipated by the clientele, types of programs, the abilities and training of maintenance personnel, available funds, priorities, and other restricting circumstances need to be considered.

The task of scheduling maintenance work to minimize user conflicts requires considerable thought and good judgment. Minimizing conflict with routine maintenance tasks can generally be handled by the coordination of schedules between the maintenance division and those responsible for programming. Admittedly there are times when an arbitrator is needed. However, the most difficult conflict problems arise when specialized maintenance is needed, when unanticipated major repair, overhaul, or reconditioning is required. Or perhaps a special type of programming requires extra attention or preparation by maintenance personnel. The basis of conflict here is associated with five major elements of management:[68]

- Communications.
- Design of facilities.
- Planning.
- Scheduling.
- Training.

All elements are dependent upon one another and all are separately important.

Communications

The importance of communications in minimizing user conflict cannot be overstressed. We need communications in four separate directions:

1. *Between the maintenance supervisor and maintenance personnel.* Maintenance personnel should be aware of regular and special program schedules in order to avoid conflicts.

2. *Between the maintenance supervisor and the program staff.* Maintenance supervisors should be informed of daily activities, schedules of program staff, and when athletic or other program areas need special preparation or attention. Remember the basic justification for the facility. Programs should routinely take priority over maintenance functions.

3. *Between the maintenance supervisor and the administration.* Too often there is a lack of understanding on the part of administrative staff (and program staff) as to the maintenance-user conflicts that are encountered by maintenance supervisors.

4. *Between all recreation system personnel and the users.* All users should be treated with courtesy. If major conflicts can be foreseen, good public relations management calls for a news release indicating the work that has to be done and when it is scheduled.

Design of Facilities

One of the more frequent complaints from the maintenance end is that the maintenance supervisor is seldom involved in the planning of new facilities or areas or in the redesign of existing facilities. The supervisor, who is directly involved in the problems that occur in user-maintenance conflicts, should be able to offer to the planner empirical information that would result in the reduction of such conflicts. Supervisors should provide suggestions regarding access and service roads, location of garbage and trash deposits or collection facilities, and sanitation around restrooms and picnic shelters. Supervisors can also be of assistance when it is necessary to redesign or relocate certain facilities by being aware of maintenance-user problems.

Planning

An efficient recreation system reflects careful planning. Planning is simply a logical approach to an objective, outlining the steps to be accomplished. Every step in the planning process must involve consideration of potential user conflicts. Road patching, tree pruning, turf irrigation, and other similar work items require advance planning and proper scheduling in order to avoid user conflicts.

Scheduling

An important aspect in minimizing user conflicts is scheduling—setting the time for starting and estimating the completion of a job. Close coordination between those responsible for user scheduling and maintenance scheduling is required. Generally, routine tasks must be performed at nonpeak use periods in order to cause a minimum of interference. Refuse collection, mowing, sweeping, and restroom cleaning, in most instances, should be done during periods of minimum use. Such tasks can best be performed early in the morning, late in the evening, and sometimes at night.

A major problem for supervisors is how to schedule the work force to accomplish their tasks during low-use hours. This calls for communications skill, proper training, and a clear explanation of duties in job descriptions.

It is sometimes necessary, however, to provide additional maintenance services during periods of peak use. This often involves the same tasks that ordinarily should be done during low-use periods. Routine checks on a regular basis are necessary to determine need. Tasks performed during peak periods of use should be accomplished by the personnel who project the best image, who take pride in their tasks, and who are capable of dealing effectively with the public.

Maintenance Personnel Training

Training can also contribute to minimizing user conflict. Maintenance personnel must be trained to perform the varied tasks assigned to them. If a worker has a thorough knowledge of the job, and how to do it, in all likelihood that person will perform in a manner that will minimize potential user conflict with maintenance operations.

In any training program for maintenance personnel, workers must be given not only technical instruction, but also must be trained to recognize the importance of the positive image that can be projected through person-to-person contacts while in the field. Conflicts can be lessened considerably if maintenance employees project a good image to the public. Every maintenance employee, either directly or indirectly, consciously or unconsciously, is engaged in public relations work.

REVIEW QUESTIONS

1. Discuss the incidence of liability lawsuits and recreation maintenance practice.
2. In order to successfully bring a legal liability suit based on negligent conduct, what elements must be proved to recover damages from the wrongdoer?
3. Discuss the current trend relative to governmental immunity.
4. Explain how the legal doctrines of "assumption of risk" and "contributory negligence" are influenced by the age of the plaintiff.
5. Cite specific park and recreation situations in which the legal charge of "nuisance" might be involved.
6. Discuss the current trends of fatalities and injuries to park visitors in the United States.
7. Cite the primary targets in any program intended to reduce visitor fatalities

in national parks.

8. Describe the three major types of fire protection equipment for buildings.
9. Discuss the problem of vandalism in U.S. park and recreation areas.
10. Indicate the justification and need for "evaluative" vandalism research for parks and recreation areas in the United States.
11. Distinguish between public relations and public relations management.
12. Explain how a recreation maintenance division should be responsive to its publics (plural) rather than public (singular).

CHAPTER BIBLIOGRAPHY

Brady, Paul T. "A Practical Approach to Vandalism." *Parks and Recreation* (April 1981): 32–35.

Christiansen, Monty L. *Vandalism Control Management for Parks and Recreation Areas.* State College, PA: Venture Publishing, 1983.

"Safety Is No Accident." *Parks and Recreation* (May 1985): 52–56.

Fazio, James R., and Gilbert, Douglas L. *Public Relations and Communications for Natural Resource Managers.* Dubuque, IA: Kendall/Hunt Publishing, 1981.

Frakt, Arthur, and Rankin, Janna S. *The Law of Park Recreation Resources and Leisure Services.* Salt Lake City, UT: Brighton Publishing, 1982.

Greenbaum, Stewart. "Safe Park Principles and Practices." *Parks and Recreation* (March 1991): 48–52.

Holford, Elizabeth, and Geyer, Leon L. "Torts on Your Turf." *Parks/Grounds Management* 99 (March 1990): 13–16.

Kotler, Philip. *Marketing Management.* Englewood Cliffs, NJ: Prentice-Hall, 1975.

National Safety Council. *Public Employee Safety Guide—Parks and Recreation.* Chicago: National Safety Council, 1974.

Accident Facts (1981 Edition). Chicago: National Safety Council, 1981.

Owyer, William O., and Murrell, Dan S. "Negligence in Visitor Security." *Parks and Recreation* (January 1985): 68–72.

Perry, Michael J. "Strategies for Combating Crime in the Parks." *Parks and Recreation* (September 1983): 49–53.

Ross, Sam. "How to Vandal Proof Your Restrooms." *Parks and Recreation.* (July 1991): 56–57.

Shattuck, Bruce. *Vandalism in Public Park Facilities.* Scottsdale, AZ: Publishing Horizons, 1987.

Sheffield, Emilyn. "Managing Depreciative Behavior." *Parks and Recreation*

(October 1988): 16.

Thayer, Ralph E., and Wagner, Fritz W. *Vandalism*. Alexandria, VA: National Recreation and Park Association, 1981.

Tiffany, Amanda. "How to Tame the Liability Monster." *Parks and Recreation* (January 1987): 64.

U.S. Consumer Products Safety Commission. *Handbook for Public Playground Safety*. Washington, DC: U.S. Consumer Products Safety Commission, 1990.

"Vandalism—A Billion Dollars a Year and Getting Worse." *U.S. News & World Report*, June 24, 1974.

"Vandalism and Outdoor Recreation." *Symposium Proceedings*, USDA Forest Service General Technical Report PSW-17, 1976.

Van der Smissen, Betty. *Legal Liability of Cities and Schools for Injuries in Recreation and Parks*. Cincinnati, OH: W. H. Anderson, 1968.

1975 Supplement to Legal Liability of Cities and Schools for Injuries in Recreation and Parks. Cincinnati, OH: W. H. Anderson, 1975.

"Trends in Personal Injury Suits," *Parks and Recreation* (May 1985): 57–83.

NOTES

1. 45 Corpus Juris 631.
2. *Balaas* v. *Hartford*, 126 Connecticut 510, 12 A(2nd) 765 (1940).
3. *Cox* v. *Des Moines*, 235 Iowa 178, 16 NW(2nd) 234 (1944).
4. Betty Van der Smissen, *Legal Liability of Cities and Schools for Injuries in Recreation and Parks* (Cincinnati, OH: W. H. Anderson, 1968), 42–43.
5. Betty Van der Smissen, *1975 Supplement to Legal Liability of Cities and Schools for Injuries in Recreation and Parks* (Cincinnati, OH: W. H. Anderson, 1975) 2–8.
6. James J. Bonifas, "See You in Court," Address delivered at the Southern District Recreation and Park Conference, Atlanta, Georgia, April 5, 1971.
7. *Orrison* v. *Rapid City*, 76 SD 145, 74 NW(2nd) 489 (1956).
8. *Kelly* v. *School District*, 102 Wash 343, 173 Pac 333 (1918).
9. *Stolpe* v. *Duquesne*, 337 Pa 215, 9 A(2nd) 427 (1939).
10. *Bennett* v. *Scranton*, 54 Lack Jur 81 (CP 1953).
11. *Maltz* v. *Board of Education*, 114 NYS (3rd) 856 (Sup Ct 1952).
12. *Scala* v. *New York City*, 200 Misc. 475, 102 NYS(2nd) 790 (Sup Ct—1951).
13. *Gottesman* v. *Cleveland*, 142 Ohio St 410, 27 Ohio Op 353, 52 NE (2nd) 644 (1944).
14. *Bennett* v. *Scranton*, 54 Lack Jur 81 Pa CP (1953).
15. *Brueen* v. *North Yakima School District*, 101 Wash 374, 172 Pac 569 (1918).
16. *Byrnes* v. *Jackson*, 140 Miss 656, 105 So 861 (1925).
17. *Cheyney* v. *Los Angeles*, 119 Cal App(2nd) 75, 258 P(2nd) 1099 (1953).
18. *Nelson* v. *Duluth*, 172 Minn 76, 214 NW 774 (1927).
19. *Turner* v. *Moverly*, 224 Mo App 683, 26 SW(2nd) 997 (1930).
20. *Woodard* v. *Des Moines*, 182 Iowa 1102, 165 NW 313 (1917).

21. *Orrison* v. *Rapid City*, 76 SD 145, 74 NW(2nd) 489 (1956).

22. *Cardinali* v. *New York*, 1 App Div(2nd) 1018, 151 NYS(2nd) 514 (1956).

23. Van der Smissen, *Legal Liability*, 103.

24. Van der Smissen, *1975 Supplement to Legal Liability*, 6.

25. *Cabbiness* v. *North Little Rock*, 228 Ar 356, 307 SW(2nd) 529 (1957); *Selden* v. *Cuyahuga Falls*, 132 Ohio St 223, 7 Ohio Op 511, 6 NE(2nd) 976 (1937); *Walker* v. *Forest Preserve Dist. of Cook County*, 27 Ill(2nd) 538, 190 NE(2nd) 296 (1963); *Cummings* v. *Nazareth*, 430 Pa 255, 242 A(2nd) 460 (1968).

26. *Lubbock* v. *Greene*, 201 F(2nd) 146 (5th Cir 1953).

27. *Emmons* v. *Virginia*, 152 Minn 295, 188 NW 561 (1922).

28. *Gottesmann* v. *Cleveland*, 142 Ohio St 410, 27 Ohio Op 353, 52 NE(2nd) 644 (1944).

29. *Schmidt* v. *Cheviot*, 31 Ohio NP 12 (CP 1933).

30. *Iacono* v. *Fitzpatrick*, 61 RI 28, 199 Atl 689 (1938).

31. *Mokovich* v. *Independent School District*, 177 Minn 446, 225 NW 292 (1929).

32. *Husband* v. *Salt Lake City*, 92 Utah 449, 69 P(2nd) 491 (1937).

33. *Ballanger* v. *Dayton*, 66 Ohio L. Abs 388, 117 NE(2nd) 469 (1952).

34. *Johnson* v. *Tennessean Newspaper, Inc.*, 192 Tenn 287, 241 SW(2nd) 399 (1951).

35. *White* v. *Charlotte*, 211 NC 186, 189 SE 492 (1937).

36. *Thrasher* v. *Cincinnati*, 28 Ohio Op 97, 13 Ohio Supp 143 (1944); *Foyston* v. *Charlotte*, 278 Michigan 255, 270 NW 288 (1936); *Rich* v. *City of Goldsboro*, 192 SE(2nd) 824 NC (1972).

37. *Fort Collins* v. *Roten*, 72 Colo 182, 210 Pac 326 (1922); *Kingsport* v. *Lane*, 35 Tenn App 183, 243 SW(2nd) 289 (1952); *Fetters* v. *Des Moines*, 260 Iowa 490, 149 NW(2nd) 815 (1967); *Pichette* v. *Manistique Public Schools*, 50 Mich App 770, 213 NW(2nd) 784 (1973).

38. *Paraska* v. *Scranton*, 122 Pa Super 1, 184 Atl 276 (1936); *McCullough* v. *Philadelphia*, 32 Pa Super 109 (1906); *Schmidt* v. *Cheviot*, 31 Ohio NP 12 (1933); *Hall* v. *Columbus Board of Education*, 32 Ohio App(2nd) 297, 61 00(2nd) 396, 290 NE(2nd) 580 (1972).

39. *Adams* v. *Schneidar*, 71 Ind App 249, 124 NE 718 (1919); *Conner* v. *Meuer*, 232 Wisc. 656, 288 NW 272 (1939); *Boyer* v. *Iowa High School Athletic Assn.*, 127 NW(2nd) 606 (Iowa 1964).

40. *Guymon* v. *Finicum*, 265 P(2nd) 706 (Okla. 1953); *Harllee* v. *Gulfport*, 120 F(2nd) 41 (5th Cir 1941); *Novak* v. *Delavan*, 31 Wis(2nd) 200, 143 NW(2nd) 6 (1966).

41. *Florey* v. *Burlington*, 247 Iowa 316, 73 NW(2nd) 770 (1955); *Bagby* v. *Kansas City*, 338 Mo 771, 92 SW(2nd) 142 (1936); *Miller* v. *Philadelphia*, 345 Pa 1, 25 A(2nd) 185 (1942).

42. *Harvey* v. *Savannah*, 59 Ga 12, 199 SE 653 (1938); *Cambereri* v. *Board of Education*, 246 App Div 127, 284 NY Supp. 902; *Tulsa* v. *Going*, 437 P(2nd) 257 (1967); *Campbell* v. *Peru* 48 Ill App(2nd) 267, 198 NE(2nd) 719 (1964); *Cumberland College* v. *Gaines*, 432 SW(2nd) 650 (Ky 1968).

43. *Snowden* v. *Kittitas County School Dist.*, 38 Wash(2nd) 691, 231 P(2nd) 621 (1951).

44. *Luan* v. *Needles Elementary School Dist.*, 154 Cal App(2nd) 803, 316 P(2nd) 773 (1957).

45. *Levine* v. *New York City*, 2 NYC(2nd) 246, 140 NE(2nd) 275 (1957).

46. *Shields* v. *School Dist.*, 408 Pa 388, 184 A(2nd) 240 (1962); *Caltavuturo* v. *Passaic*, 124 NJ Super 361, 301 A(2nd) 114 (1973).

47. *Carradine* v. *New York City*, 16 App Div(2nd) 928, 229 NYC(2nd) 328 (1962).

48. *Ackeret* v. *Minneapolis,* 129 Minn 190, 151 NW 976 (1915); *Bingham* v. *Board of Education,* 118 Utah 582, 223 P(2nd) 432 (1950); *State* v. *San Mateo Co.,* 69 Cal Rptr. 683, 263 Cal App(2nd) 396 (1968); *Peterson* v. *Honolulu,* 496 P(2nd) 5 (Hawaii 1972).

49. *Kilbourn* v. *Seattle,* 43 Wash(2nd) 373, 261 Pa(2nd) 407 (1953); *Pietz* v. *Oskaloosa,* 250 Iowa 374, 92 NW(2nd) 577 (1958); *Smith* v. *United States,* 117 F Supp 525 (So Cal 1953).

50. *Rockett* v. *Philadelphia,* 256 Pa 347, 100 Atl 826 (1917).

51. *Sapula* v. *Young,* 147 Okla 179, 296 Pac 418 (1931).

52. *Houston* v. *George,* 479 SW(2nd) 257 Tex Supp (1972); *Mahoney* v. *Elmhurst Park Dist.,* 47 Ill(2nd) 367; 265 NE(2nd) 654 (1971).

53. American National Standards Institute, "Method of Measuring and Recording Patron and Non-Employee Injury Statistics," (ANSI Standard Z 108.1), 1430 Broadway, New York, NY 10018.

54. American National Standards Institute, "Specifications for Making Buildings and Facilities Accessible to and Usable by the Physically Handicapped," (A. 117.1), 1430 Broadway, New York, NY 10018.

55. "Vandalism—A Billion Dollars a Year and Getting Worse," *U.S. News & World Report,* June 24, 1975, 39.

56. Todd Wilkenson, "Raiders of the Parks," *National Parks,* (September/October 1991): 30–35.

57. NRPA Southern Regional Conference, "Vandalism Survey, Southern Regional States," A report, Biloxi, Mississippi, March 1981.

58. Frank A. Butts and Randy Boren, "A Study of Vandalism Patterns," Vicksburg District, U.S. Corps of Engineers, Vicksburg, Mississippi, 1981.

59. "Vandalism—A Billion Dollars a Year," 39.

60. Roger N. Clark, "Control of Vandalism in Recreation Areas—Fact, Fiction, or Folklore?" in *Vandalism and Outdoor Recreation: Symposium Proceedings,* USDA Forest Service General Technical Report PSW-17/1976, 63.

61. Roger N. Clark et al., "Depreciative Behavior in Forest Campgrounds: An Exploratory Study," USDA Forest Res. Note PNW-161, Pacific Northwest Forest and Ranger Experiment Station, Portland, Oregon, 1971.

62. Monty Christiansen, "Vandalism," *Park Maintenance,* 32, no. 9 (September 1979): 10–12.

63. C. Ray Jeffery, *Crime Prevention Through Environmental Design* (Beverly Hills, CA: Sage, 1971), 290.

64. L. W. Burton, "School Protective Systems." Address delivered at the Bicentennial Conference of the National Association of School Security Directors, Alexandria, Virginia, July 1976.

65. Clark, "Control of Vandalism in Recreation Areas," p. 69.

66. Lawrence A. Appley, *Management in Action* (New York: American Management Association, 1956), 53.

67. Oka T. Hester, "Let's Take a Look," in *Public Relations Manual* (Greensboro, NC: Greensboro Park and Recreation Department, 1974).

68. Hans G. Uhlig, "Minimizing User Conflicts," Monograph prepared for the Park and Recreation Maintenance Management School, North Carolina State University, Raleigh, North Carolina, 1975.

INDEX